A Journey into the *Zohar*

A Journey into the *Zohar*

An Introduction to
The Book of Radiance

NATHAN WOLSKI

SUNY
PRESS

Cover art, page from Bodleian manuscript, courtesy of the Bodleian Library, University of Oxford, MS. Opp Add. Fol. 61, fol. 201b.

Published by State University of New York Press, Albany

For information, contact State University of New York Press, Albany, NY
www.sunypress.edu

Production by Kelli Williams
Marketing by Michael Campochiaro

Library of Congress Cataloging-in-Publication Data

Wolski, Nathan.
  A journey into the Zohar : an introduction to the book of radiance / Nathan Wolski.
     p. cm.
  Includes bibliographical references and index.
  ISBN 978-1-4384-3053-9 (hardcover : alk. paper)
  ISBN 978-1-4384-3054-6 (pbk. : alk. paper) 1. Zohar. 2. Cabala.
3. Mysticism—Judaism. I. Title.

BM525.A59W65 2010
  296.1'62—dc22

                                                            2009022695

10   9   8   7   6   5   4   3   2   1

For Merav

מים רבים לא יוכלו לכבות את האהבה
Great seas cannot quench love
—Song of Songs 8:7

Heylik di vegn, nor heyliker geyers;
gebentsht iz der gang un gebentshter dos geyn

Holy are the ways, even holier the wanderers;
blessed is the walk and more blessed the walking
—Der Nister, "Der nozir un dos tsigele"

Contents

Acknowledgments

I wish to acknowledge here my friend and teacher Dr. Melila Hellner-Eshed. As all of her students can attest, the *Zohar* shines most brilliantly in her. Melila graciously read earlier drafts of this book and provided valuable feedback. I am grateful to my friend and colleague Dr. Michael Fagenblat, who also read earlier drafts of this work and whose support has accompanied this project from the beginning. Above all, however, my thanks and gratitude to my wife, Merav Carmeli, who first introduced me to the *Zohar* and its wondrous delights. May we continue to explore its enchanted world together! Our children, Layla, Ella, and now Lev, also deserve my thanks for their love and humor. Chapter 9 is a modified version of an article that appeared in the journal *Prooftexts* 28, 2008. I thank Indiana University Press for permission to revise and reprint the article they first published. I also wish to acknowledge the team at SUNY Press, Nancy Ellegate, Kelli Williams-Leroux and Michael Campochiaro. Finally, my thanks to my colleagues at the Australian Centre for Jewish Civilisation and the School of Historical Studies, Monash University, Australia.

Note on Translation

Unless stated all the *Zohar* translations in this book are my own and are based on standard printed editions of the *Zohar*. On occasion, I have also drawn upon the translations of Daniel Matt (*The Book of Enlightenment* and the emerging Pritzker edition of *The Zohar*), as well as the translations of Isaiah Tishby and David Goldstein from *The Wisdom of the Zohar*. These are all indicated in the text. Bible translations are based largely on the *JPS Hebrew-English Tanakh* as well as Robert Alter's translation of *The Five Books of Moses*, though I have frequently modified these in accordance with the *Zohar*'s reading. I have also benefited from Ariel and Chana Bloch, *The Song of Songs: A New Translation*. Translations of passages from the Talmud and from *Midrash Rabbah* have primarily been taken and occasionally modified from the Soncino English translation.

•◆•

CHAPTER ONE

The Way of the *Zohar*

> When you study, study by a river, so as the waters flow, your teachings may flow.
>
> —Babylonian Talmud, *Horayot* 12a

The *Zohar* is a curious book, if we can even call it that. *The Book of Radiance*, the great work of the Spanish Kabbalah, defies simple classifications. Part commentary on the Torah, both conventional midrashic and kabbalistic, and part narrative, although the stories found throughout the *Zohar* are in no particular order, the *Zohar* is unlike any other work in the Jewish canon. Written in the main in an enigmatic yet strangely poetic Aramaic, the *Zohar*'s thousands of pages tell two stories simultaneously. The first tale—magical and enchanted— is the story of the Companions, the wandering mystics headed by the grand master, Rabbi Shimon bar Yoḥai. As Gershom Scholem noted long ago, the *Zohar* is a "proto-novel" and recounts the adventures of ten itinerant sages as they wander across the landscape of the second-century land of Israel. By a brook, under the shade of a tree, in the inner recesses of a cave, or just on the road, these wandering mystic masters walk and talk, and together pour forth the deepest secrets and mysteries of the Torah, the cosmos, and God. On their many journeys, some of which seem to have no particular destination, the Companions encounter anonymous donkey drivers and small children, as well as an extended cast of liminal types who themselves turn out to be the bearers of profound mystical teachings. The narratives recounting this mystical epic are surely among the great accomplishments of medieval Jewish literature, and artfully fuse humor, adventure, desire, irony, and pathos. The second tale recounted by the *Zohar* is equally extraordinary—the story of God. Employing an impressive array of kabbalistic symbolism, the *Zohar* reads the verses of the Torah according to the "mystery of faith," *raza de-mehemenuta*, a figural mode of reading whereby the Torah is transformed from a book of narratives and laws into a story relating the deepest life of divinity. Under their loving gaze, the words of scripture are read by the Companions as signifying the ultimate reality of God in all its complexity and wonder. From the primal breakthrough, as divinity bursts forth from its own nothingness to bring forth the incredible diversity of being, to the erotic relations between the male and female elements of the divine, the *Zohar* delights in reading the words of Torah as nothing less than the continually unfolding biography of God.

Yet beyond recounting these two tales—which are invariably interwoven on every page—the *Zohar* invites the reader to actively participate in its mythical adventure. This active participation sometimes takes the form of direct calls to awaken to the reality of divinity and the divinity of reality, while other times, our participation as readers is more subtle, arising through the difficult work of interpreting the *Zohar*'s symbolic network and interpretative moves. Whatever the strategy, the *Zohar* has the unique capacity to draw us into its world and, most importantly, to bring us into contact with and consciousness of the flow of divinity. This performative aspect is pivotal, for the *Zohar* is not merely a work about Jewish mysticism but is a work written from within the horizons of mystical experience that aims to regenerate our mystical awareness of God, Torah, and reality as a whole.

That reading, or more precisely, interpreting, might have the power to bring about revelatory experience is in fact one of the central assumptions of classical rabbinic culture. A short tale appearing in *Song of Songs Rabbah*, a late midrashic compilation from the Talmudic era, presents what might best be described as a rabbinic or Jewish account of reading as the experience of revelation:

> Ben Azzai was sitting and interpreting and the fire surrounded him.
>
> They went and told Rabbi Akiva: Rabbi, Ben Azzai is sitting and interpreting and the fire is burning around him.
>
> He went to him and said to him: I have heard that you were interpreting and the fire was burning around you.
>
> He said to him: Indeed.

He said to him: Perhaps you were occupied in the study of the chambers of the chariot?

He said to him: No, but I was sitting and stringing together words of Torah, and words of the Torah to the Prophets, and the Prophets to the Writings, and the words were as joyous as when they were given from Sinai, and they were as sweet as their original giving. Were they not originally given in fire, as it is written, *The mountain was ablaze with flames to the heart of the heavens* (Deut. 4:11)?

—*Song of Songs Rabbah* 1:10[1]

Here, Ben Azzai, one of the "four who entered the orchard" (BT *Ḥagiga* 14b), is able to attain an experience comparable to the original Sinaitic moment, though significantly he does so not through any esoteric practice but merely through the normative act of studying the Torah. The great bead game of *midrash*, which as Elliot Wolfson reminds us has a numerical value equaling the word *niftehu*, "were opened," from the phrase in Ezekiel, "the heavens were opened and I saw visions of God" (Ezek. 1:1), is thus capable of bringing us to the same experiential space as the giving of the Torah at Mount Sinai.[2] In my view, the *Zohar* accomplishes this midrashic-mystical quest like no other work before it or indeed since.

As befits a work of great mystery, the origins of the *Zohar* are shrouded in legend, rumor, and enigma. While the *Zohar* presents itself as a work from the second century of the Common Era, setting itself within the tannaitic landscape of the sages of the Mishnah, scholars today are unanimous in their view that the composition is the product of thirteenth-century Spain. In fact, ever since its first appearance there have been those—both opponents of the *Zohar* and its devotees—who have questioned the second-century provenance of the work. Thanks largely to the pioneering efforts of Gershom Scholem and more recently Yehuda Liebes and Ronit Meroz, we now have a picture, still fuzzy in parts but visible nevertheless, of the origins of this masterpiece of mystical literature. While the precise details of the authorship of the *Zohar* remain a matter of debate, there seems little doubt that the major portion of the work we call *Sefer ha-Zohar* (The Book of Radiance) is to be associated with the Castilian kabbalist, Rabbi Moses de Leon. Although we do not know as much about this important figure as we would like, we do possess a number of his Hebrew writings, which treat all manner of kabbalistic themes and which, importantly, bear striking resemblance to passages in the *Zohar*. Indeed, Gershom Scholem was of the opinion that the entirety of the *Zohar*, excluding only the later strata, was to be

attributed solely to de Leon. Recent scholarship, however, while accept-
ing the centrality of Moses de Leon in the zoharic enterprise, has suggested instead that we view the *Zohar* as the work of numerous hands
and perhaps even numerous generations, a kabbalistic school or group,
not unlike the Companions themselves, who may well be a fictional representation of an actual kabbalistic fraternity from late thirteenth- and
early fourteenth-century Spain.[3] Whatever the case—and part of the joy
of the *Zohar* is that we just don't know—the composition is clearly a
pseudo-epigraphy, a work from one historical epoch (in this case, thirteenth-century Spain) that claims to hail from another (in this case,
second-century Palestine). That the work is a pseudo-epigraphy does
not of course make it a "great lie" or a "pious fraud," as Jewish histori-
ans of the nineteenth century maintained. In setting their masterpiece in
the world of the rabbis, whoever it was that wrote the *Zohar* was certainly not trying to pull the wool over our eyes. Modern notions of
authorship are very different from medieval and ancient notions of
authorship and the literary strategy of placing one's new words in the
mouth of someone old—new/ancient words as the *Zohar* would say—
has a long history in Jewish literature. In fact by placing their words in
the world of the Mishnah, the authors of the *Zohar* make a bold comment about their own work, equal in authority to the founding document of rabbinic Judaism. As Yehuda Liebes has suggested, this literary
choice reveals a certain renaissance attitude and indicates the zoharic
authors' desire to reconnect with the creative spirit of the giants of the
Mishnah.[4] As one cannot but notice upon beginning to read the composition, the *Zohar* is not a humble work but boldly proclaims its teachings, aware of its own originality and brilliance, and dares to claim as
much authority as the Mishnah and even the Torah itself.

> Happy is the generation in which Rabbi Shimon abides. Happy
> is its portion in the upper and lower worlds.
>
> About him it is written, *Happy are you O land for your
> king is a free man* (Eccles. 10:17).
>
> What is *a free man*? One who lifts his head to reveal and
> interpret things and does not fear, like one who is free and says
> what he pleases and does not fear.
>
> What is *your king*? This is Rabbi Shimon bar Yoḥai, the
> master of Torah, the master of wisdom!
>
> —*Zohar* 3:79b

> Rabbi Shimon said: All you luminaries, Companions who enter
> the holy circle, I call to witness the highest heavens and the

highest holy earth that I now see what no man has seen since
Moses ascended Mount Sinai for the second time.

For I see my face shining like the powerful light of the sun
. . .

And what's more, I know that my face is shining, while
Moses did not know, nor did he contemplate, as it is written,
Moses was not aware that the skin of his face was shining
(Exod. 34:29).

—*Zohar* 3:132b

Far from undermining our estimation of the *Zohar*, the fact that its
authors were able to convince generations of readers who thought the
work an authentic document of the second century is testament to the
literary and spiritual genius of the composition.

The *Zohar*, it should be remembered, was by no means the first
kabbalistic work. By the time it appears in the mid-1280s, Kabbalah
and the kabbalistic way of thinking and speaking about God had
already captivated the hearts and minds of Provençal and then Spanish
rabbinic elites. While the origins of Kabbalah remain shrouded in mystery, scholars today have a fairly good understanding of the spread of
this revolution within rabbinic Judaism. From *Sefer ha-Bahir* (The Book
of Brilliance), which first appeared toward the end of the twelfth century, to Nahmanides' famous yet cryptic Torah commentary "according
to the way of truth," to a variety of kabbalistic circles active in Gerona
and Castile in the middle and later parts of the thirteenth century, the
classical Kabbalah had already crystallized for nearly one hundred years
before the arrival of the *Zohar*.[5] The *Zohar* thus inherited a language
and a way of thinking and reading derived from the great works of the
earliest phase of the Spanish Kabbalah. It is to these works that we owe
the kabbalistic conception of God, at once hidden and inscrutable,
beyond the horizons of human cognition and experience—*Ein Sof*, the
infinite One—the God known only through negation, as well as a God
seeking intimacy with humanity and the world, a God complex in
nature, comprising ten powers or aspects—the sefirot—yet whose complexity is somehow close to our own human nature.

While the *Zohar* never employs the word *sefirot*, preferring instead
more colorful designations such as "levels," "rungs," "colors,"
"lights," and so forth, sefirotic language lies at the heart of the *Zohar*
and its conception of divinity. Like the kabbalists before them, the
authors of the *Zohar* experienced God as a complex and dynamic mystery. In addition to *Ein Sof*, the hidden One, "the God beyond god" to
borrow Meister Eckhart's phrase,[6] the kabbalists of the *Zohar* spoke

about divinity as a complex being. In contrast to Maimonides' absolute unity (see *Hilkhot Yesodei ha-Torah* 2:10), the *Zohar* understands divine being to be comprised of ten powers or hypostases. These powers, it should be stressed, are not merely the means through which divinity engages with the world but constitute, rather, the divine organism itself. These ten sefirot (the word derives from *Sefer Yetsirah*, an ancient work of Jewish mysticism where it means "number" or "cipher") are gendered and dynamic and it is their interrelations, figured in part as a love story full of desire, union, and separation, which drives the great drama of God. Although sefirotic language and sefirotic thinking enable an exciting and challenging way of speaking about divine reality, the language of Kabbalah can be quite complicated, especially to the neophyte.[7] It can take years of study before one cultivates an intuitive understanding of this unique mode of thinking about God without the technical details of this formal yet fluid language getting in the way. While there are any number of ways one can think about the sefirot, it can be helpful to conceptualize them as both different aspects of the divine personality (just as we are complex beings with different parts to our psyche and consciousness), as well as different moments in the passage from infinity to finitude. The sefirot thus mark the various stages in the divine unfolding, from pure infinity and nothingness into differentiated reality.

As we shall see repeatedly throughout this book, the *Zohar* understands God as a dynamic being, constantly in the process of becoming. Not unlike contemporary cosmology that views the Big Bang as an ongoing event, the God of the *Zohar* is always emerging, seeking to flow out of itself into our reality. Indeed, one of the great accomplishments of sefirotic language is precisely its ability to bring us into an awareness of the becoming of being. While we tend to think of reality as fixed and ready-made, the *Zohar* insists that God, and by extension being, is always and continuously generated from nothingness.

Lest these ideas remain abstract and mystifying, let us consider by way of example two short passages:

> Rabbi Shimon opened: *The House, in its being built, was built of stone dressed in the quarry, so no hammer, axe, or any iron tool was heard* (1 Kings 6:7) . . .
>
> When it arose in the will of the Blessed Holy One to fashion glory for Its glory, from the midst of thought a desire arose to expand—expanding from the site of concealed thought, unknown, expanding and settling in the larynx, a site continuously gushing in the mystery of the spirit of life.

When thought expanded and settled in this site, that thought was called *Elohim Ḥayyim*, Living God: *He is Living God* (Jer. 10:10).

It sought to expand and reveal Itself further; thence issued fire, air, and water, merging as one. Jacob emerged, Consummate Man, a single voice issuing audibly. Hence, thought, having been concealed in silence, was heard, revealing itself.

Thought expanded further revealing itself, and this voice struck against lips. Then speech issued, consummating all, receiving all. It is perceived that all is concealed thought, having been within, and all is one.

Once this expansion ripened, generating speech through the potency of that voice, then, *The House in its being built.*

The verse does not read, *when it was built*, but rather, *in its being built*, every single time.

—*Zohar* 1:74a (Matt, *The Zohar*)

Here, Rabbi Shimon, the grand master of the zoharic mystical fraternity, outlines the structure of divine being (i.e., the sefirot) and its expansion out of its own nothingness. The *Zohar* delights in telling this never-ending story, and repeatedly throughout the *Zohar* we find accounts of the "birth of God" as knowable divinity emerges out of the inner recesses and depths of its own nothingness. Rather than employing the formal names of the sefirot (*Ḥokhmah, Binah, Tiferet, Malkhut*, etc.), the *Zohar* here prefers their symbolic designations, Thought, Voice, and Speech, to convey the emergence of the House of God and the House of Being. While not always the case, the sefirotic symbolism informing this passage can be easily decoded. From concealed thought (*Ḥokhmah*), to the site continuously gushing (*Binah*), to Voice (*Tiferet*), and finally on to Speech (*Malkhut*), the sefirotic codes are precise and clear. The "accomplishment" of this passage, however, does not lie merely in the formal sefirotic information it conveys, but rather in its ability to help us understand the key process and dynamic of divinity— its continuous emergence and manifestation from concealment. Just like our own thinking processes that we might imagine as beginning mysteriously in the unconscious before moving to consciousness, then undergoing finer and finer articulation from voice to communicable speech, so the divine being moves from a state of mysterious concealment to actualization. This movement, our passage notes through a close reading of the verse describing the construction of the temple of Solomon that employs an unusual verbal form in the continuous present ("in its being built"), is not a singular event. It is not that divinity and reality are "born" once and for all. The mystical process of becoming, rather, is ongoing, happening here and now. As we shall see on numerous occasions in this book, the zoharic quest and the Companions' contemplative mystical goal is precisely to attain in thought and come into live contact with this quality of the becomingness or unfolding of reality.

The *Zohar* is a work of exegetical or interpretative genius, much of whose charm, besides its profound religious insights and touching narratives, lies in the way the Companions find in the verses of the Torah this extraordinary tale of divinity. It must not be forgotten that the *Zohar* is a commentary on the Torah, and the Companions uncover the hidden life of God through creative and virtuoso interpretations of scripture. Even verses seemingly devoid of mystical content are readily transformed by the wandering sages into vehicles bearing the flow of divinity. Under the Companions' "open-eyes" the verses of scripture undergo what Moshe Idel has termed a process of dynamization,[8] as static verbal combinations are enlivened, and assume a dynamic and at times quite erotic signification. Indeed the experience of understanding the *Zohar*'s reading of a particular verse is one of the great joys awaiting the *Zohar* reader. Before our very eyes the words of scripture open to a different dimension of being and grant us access to the realm of divine unfolding. The experience is a bit like looking at a computer-generated "hidden image stereogram," where at first you can't see the image that is hiding in the background, but then, when you attune your gaze (actually one needs a soft gaze or soft consciousness and this is not unlike reading the *Zohar*) you encounter a hitherto hidden world. The following more complex passage, one of hundreds that we might have chosen, illustrates this quality of zoharic interpretation:

> Rabbi Aḥa was walking on the way and Rabbi Ḥiyya and Rabbi Yose met him.
> Rabbi Aḥa said: Certainly we are three and are now fit to receive the face of *Shekhinah*.
> They joined as one and walked on.
> Rabbi Aḥa said: Let everyone say a word of the knot of Torah while we walk.
>
> Rabbi Ḥiyya opened, saying: *Pour down, O heavens, from above. Let the skies rain down righteousness. Let the earth open up and salvation sprout and let righteousness spring up together* (Isa. 45:8).
> This verse is a mystery of wisdom that we have learned from the Holy Luminary . . .

Pour down, O heavens, from above—it is written, *from above*. From *above* indeed! From the Holy Ancient One does it come, and not from the site called *heavens* . . . but from *above*, precisely.

Let the skies rain down (yizlu) righteousness—when the *heavens* receive from *above*, from the supernal site that abides above them, then *the skies rain down righteousness*.

What are *the skies*? The site where they grind manna for the righteous . . .

For whom? For the site called *Righteous One*, for they grind the manna that comes from *above*, and all the goodness is gathered in them to bestow it on the rung of *Righteous One*, so that *Righteousness* will be blessed from their flow (*nezilu*) . . .

Who are the righteous? This is *Righteous One (Tzaddik) and Righteousness (Tzedek)*, Joseph and Rachel, for when they unite as one, they are called righteous (*tzaddikim*) . . .

Then, *let the earth open up*—below,

and salvation sprout—for the people of the world.

And let righteousness (tzedakah) spring up together—all love and all the goodness of the world increase and humankind's nourishment abounds in the world. Then joy is added to joy and all the worlds are blessed.

Rabbi Aḥa said: Had I come only to hear this, it would be enough!

—*Zohar* 3:25b–26a

In this brief exegetical narrative we find once again the story of the downward flow of divinity—from *above*, the Holy Ancient One, the most recondite aspect of divinity, through the *heavens*, the sefirah *Tiferet*, onward to the *skies*, the sefirot *Nezaḥ* and *Hod*, into *righteous one*, the divine phallus and conduit of the divine flow, and finally, into *righteousness*, the last sefirah *Malkhut*, from which the divine being pours down into our reality. This outpouring of divinity is also erotic, predicated on the sexual union of Joseph and Rachel, the male and female aspects of God. The beautiful verse from Isaiah—"Pour down O heavens from above, let the skies rain down righteousness"—thus becomes for Rabbi Ḥiyya a portal into a dynamic and erotic realm, recounting the flow of being through the various grades of divinity and on to humanity below. Like Rabbi Aḥa the reader too is overwhelmed by the ingenuity of Rabbi Ḥiyya's exegetical craft.

If the *Zohar*'s interpretations of Torah are brilliant and daring, its broader literary setting—a group of sages wandering across the landscape—is equally original and exciting. One of the exceptional features of the *Zohar* is without doubt the location of its many narratives and homilies. Not even once throughout its more than a thousand folio pages do we encounter the Companions in a traditional Jewish setting—the house of study or the house of prayer. Rather, we find the Companions in one of two situations—studying Torah from midnight till dawn or walking on the way. *Zohar* scholars have analyzed this curious literary choice—to set the deepest mysteries of Torah away from the key institutions of Jewish life—from numerous perspectives.[9] Some have seen in this literary strategy a critique of the kind of text study and Jewish learning regnant in the *Zohar*'s day—legalistic, confined to the *beit midrash*, and devoid of real contact with life, the world and God—while others have viewed the recourse to the way as a literary analogue to the *Zohar*'s interpretive and religious spirit—wandering, open to innovation and surprise, fluid and dynamic. Although the *Zohar* is certainly the first Jewish work to celebrate the way or the journey as *the* primary locus for mystical knowledge and insight, there is, nevertheless, a Jewish prehistory to this idea. The *Shema*, the Jewish catechism and proclamation of divine unity recited twice daily, already contains the injunction to speak words of Torah "when you sit in your house and when you walk on the way" (Deut. 6:4–9), to which the rabbis of the Talmud added their own distinctive formulations.[10] The prototype for the zoharic journey narrative, however, is to be found in a well-known tale appearing in the Babylonian Talmud in tractate *Ḥagiga* (14b), in the chapter describing the "Work of the Chariot" and the "Work of the Beginning," the rabbinic terms for esoteric mystical teachings. In this short and wonderful account, we find many of the characteristics of the mystical narratives as they will appear in the *Zohar*—two or more sages on a journey, Torah learning that brings about the presence of the *Shekhinah*, as well as considerable pathos.

> Our rabbis taught: A story of Rabbi Yoḥanan ben Zakkai who was riding on a donkey when going on a journey, and Rabbi El'azar ben Arakh was driving the donkey from behind.
>
> [Rabbi El'azar] said to him: Master, teach me a chapter of the Work of the Chariot.
>
> He said to him: Have I not taught you thus: Nor the Work of the Chariot in the presence of one, unless he is a sage and understands of his own knowledge?

[Rabbi El'azar] said to him: Master, permit me to say before you something that you have taught me.

He said to him: Say.

Immediately Rabbi Yoḥanan dismounted from the donkey and wrapped himself [in his prayer shawl] and sat upon a stone beneath an olive tree.

[Rabbi El'azar] said to him: Why did you dismount from the donkey?

He answered: Is it proper that while you are expounding the Work of the Chariot and the *Shekhinah* is with us and the ministering angels accompany us, I should ride on the donkey?!

Immediately Rabbi El'azar began his exposition of the Work of the Chariot and fire came down from heaven and encompassed all the trees in the field that burst into song . . .

Rabbi Yoḥanan ben Zakkai rose and kissed him on his head and said: Blessed be the Lord, God of Israel, who has given a son to Abraham our father, who knows to speculate upon, to investigate, and expound the Work of the Chariot!

In setting their own esoteric lore on the way, the authors of the *Zohar* thus position themselves within the oldest mystical tradition of Judaism, a tradition extending back to Yoḥanan ben Zakkai, the founder of Rabbinic Judaism, about whom it is written that he knew "the speech of the ministering angels and the speech of the palm trees" (BT *Sukka* 28a).

Whatever the origins of this literary motif, it is, as Melila Hellner-Eshed has so beautifully observed, the consciousness of the way that is decisive.[11] According to the *Zohar*, the world is best experienced from the changing vantages of a wanderer. Only the traveler has the fresh eyes, the unique perspective, from which the deepest dimensions of reality and Torah can be fathomed. One must know how to read the Torah *be-oraḥ keshot*, according to the true way, and to do so, one must *azil be-orḥa*, walk the way. Not unlike a thirteenth-century *Zen and the Art of Motorcycle Maintenance*, the *Zohar* encourages us to step out, open our eyes, and experience the diversity of being. A well-known passage presents this experiential manifesto of the *Zohar* most beautifully:

But the path of the righteous is like radiant sunlight, ever brightening until noon, the way of the wicked is all darkness (Prov. 4:18–19) . . .

The path of the righteous—what is the difference between path and way?

They have already clarified the matter, but a path is that which has just now been opened and revealed, and was made in that place a path, where no feet have trodden before.

Way (derekh), as it is written, *as one who treads (dorekh) in the winepress* (Isa. 63:1), where the feet of all who wish tread.

That is why where the righteous walk is called *path (orah)*, since they were the first to open that place. And even when others, the people of the world, walk in that place, now that the righteous walk there it becomes a new place, for now that place is new as though never trodden on by any before, because the righteous invigorate that place through the sublime words in which the Blessed Holy One delights.

And what's more, the *Shehkinah* goes in that place, which was not the case before. And that is why it is called *the path (orah) of the righteous*, because the sublime holy guest (*oreah*) visits there.

—*Zohar* 2:215a

Unlike the biblical verse that is built on the opposition between the righteous and the wicked, Rabbi Shimon's exposition turns on his distinguishing between path (*orah*) and way (*derekh*). Where the wicked walk the road more traveled, the righteous—the mystics—are trailblazers who seek interpretative and experiential originality. God, according to this text, delights in newness and innovation and the mystical-creative task is thus "to boldly go where no one has gone before." Our creativity, the "sublime words" we innovate on the way, brings about the indwelling of the *Shekhinah*, the divine presence in the world. As expressed in the beautiful formulation of this passage: we walk the path (*orah*) to bring about the presence of the guest (*oreah*). We are thus the means through which the divine acquires new knowledge and experience of being. We are, as it were, the eyes of God.

In addition to the setting of the *Zohar's* many narratives, the formal structure of these compositions also plays an important role in conveying the *Zohar's* mystical goals. As we shall see, although *Zohar* narratives are frequently surprising and the homilies contained within them playful, even improvisational, zoharic narratives do, nevertheless, follow a tight structure. The classical zoharic narrative, of which there are dozens if not hundreds, conventionally begins with two or more of the Companions walking on the way. Either in response to some event that befalls them on their journey or, more simply, in the course of their wanderings, one of the sages invites his fellow traveler to "engage words of Torah, words of the Ancient of Days" as one passage puts it. The Companions then begin to discuss Torah, examining and interpreting her verses in new and surprising ways. Usually, after a series of expositions, the Companions chance upon another wanderer, in the main not associated with the zoharic fraternity. Be it an encounter with an old man, a donkey driver, a desert hermit, some traveling merchants, or even, as happens on numerous occasions, a young child, *Zohar* narratives are punctuated by a key turning point where some "external" force enters the back and forth of the Companions' expositions and alters the course of the unfolding interpretative events. The Companions, for their part, usually greet these anonymous wandering types with scorn and derision, assuming that they cannot possibly have anything to learn from anyone outside their own elite circle. It is then—on cue every time—that the tables are turned and, in what has been aptly described as a carnivalesque switch, the outsiders become the masters, revealing a new insight, more subtle and profound than that uncovered by the Companions themselves. As readers we await and then delight in this narrative twist, sharing the Companions' response of surprise as we too experience the new apprehension of the verses or themes being discussed. Zoharic narratives thus possess a structure of intensification, a deepening, an "aha" moment, as along with the Companions and thanks to the outsider, we see something we didn't see before. By way of example, let us consider a short narrative unit, which aside from demonstrating the format and mode of zoharic narrative, also presents the central theurgic task to adorn and beautify God through mystical-poetic creativity.

Rabbi Yose and Rabbi Ḥiyya were walking on the way and a donkey driver was goading behind them.

Rabbi Yose said to Rabbi Ḥiyya: We should engage and ply words of Torah, for the Blessed Holy One goes before us; therefore it is time to make an adornment for Him with us on this way.

Rabbi Ḥiyya opened, saying: *Time to act for YHVH, they have violated Your Torah* (Ps. 119:126). This verse has been established by the Companions.

But, *Time to act for YHVH (et la-asot le-YHVH)*—whenever Torah abides in the world and human beings engage her, the Blessed Holy One, so to speak, rejoices in the work of His hands, and rejoices in all the worlds, and heaven and earth abide in their place.

What's more, the Blessed Holy One assembles His entire court and says to them: Look at the holy people I have on the earth, for My Torah is adorned by them. Look at the work of My hands, about whom you said, *What is man that You are mindful of him?* (Ps. 8:5).

And these, when they see the joy of their Master in His people, immediately open and say, *Who is like Your people Israel, a unique nation on earth!* (2 Sam. 7:23).

But when Israel desists from Torah, His strength, so to speak, is weakened, as it is written, *You have weakened the rock that bore you* (Deut. 32:18) . . . and therefore, *It is time to act for YHVH.*

The remaining righteous must gird their loins and perform good deeds so that the Blessed Holy One will be strengthened through them . . . What is the reason? Because *they have violated Your Torah,* and the people of the world do not engage her fittingly.

The donkey driver who was goading behind them said to them: If it pleases you, there is one question I wish to know.

Rabbi Yose said: Certainly the way is adorned before us! Ask your question.

He said: Regarding this verse, were it written *one must act* or *we will act,* I would say so. But what is *time [to act for YHVH]?*

Furthermore, *to act for YHVH?* It should have said, *before YHVH.* What is the meaning of *to act for YHVH?*

Rabbi Yose said: With numerous hues the way is adorned before us! First, for we were two and now are three and the *Shekhinah* is included with us. Second, for we thought that you were nothing but a parched tree, yet you are fresh like an olive. And third, for you have asked fittingly, and since you have begun a word, say on.

He opened, saying: *Time to act for YHVH, they have violated Your Torah.*

Time to act for YHVH (et la-asot le-YHVH)—there is a time and there is a time, *a time to love and a time to hate* (Eccles. 3:8). There is a time above, and this time is a mystery of faith, and it is called, *a time of favor (et ratzon)* (Ps. 69:14). And this is that a person is required to love God constantly, as it is said, *And you shall love YHVH your God* (Deut. 6:5).

Therefore, *a time to love*, this is the time that a person is required to love.

There is another time that is the mystery of other gods that a person is required to hate, and his heart should not be drawn after it. Therefore, *a time to hate*. And because of this it is written, *Tell your brother Aaron that he is not to come at any time into the sanctuary* (Lev. 16:2).

When Israel engage Torah and the commandments of the Torah, this *time*, the mystery of holy faith, is arrayed in her arrayal and adorned in perfection as is fitting.

And when Israel desist from Torah, this *time*, so to speak, is not arrayed and does not abide in perfection and light, and then, *Time to act for YHVH*.

What is *to act for (la-asot)*? As it is said, *that Elohim created to make (la-asot)* (Gen. 2:3). What is *to make*? The bodies of the demons remained, for the day had been sanctified and they had not been made, and they remained *to make,* spirits without bodies. So here, *time to act* remains un-arrayed and without perfection. What is the reason? For *they have violated Your Torah*—because Israel desisted below from words of Torah; because this *time* abides, either ascending or descending, on account of Israel.

Rabbi Yose and Rabbi Ḥiyya came and kissed him on his head.

Rabbi Yose said: Certainly it is not right that you goad behind us! Blessed is this way that we merited to hear this! Blessed is the generation in which Rabbi Shimon abides, for even among the mountains wisdom is found!

Rabbi Yose and Rabbi Ḥiyya dismounted and the three of them walked on the way . . .

—*Zohar* 2:155b–156a

This particular narrative, which in fact extends beyond the portion we have excerpted here, begins in classical zoharic fashion. Rabbi Ḥiyya and Rabbi Yose, two of the more colorful characters in the mystical fraternity, are walking on the way accompanied by an anonymous donkey driver to whom they of course pay no attention. The invocation to ply Torah is here embellished with the additional mystical-mythical expression of providing an adornment, a *tikkun*, for the Blessed Holy One. The word *tikkun*, now part of contemporary Jewish language through the expression *tikkun olam*, healing the world, means something quite different in the *Zohar* where its semantic range spans adornment, garment, arrayal, and rectification. The Companions' central preoccupation throughout the *Zohar* is to bring about the unification of the male and female aspects of divinity, a task they accomplish primarily through their interpretations of Torah. Exegesis in the *Zohar* is a creative affair and the Companions seek not only to create new Torah, to uncover hidden dimensions in her verses, words, and coronets, but also to create an adornment, to array and beautify *Malkhut*, the *Shekhinah*, the female aspect of God, in preparation for union with her partner the Blessed Holy One, the male grade of divinity. According to the *Zohar*, the Companions' mystical-poetic creativity actually impacts upon the divine world and stimulates the sexual union of the male and female within God. That human beings have the capacity (and responsibility) to influence divinity is one of the radical innovations of kabbalistic thought. Far indeed from the God of Maimonides who, like Aristotle's unmoved mover, is not influenced one jot by the affairs of humanity—"for all beings are in need of Him, but He, blessed be He, is not in need of them"[12]—the God of the *Zohar* is intimately involved with our lives and in fact depends on humanity for perfection, union, and actualization. The divine destiny is in our hands and astonishingly depends on our literary creativity and ingenuity for its fulfilment.

Following the opening narrative frame, Rabbi Ḥiyya begins his exposition, taking as his verse, "time to act for YHVH, they have violated Your Torah" (Ps. 119:126). This verse has a fascinating history. It was expounded by the rabbis to permit the violation of the Torah under certain circumstances—"time to act for YHVH, violate Your Torah!"—and was even used by Maimonides in the introduction to *The Guide of the Perplexed* to justify his disclosure of concealed matters.[13] In fact, in the *Idra Rabba* (*Zohar* 3:127b), the pinnacle moment of the entire *Zohar* narrative, when the Companions all assemble for a never to be repeated disclosure of mysteries, Rabbi Shimon too begins his address with the same stirring verse. Rabbi Ḥiyya's interpretation, however, pursues a different tack and takes us to the heart of the mutually dependent relationship between God and the people of Israel, as God both delights in and is strengthened by the act of Torah study below. In the theurgic language of our passage, "heaven and earth abide in their place," signifying both the maintenance of the cosmos as a whole as well as harmony between the male and female elements of divinity. One must thus act *for YHVH*, because divinity is dependent on humanity and in particular on our Torah adornments. Not to do so, to *violate Your Torah*, is to weaken and detract from the divine essence. Indeed, it is because the majority of the world "does not engage her fittingly" and she, the Torah, lies unadorned that Rabbi

Ḥiyya and Rabbi Yose must now *act for YHVH*. While theurgy—the idea that what we do below impacts on high in the divine realm—is often thought of as a kabbalistic innovation, we can find fragments of this mythological view in the world of rabbinic culture. As Moshe Idel has convincingly demonstrated, the rabbis too, on occasion, understand their actions to influence the divine destiny.

> Rabbi Azariah said in the name of Rabbi Yehuda bar Simon: So long as the righteous act according to the will of heaven, they add power to the Dynamis, as it is written, *And so, let the Lord's power, pray, be great* (Num. 14:17). And if they do not act accordingly it is as if *you have weakened the Rock that formed you* (Deut. 32:18).
>
> —*Pesikta de-Rav Kahana* 26[14]

In the *Zohar*, of course, this view becomes central and the idea that the destiny of God lies in our hands runs through the entire composition.

Although Rabbi Ḥiyya's opening exposition is neat and nice and even very zoharic it is by no means dazzling. Aside from conveying the important zoharic principle of human-divine interdependence mediated by our mystical-poetic creativity, there are no astonishing insights into the words of the verse he expounds. It is then to the donkey driver that the deepest revelations and innovations belong. Overhearing the sages' mystical discourse, the donkey driver interjects and insists on an explanation for the precise wording of the verse just expounded. Why does the verse, he asks, use the expression *to act for* and why the word *time*? There must be a deeper meaning to this arrangement. The donkey driver's exposition is, as we come to expect, surprising, innovative, and exegetically precise. In fact, by the time he completes his thought, we have an entirely new appreciation of the verse from Psalms, which we now understand refers to subtle processes within the Godhead. The word *time, et* / עת, the donkey driver says, is "a mystery of faith," by which he means that it symbolizes a particular sefirah within the divine being. As we find elsewhere in the *Zohar*, *time* is one of the key designations for *Malkhut*, the partner of *Tiferet* symbolized chiefly through the epithet *YHVH*, and Israel's theurgic task is none other than to array and adorn this *time*, the *Shekhinah*, through Torah study and performance of the commandments. (Paralleling this *time to love*, that is the time that we are commanded to love, is a *time to hate*, the shadowy evil double of the divine—"other gods"—the realm of the demonic and impure.) The last of the sefirot and the aspect of divinity with which the human being most readily comes into contact, the *Shekhinah/Malkhut* is the great heroine of the *Zohar*, and it is her existential situation spanning desire, delight, union, longing, exile, alienation, and pain that perhaps marks the central drama in the composition. Positioned at the limits of divinity, the divine female is the most dynamic (and interesting) aspect of God. Like the ever changing moon, which possesses no light of its own but reflects the brilliance of the sun, *Malkhut* is dependent on the influx of the sefirot above her for illumination. She is also dependent on the mystics below, "her handmaidens" as one text calls them, to protect, sustain, and beautify her in preparation for her union with *YHVH*, the Blessed Holy One, the male face of divinity. It is she that the Companions must always tend to and *act for* and it is she who is referred to by the word *time* in the verse from Psalms.

Having uncovered the deeper meaning of the opening word in Rabbi Ḥiyya's verse, the donkey driver proceeds to explain the mystical significance of the expression, *to act for*, *la-asot*. Like the word *time*, this word has a mystical signification, and in explicating it the donkey driver sends us to a well-known verse from Genesis recounting the completion of creation: "And God blessed the seventh day and declared it holy, because on it He ceased from all His work that God created to make (*la-asot*)" (Gen. 2:3). While the verse from Genesis is well known and is recited as part of the Friday night Kiddush ceremony, the verse is actually quite enigmatic. The last word, *la-asot*, to make, seems out of place, superfluous, and incomplete. The rabbis of late antiquity also noticed this oddity from which they derived the following fascinating mythical theme:

> It is not written here, *that God created and made*, but rather *to make* (Gen. 2:3), for the Sabbath came first, with the work not yet completed.
>
> Rabbi Benaya said: This refers to the demons, for He created their souls, and as He was creating their bodies, the Sabbath day was hallowed. He left them and they remained soul without body.
>
> —*Tanḥuma* (Buber), Genesis 17[15]

The rabbis thus find in the "dangling" and incomplete *la-asot* a reference to the incompleteness of creation—creation is a task to be completed by us—as well as more specifically a reference to demons, who are themselves understood as a kind of incomplete creation, souls without bodies. In a display of exegetical ingenuity, the donkey driver connects this notion of *la-asot* as incompleteness and that which remains to be done with *time*, the sefirah *Malkhut*, herself incomplete and un-arrayed, dependent on the people of Israel for her perfection, "because this *time* abides, either ascending or descending, on account of Israel." The verse from Psalms, "time to act for YHVH," having been adequately expounded by Rabbi Ḥiyya, is now revealed to contain something more, encoding the mystical quest to array and beautify *time*, the *Shekhinah*, who on account of her imperfection and incompleteness needs to be *acted for* to bring her into union with the Blessed Holy One, *YHVH*. The donkey driver thus takes our understanding to another level—zooming in on a detail that we previously did not notice, and before our eyes the verse morphs and is revealed to contain a profound secret. This structure of intensification is repeated hundreds of times throughout the *Zohar* and is one of the key performative strategies of the composition, reminding us as readers of the ever present possibility of a deeper consciousness and apprehension of both the verses of the Torah and reality as a whole.

·•·

The *Zohar* is a work of great beauty, of spiritual subtlety, depth, and abiding relevance, yet it remains largely unknown and inaccessible beyond the confines of the academic world. There are good reasons for this. The *Zohar* is, as we have begun to see, an extremely complex work, written in a specialized symbolic language that treats of the greatest mysteries of God and the Torah. Deciphering a *Zohar* passage requires a deep familiarity with the Bible, rabbinic literature, and medieval Jewish thought, not to mention an intuitive and hard-won familiarity with kabbalistic language. That the *Zohar*'s teachings should remain solely in the scholarly domain is a great shame, as the *Zohar* offers us today, as it has to its readers for more than seven hundred years, a view of religious life unrivaled (at least in the Jewish canon) in its imagination, daring, and insight. Although the *Zohar* has been blessed with an awesome cadre of commentators—both medieval and modern—the general reader has nearly no way of accessing this mystical classic, despite some notable exceptions.[16] *Zohar* scholarship, which has attracted some of the greatest minds in Jewish studies, has not concerned itself with making its insights and discoveries amenable to a general readership and has been concerned instead with the kinds of questions that are quite properly the focus of academic work. This book seeks to redress this void and aims to open the mysterious, wondrous, and at times bewildering universe of one of the masterpieces of world mystical literature. Given the great luminaries who have explicated the world of the *Zohar*, it is not the intention of this study to present any radically new thesis about the *Zohar*. My aim, rather, is to mediate the

Zohar itself, as well as the body of fascinating scholarship surrounding it—a body of literature beginning with the pioneering works of Gershom Scholem and Isaiah Tishby and continuing in our days with the works of Moshe Idel, Yehuda Liebes, Elliot Wolfson, and my teacher Melila Hellner-Eshed. My focus on zoharic exegetical narrative with particular emphasis on the literary and performative elements of the composition does, however, offer a new mode of *Zohar* analysis and has the additional advantage of providing nonspecialists a much clearer view into the world of the *Zohar* than is currently available.[17]

That spiritual seeking ought to be mediated by critical scholarship might seem puzzling to some. Religion is often hostile to such scholarship, which tends to historicize, categorize, and relativize religious texts, often at the expense of the wonder that lies at the heart of the spiritual life. We are, as Nietzsche said, "by nature winged creatures and honey-gatherers of the spirit,"[18] and we need spiritual guides and spiritual works. Spiritual heights, however, especially when they border on the super-rational, must be mediated by responsible and critical scholarship. Religious life need not be naïve but can and ought to be informed by the best of scholarly research, just as the wonder of the cosmos is intensified by the dazzling discoveries of scientific research. Of course, scholarship can get in the way and religious insights—philosophical and mystical—are all too often hidden and buried in scholarly literature. Yet the attempt to produce readings informed by critical-historical scholarship, but which seek, nevertheless, to access the profound teachings found in religious texts strikes me as more important now than ever before. It is this sense of a mystery without mystification that this book seeks to present.

More than fifty years ago the great scholar-mystic-activist Abraham Joshua Heschel reminded us, as Plato already said, that everything begins or ought to begin in wonder.[19] To be authentic and alive religious life must, he argued, find its way back to the sense of mystery and radical amazement at being. According to Heschel, modern man is in a state slumber—"sleep is in their sockets," as the *Zohar* says—and the need of the hour is to awaken and arouse to the primal mystery of reality. For many Jews, and I suspect for many non-Jews raised with traditional religious upbringings, religion, at least the way we encounter it in school, the synagogue, church, or mosque, is devoid of wonder and mystery. Religions tend to present themselves as ready-made truths, static statements of belief, and inflexible codes of action. But religious life is a journey, full of surprise and wonder. More than any Jewish work I know, the *Zohar* has the capacity to open us to these dimensions of experience. As the *Zohar* says repeatedly, "the world abides because of the mystery."

The last decade has, as is well known, seen an explosion of Kabbalah into popular culture. One cannot go into a bookstore today without encountering dozens of books on the Kabbalah. Kabbalah, it has been said, is to the first decade of the twenty-first century what Tibetan Buddhism was to the eighties and nineties of the last century.[20] I certainly do not wish to criticize this New Age Kabbalah. I know that there are both traditionalists and scholars who scoff at this movement. And while I understand their reservations and am yet to be convinced of the depth and profundity of these New Age kabbalistic fusions, I see no reason why people of all faiths and backgrounds should not find what they can in the kabbalistic tradition. For more than five hundred years, ever since the first Christian kabbalists and the Hermetic Qabbalists who succeeded them, people of all kinds have turned to the Kabbalah for inspiration to create their own contemporary Kabbalahs. But this is best done by going back to the source—and the *Zohar* is most definitely the source of sources, the root of roots—which outshines and outdazzles all contemporary distillations. The *Zohar* is much more than a work of kabbalistic doctrine, and the experience of reading the *Zohar* cannot be reduced to teachings, concepts, or spiritual guidebooks, however well intentioned.

Each chapter of this book presents an extended zoharic narrative followed by a discursive commentary. Zoharic narratives are rarely presented as integral literary units (scholars tend to examine isolated themes, motifs, and principles), yet it is precisely in the zoharic narrative flow, as story and exegesis fuse, that the charm of the *Zohar* is most apparent. It is this flow that I have sought to present. The narratives were all selected primarily because of their beauty as well as their capacity to demonstrate the diversity of the zoharic world. I have also chosen short to mid-length zoharic units; the longer and more complex narratives in the *Zohar*, some of which extend for dozens of folio pages, too unwieldy for a work of this kind. The commentary is intended as a step-by-step guide through the labyrinth of these passages, pointing out the subtle moves of the text, its exegetical strategies, symbolic terms, enigmatic turns of phrase, and thematic connections. While the chapters do, to a degree, flow on from one another and build on themes encountered earlier, one need not read them in sequence. Each chapter may be considered a stand alone mystical meditation. It is, however, important to read each narrative carefully and slowly. The *Zohar* is a literary delight and beyond its specific teachings, ought to read by savoring its brilliant and diverse images and subtle insights. *Zohar* texts do not yield their secrets easily and the reader must persevere, patiently encountering their multiple levels of meaning.

The translations presented here are all my own and are based on standard printed editions of the *Zohar*. Two of the narratives are, as far as I know, appearing in English for the first time, while the remainder have only been partially or inadequately rendered in the past. As anyone who has ever tried to translate the *Zohar* can attest, one does so only with considerable trepidation. The *Zohar* has its own unique cadence and rhythm, a special feel, which one fears is lost in translation. I am reminded of Cervantes' wonderful observation in *Don Quixote*, another and in some sense similar Spanish book of journeys, where *el caballero andante*, the wandering knight, beautifully captures our problem:

> It seems to me that translating from one language to another . . . is like viewing Flemish tapestries from the wrong side, when, although one can make out the figures, they are covered by threads that obscure them, and one cannot appreciate the smooth finish of the right side.[21]

The difficulties in translating the *Zohar* are made all the more acute in light of the wonderful English translation that is now emerging, volume by volume, by Daniel C. Matt.[22] Matt's poetic translations, about which we can only say, "the voice of the turtledove is now heard in our land" (Song of Songs 2:12), are unparalleled, and will surely become canonical in the English-speaking world. However, the completion of Matt's project is still some ten or more years off and at present only the first third of the *Zohar* has been translated. My own translations follow many of Matt's innovations and novel solutions to particular zoharic problems and I am heavily indebted to him. In these translations I have not tried to smooth out some of the curious, odd, and sometimes down-right bizarre verbal and syntactical constructions often encountered in the *Zohar*. While the *Zohar* should be accessible, it should also be strange and foreign—other-worldly—as befits a work of great mystery and enigma.

The Baal Shem Tov, the founder of the Hasidic movement, once commented that the original radiance of creation, the light concealed by God for the righteous in the world to come, is actually hidden within the pages of the *Zohar*.[23] While we read the *Zohar* for many different reasons—to learn, to be challenged intellectually, to be amused, and to be delighted—we read it above all because it has the capacity to generate within us an experience of something wonderful and profound, that original radiance of creation.

Let us now begin to walk on the way . . .

•◆•

CHAPTER TWO

In the Mountains of Kurdistan

Reading Torah with the Companions

Zohar 3:149a–150b

Rabbi El'azar, Rabbi Yose, and Rabbi Yitzḥak were walking on the way.

They encountered the mountains of Kurdistan.

While they were walking, Rabbi El'azar raised his eyes and saw those high mountains and they were dark.

They were seized with fear.

Rabbi El'azar said to the Companions: Were father here I would not be afraid but since we are three and words of Torah are between us judgment is not present here.

Rabbi El'azar opened, saying: *In the seventh month on the seventeenth day of the month, the ark came to rest on the mountains of Ararat* (Gen. 8:4).

How beloved are the words of Torah?! For in each and every word there are supernal mysteries, and the Torah is called the supernal principle (*kelala ila'a*).

And we have learned in the thirteen attributes of Torah—*anything that was included in a general statement (kelal) but was then singled out from the general statement in order to teach something, was not singled out to teach only about itself, but to apply its teaching to the entire generality.*

23

As for the Torah, which is the supernal principle, even though a story of the world is singled out from it, it certainly does not come to present that story, but rather to present supernal matters, supernal mysteries; and *it was not singled out to teach only about itself but to apply its teaching to the entire generality,* because that story of Torah, or that narrative, even though it was singled out from the generality (*kelal*) of Torah, was not singled out to present only about itself, but rather was singled out to present about the supernal principle of Torah in its entirety.

Like that which is written, *In the seventh month on the seventeenth day of the month, the ark came to rest on the mountains of Ararat* (Gen. 8:4).
Certainly this verse was singled out from the generality of Torah and comes in a story of the world.
What does it matter to us if it rests here or there?! It must have rested somewhere!
But to apply its teaching to the entire generality.
Happy are Israel for they have been given a supernal Torah, a Torah of truth!
As for the one who says that the story of Torah comes only to present that story alone—may his spirit deflate!
For if it were so she would not be a supernal Torah, a Torah of truth.
Ah, but certainly the Torah is holy, supernal; she is a Torah of truth.

Come and see:
A king of flesh and blood—it is not dignified for him to speak of common matters, all the more so to write them.
If it should enter your mind that the supernal king, the Blessed Holy One, had no supernal matters to write and with which to make a Torah, but gathered all the words of commoners [or: ordinary words], like the words of Esau, the words of Hagar, the words of Laban with Jacob, the words of the ass, the words of Bilaam, the words of Balak, the words of Zimri, and assembled them and all the other stories that are written and made from them a Torah, if so, why is she called a *Torah of truth* (Mal. 2:6)?
The Torah of YHVH is perfect . . . the testimony of YHVH is enduring . . . the precepts of YHVH are just . . . the instruction of YHVH is lucid . . . the fear of YHVH is pure . . . the judgments of YHVH are true (Ps. 19:8–10); and it is written, *more desirable than gold, than much fine gold* (ibid.:11).
These are the words of Torah.

Certainly the Torah is holy, she is supernal, a Torah of truth.
The Torah of YHVH is perfect—each and every word comes to present supernal matters, and that word of that story does not come to present itself alone, but rather comes to present the generality, as we have established.

Come and see:
In the seventh month on the seventeenth day of the month, the ark came to rest on the mountains of Ararat (Gen. 8:4).
So it is with this verse, how much more so with others!
At the time when judgment hovers over the world and judgments abide, and the Blessed Holy One sits on His throne of judgment to judge the world, within that throne, the treasury of the King, numerous records are inscribed and numerous notes are concealed.
All the books that are opened are concealed there; and therefore nothing is forgotten by the King.
This throne is not arrayed and does not abide except in the seventh month, which is the day of judgment, a day on which all the people of the world are reckoned.
They all pass before that throne.
About this [it is written], *In the seventh month . . . the ark came to rest*—in the seventh month, indeed, for it is the judgment of the world.
On the mountains of Ararat—those masters of judgment, masters of the groan and moan, and they all are present on that day before the Blessed Holy One.
Many shield-bearing warriors are aroused on that day and all stand beneath the throne in judgment on the world.
On that day Israel offer up prayer and plead and beseech before Him, they blow the shofar and the Blessed Holy One has mercy on them and transforms judgment into mercy.
All the upper and lower realms open and say: *Happy is the people who know the joyful shout (tru'ah)* (Ps. 89:10).
Therefore it is necessary on that day that the one who performs the trumpeting know the essence of the matter and direct his mind in the *tru'ah* and perform the matter with wisdom.
Therefore it is written, *Happy is the people who know the joyful shout* and not who perform the joyful shout, as has been said.

They walked on that entire day.
When night fell they ascended to a certain place and found a cave.
Rabbi El'azar said: Let someone enter the cave if perchance he may find a site that is more fittingly arrayed.

Rabbi Yose entered and saw another cave within, the light of a candle glowing inside.

He heard a voice saying: *Be-ha'alotekha, When you light the lamps, the seven lamps will give light at the front of the lamp stand* (Num. 8:2).

Here the Assembly of Israel receives the light and the Supernal Mother is crowned and all the lights radiate from Her.

In Her two small glowing marshals fly, wedding attendants, linking all upward and from there below.

Rabbi Yose heard and rejoiced and approached Rabbi El'azar.

Rabbi El'azar said to him: Let us enter for the Blessed Holy One has appointed for us this day that miracles befall us.

They entered.

When they entered they saw two people plying Torah.

Rabbi El'azar said: *How precious is Your loving-kindness O God, human beings shelter in the shadow of Your wings* (Ps. 36:8).

They [the two people] arose and they all sat down and rejoiced.

Rabbi El'azar said: *How precious is Your loving-kindness O God*—that I found you.

The Blessed Holy One has shown us loving-kindness in this place.

Now light the lamps!

Rabbi Yose opened, saying:

Be-ha'alotekha, When you light the lamps—*be-ha'alotekha, when you elevate*, literally, [that is] when you light.

For behold the priest performs two services as one, a single bond.

And what are they?

Oil and incense, as it is written, *Oil and incense rejoice the heart* (Prov. 27:9).

It is written, *Aaron shall burn upon it aromatic incense, morning after morning, when he dresses (be-heitivo) the lamps he shall burn it* (Exod. 30:7) and it is written, *And when Aaron lights (be-ha'alot) the lamps at twilight he shall burn it* (ibid. 30:8).

What is the difference between what is written here, *when he dresses (be-heitivo)*, and what is written there, *when he lights (be-ha'alot)*?

Rabbi Yehudah said: It is all one.

Rabbi Yose said: *Be-heitivo, when he dresses*—as it is said, *For your loving is better (tovim) than wine* (Song of Songs 1:2).

Tovim—saturated with wine, as it is said, *For we were satiated and were good (tovim)* (Jer. 44:17).

Rabbi Yehudah said: *Hatavah, dressing / making good*, literally, as it is said, *a good-hearted person is a continuous feast* (Prov. 15:15).

When he lights (be-ha'alot)—when they are watered and saturated from the waters of the river, then the supernal beings elevate (*ila'in iluya*) and blessings are found in all of them and joy in all, and therefore it is written, *be-ha'alot—when he elevates.*

Rabbi Aḥa said: When the Depth of All illuminates it irradiates the river, and the river flows on in a straight path to water all.

Then it is written, *be-ha'alot, when he elevates,* (alt., *be-heitivo,* when he dresses) for from the Depth of All they issue forth;

be-ha'alot, when he elevates, which comes from the supernal facet of the Depth of All that is called Thought.

It is all one matter.

Then the Assembly of Israel is blessed and blessings are found in all the worlds.

Commentary on *Zohar* 3:149a–150b

In the zoharic unit known as *Rav Metivta*, the Master of the Academy, we find a short yet particularly beautiful paean to the Torah uttered by Rabbi Shimon, the grand master of the zoharic mystical fraternity.[1] In a rare moment of solitude, Rabbi Shimon weeps as he contemplates the sublime nature of the Torah, and for a brief moment we are granted a glimpse of his private yearning:

> Rabbi Shimon cried and wept.
> He opened, saying: *A loving doe, a graceful mountain goat. Let her breasts satisfy you at all times, be infatuated with love of her always* (Prov. 5:19).
> Torah, Torah, light of all worlds!
> How many oceans and streams, springs and fountains spread forth from you in all directions?!
> All is from you, on you depend the upper and lower realms, a supernal light issues from you.
> Torah, Torah, what can I say to you?
> You are a loving doe and a graceful mountain goat.
> Above and below are your lovers.
> Who will merit to suckle from you as is fitting?
> Torah, Torah, delight of your Master,
> Who is able to reveal and utter your secrets and mysteries?!
> He cried and placed his head between his knees and kissed the earth.
>
> —*Zohar* 3:166b

Rabbi Shimon's paean displays many of the *Zohar*'s fundamental attitudes toward the Torah. Far from being merely a book of narratives and legal injunctions, the Torah is presented here as both beloved and mother, the ultimate object of Rabbi Shimon's erotic desires as well as the source of his spiritual nourishment. Following rabbinic precedent, the Torah is termed the "delight" of God, the preexistent companion of the Blessed Holy One through whom the world was created,[2] and is at once the light of all worlds and an overflowing spring, brimming with the secrets of all existence. For the Companions of the *Zohar*, not only is the Torah the ultimate repository of all the mysteries of the cosmos, but he who knows how to read her verses gains access to a world of live contact with God.

The passage at the beginning of this chapter (*Zohar* 3:149a–150b) contains one of the *Zohar*'s more extended reflections on the Torah.

Through a delightful narrative featuring many of the *Zohar*'s favored and most charming literary motifs—wandering sages, mountains, caves, the passage from day to night and fear to deliverance, as well as mysterious mystical cave dwellers—the *Zohar* presents us with a wonderful illustration of the Companions' engagement with Torah. The *Zohar* does not merely present here a "theory of Torah," but rather a demonstration of the varied encounters with her words, culminating as we will soon see with mystical ecstasy.

The narrative begins in classical zoharic fashion:

> Rabbi El'azar, Rabbi Yose, and Rabbi Yitzhak were walking on the way.
> They encountered the mountains of Kurdistan.
> While they were walking, Rabbi El'azar raised his eyes and saw those high mountains and they were dark.
> They were seized with fear.
> Rabbi El'azar said to the Companions: Were father here I would not be afraid, but since we are three and words of Torah are between us, judgment is not present here.

As we have noted, "the way" is the preferred location for many zoharic narratives. In this case, the journey is particularly fantastic, as the companions find themselves in the mountains of Kurdistan, in Asia Minor. The Aramaic words for "mountains of Kurdistan," *turei kardu*, are taken from the Aramaic translation to Genesis 8:4, where Onkelos, the famous proselyte translator of the Torah, renders "mountains of Ararat" as "mountains of Kurdistan," and it is this association that leads Rabbi El'azar to begin expounding the verse about the resting place of Noah's ark.[3] Seized with fear, the wandering companions do what they do best: they walk and talk Torah, their being together, and their being with her—the Torah/*Shekhinah*—enveloping them in a shield of grace.[4]

> Rabbi El'azar opened, saying: *In the seventh month on the seventeenth day of the month, the ark came to rest on the mountains of Ararat* (Gen. 8:4).
> How beloved are the words of Torah, for in each and every word there are supernal mysteries, and the Torah is called the supernal principle (*klela ila'a*).
> And we have learned in the thirteen attributes of Torah—*anything that was included in a general statement (kelal) but was then singled out from the general statement in order to*

*teach something, was not singled out to teach only about itself,
but to apply its teaching to the entire generality.*[5]

As for the Torah, which is the supernal principle, even
though a story of the world is singled out from it, it certainly
does not come to present that story, but rather to present supernal matters, supernal mysteries; and *it was not singled out to
teach only about itself but to apply its teaching to the entire
generality,* because that story of Torah, or that narrative, even
though it was singled out from the generality of Torah, was not
singled out to present only about itself, but rather was singled
out to present about the supernal principle of Torah in its
entirety.

Like that which is written, *In the seventh month on the seventeenth day of the month, the ark came to rest on the mountains of Ararat* (Gen. 8:4).

Certainly this verse was singled out from the generality of
Torah and comes in a story of the world.

What does it matter to us if it rests here or there?! It must
have rested somewhere!

But to apply its teaching to the entire generality.

Happy are Israel for they have been given a supernal Torah,
a Torah of truth!

As for the one who says that the story of Torah comes only
to present that story alone—may his spirit deflate!

For if it were so she would not be a supernal Torah, a
Torah of truth.

Ah, but certainly the Torah is holy, supernal; she is a Torah
of truth.

Before beginning to expound his verse that relates the date and
location of the resting of the ark, Rabbi El'azar begins with an extended
celebration of the Torah and its wondrous properties. His comments
remind the reader that the Torah is no ordinary book; all her words
contain mysteries, and while it might appear that she is merely relating
a seemingly irrelevant piece of historical or narrative information, when
coming to expound her verses, one must remember what she is—a
Torah of truth, the supernal principle, the name of God. "The whole of
the Torah is the name of the Blessed Holy One and he who studies it is
like one who studies the holy name, since the whole Torah is one holy
name, a supernal name, a name that comprises names" (*Zohar*
2:124a).[6] The stories of the Torah, as edifying or interesting as they may
be, are not the source of the Torah's truth or holiness. It is, rather, that

which they point to, or what lies behind them, *the entire generality*, the flowing and mysterious world of divinity, which the mystic seeks. A few pages after this passage, the *Zohar* offers one of its most beautiful reflections on the stories of the Torah and, as in our narrative, contains the stern warning: "Woe to the human being who says that Torah presents mere stories and ordinary words!"

> Come and see:
> There is a garment visible to all.
> When those fools see someone in a good-looking garment they look no further.
> But the essence of the garment is the body; the essence of the body is the soul.
> So it is with Torah.
> She has a body: the commandments of Torah, called "the embodiment of Torah."
> This body is clothed in garments: the stories of the world.
> Fools of the world look only at the garment, the story of Torah; they know nothing more.
> They do not look at what is under that garment.
> Those who know more do not look at the garment, but rather at the body under that garment.
> The wise ones, servants of the King on high, those who stood at Mt. Sinai, look only at the soul, root of all, real Torah!
> . . .
>
> —*Zohar* 3:152a (Matt, *Book of Enlightenment*)

The mystics know that the real Torah, *oraita mamash*, lies beneath the garment of Torah—the stories, and beneath the body of Torah—the commandments. Real Torah—the soul of Torah—lies hidden, and the Companions' hermeneutical (and erotic) quest is to see Torah "from beneath the garment." While the stories may be necessary "as wine must sit in a jar," the mystic must never forget the true object of his desire, the inner core of Torah that treats of the grand story of the divine being, the divine generality lying behind the particular Torah narrative. On numerous occasions the *Zohar* cites the verse from Psalms (119:18), "Open my eyes so I can see wonders out of Your Torah" as a kind of call or reminder that that which we seek lies hidden within the Torah's words, and repeatedly castigates those who, unaware of the Torah's multidimensionality, mock and ridicule her. The Companions' relationship with the Torah is a chivalric romance between a knight and his lover, and the Companions (and indeed the Torah herself) desire the total unmediated intimacy of lovers. As we find in the zoharic composition *Sabba de-Mishpatim*, where two of the Companions learn from an old donkey driver the secrets of Torah interpretation, the mystical quest is to unveil the Torah, lovingly and persistently pursuing her, till "she reveals herself face to face . . . [revealing] all her hidden secrets, all her hidden ways, since primordial days secreted in her heart" (*Zohar* 2:99b).[7]

The Companions, however, do not read the Torah only to discover the wondrous mysteries secreted therein. The mystical engagement with Torah contains a strong experiential component, and beyond any doctrinal content—sefirotic or otherwise—that the Torah seeks to convey, the Companions' encounter with Torah is also intended to bring them into contact with the living, dynamic, and pulsating aspect of divinity as it unfolds and flows through reality. "The world that is coming," *alma de-atei*, while referring specifically to the sefirah *Binah*, is also used by the *Zohar* more generally, to signify the flowing aspect of the divine with which the human being seeks to come into contact. According to the *Zohar*, divinity is always in motion, always changing, and always unfolding, and the task of the mystic is to experience this flow through the words of the Torah. A short passage appearing just before our own narrative beautifully conveys this idea:

> Rabbi Yehudah opened . . . Happy is the portion of Israel, for the Blessed Holy One desired them and gave them a Torah of truth, the Tree of Life, through which a person inherits life in this world and life in the world that is coming. For whoever engages Torah and cleaves to her possesses life, while whoever abandons words of Torah and separates from Torah, is as though he separates from life, for she is life and all her words are life, as is written, *They are life to him who finds them, healing for his whole body* (Prov. 4:22), and it is written, *She will be a cure for your body, a tonic (shikui) for your bones* (Prov. 3:8).
>
> —*Zohar* 3:148b

The Torah then is ultimate life leading like a gateway to "the world that is coming." We shall return once again to the Torah's capacity to arouse mystical consciousness in our exploration of Torah and wine later (see chapter 5).

Back to our narrative:

In the continuation of his opening exhortation of the Torah, Rabbi El'azar makes explicit the apparent chasm between the stories found in the Torah and the view of the Torah as supernal and holy:

Come and see:

A king of flesh and blood—it is not dignified for him to speak of common matters, all the more so to write them.

If it should enter your mind that the supernal King, the Blessed Holy One, had no supernal matters to write and with which to make a Torah, but gathered all the words of commoners [or: ordinary words], like the words of Esau, the words of Hagar, the words of Laban with Jacob, the words of the ass, the words of Bilaam, the words of Balak, the words of Zimri, and assembled them and all the other stories that are written and made from them a Torah, if so, why is she called a *Torah of truth* (Mal. 2:6)?

The Torah of YHVH is perfect . . . the testimony of YHVH is enduring . . . the precepts of YHVH are just . . . the instruction of YHVH is lucid . . . the fear of YHVH is pure . . . the judgments of YHVH are true (Ps. 19:8–10); and it is written, *more desirable than gold, than much fine gold* (ibid.:11).

These are the words of Torah.

Certainly the Torah is holy, she is supernal, a Torah of truth.

The Torah of YHVH is perfect—each and every word comes to present supernal matters, and that word of that story does not come to present itself alone, but rather comes to present the generality (*kelal*), as we have established.

If the Torah is really from heaven, why then does it include such trivial matters? Surely the Master of the Universe had more interesting things to convey to humanity than irrelevant narrative details, genealogies and the like! Where is the philosophy? Where are the truths of the cosmos and of being? The answer, of course, is that these stories are merely the external layer of Torah, and the mystic must cast his "open eye"[8] and penetrate the Torah's veils to discover how "each and every word comes to present supernal matters." Writing a generation or so before the *Zohar*, Rabbi Azriel of Gerona, one of the leading kabbalists of his day, commented that without an understanding of their hidden meaning, "certain sections and verses of the Torah seem fit to be thrown into the fire." Only one who has gained mystical insight can appreciate that "no essential distinction can be drawn between the section of Genesis 36, setting forth the generations of Esau, and the Ten Commandments, for it is all one whole and one edifice."[9]

The kabbalists, it should be noted, were not the first to raise concerns about some of the seemingly banal details found in the Torah. In tractate *Sanhedrin* in the Babylonian Talmud, in a famous discussion about those who forfeit life in the world to come, the sages counted he who denies the principle of "Torah from heaven."

> MISHNAH: All Israel have a portion in the world to come . . . but the following have no portion in the world to come . . . he who says that the Torah is not from heaven . . .

> GEMARA: Our rabbis taught: *Because he spurned the word of the Lord and violated His commandment, that person shall be cut off* (Num. 15:31). This refers to one who maintains that the Torah is not from heaven . . .
> Another baraita taught: *Because he spurned the word of the Lord*—this refers to the one who maintains that the Torah is not from heaven. And even if he asserts that that whole Torah is from heaven, excepting a particular verse, which [he maintains] was not uttered by God but by Moses himself, he is included in *because he spurned the word of the Lord*. And even if he admits that the whole Torah is from heaven, excepting a single point, a particular a fortiori, or a particular argument by analogy—he is still included in *because he spurned the word of the Lord* . . .
> Our rabbis taught: *But the person who acts defiantly* (Num. 15:30)—this refers to Manasseh the son of Hezekiyah, who examined [biblical] narratives to prove them worthless. He jeered: Has Moses nothing to write but, *And Lotan's sister was Timna* (Gen. 36:22), *And Timna was concubine to Eliphaz* (ibid.:12), *And Rueben went in the days of the wheat harvest and found mandrakes in the field* (Gen. 30:14)?
> —BT *Sanhedrin* 99a–b (Soncino, modified)

Through the figure of Manasseh the son of Hezekiyah, the rabbis express their astonishment at the content of the Torah, seemingly at odds with a view of *Torah min ha-shamayim*, Torah from heaven. Where the rabbis found ethical teachings in these "irrelevant" passages, the Companions of the *Zohar* find the story of God in all its wonder and magnificence.

In answering his own query about the surprising content of Torah, Rabbi El'azar cites a number of verses from Psalm 19. Beyond confirming the view of the perfection of the Torah, the recitation of the verses has a mantra-like effect, refining the reader's consciousness and attuning him to the appropriate mode of Torah interpretation. While the verses are cited in shorthand only, when read in their complete form, they reveal many of the *Zohar*'s fundamental assumptions about the nature of Torah and her relationship with her lovers:

> The Torah of YHVH is perfect, renewing life;
> The decrees of YHVH are enduring, making the simple wise (*maḥkimat peti*).
> The precepts of YHVH are just, rejoicing the heart;
> The instruction of YHVH is lucid, enlightening the eyes . . .
> sweeter than honey, than drippings of the comb.
>
> —Psalms 19:16–17

The words of the Torah are sweet and flowing, the source of ultimate life, illumination, joy, and wisdom. The stress on the verse "The Torah of YHVH is perfect" is of particular significance. In *Sha'arei Orah*, one of the most important kabbalistic works from the same period as the *Zohar*, and written by Joseph Gikatilla, a colleague of Moses de Leon and perhaps also one of the people responsible for the composition of the *Zohar*, we find this verse cited in a particularly important passage addressing the Torah:

> . . . know the Written Torah is the essence of this Name which is called YHVH, may He be blessed. Thus it is written: *The Torah of YHVH is perfect* (Ps. 19:8). Now let me explain, know that all of the Torah is like the essence of the form of YHVH, may He be blessed, and if God forbid, there would be a letter missing or a letter added, it would not be the Torah of YHVH, for the form of this truth would not be YHVH. You already know what I have told you in this gate that the great Name YHVH, may He be blessed, is the root and the trunk of the tree while the other Holy Names are branches that extend from the tree from all sides, and the Cognomens are woven through the Holy Name which are known as branches; if this is so, all the Torah is like the attribute which is the essence of YHVH, may He be blessed. If this is so, keep this with you, for it is a great principle, and you will understand that the written Torah is the essence of His great Name.[10]

According to Gikatilla, like Nahmanides before him, the entire Torah is comprised of divine names, and these names are all permutations and combinations of the one ineffable name, YHVH. As he writes in his introduction: "Thus all the Torah is woven with [the strands] of YHVH and it is for this reason that it is stated, *The Torah of YHVH is perfect.*[11] As Gershom Scholem pointed out in his seminal essay on the kabbalistic view of the Torah, the words "Torah of YHVH" are not merely taken to indicate the divine source of the Torah but to convey the idea of the Torah as that which explains YHVH, or the Torah that is about YHVH.[12]

With these theoretical reflections on the nature of the Torah completed, Rabbi El'azar now comes to expound the verse about the ark, and in so doing, demonstrates how the Torah ought to be read:

Come and see:
In the seventh month on the seventeenth day of the month, the ark came to rest on the mountains of Ararat (Gen. 8:4).
So it is with this verse, how much more so with others!
At the time when judgment hovers over the world and judgments abide, and the Blessed Holy One sits on His throne of judgment to judge the world, within that throne, the treasury of the King, numerous records are inscribed and numerous notes are concealed.
All the books that are opened are concealed there; and therefore nothing is forgotten by the King.
This throne is not arrayed and does not abide except in the seventh month, which is the day of judgment, a day on which all the people of the world are reckoned.
They all pass before that throne.
About this [it is written], *In the seventh month . . . the ark came to rest*—in the seventh month, indeed, for it is the judgment of the world.
On the mountains of Ararat—those masters of judgment, masters of the groan and moan, and they all are present on that day before the Blessed Holy One.
Many shield-bearing warriors are aroused on that day and all stand beneath the throne in judgment on the world.
On that day Israel offer up prayer and plead and beseech before Him, they blow the shofar and the Blessed Holy One has mercy on them and transforms judgment into mercy.
All the upper and lower realms open and say: *Happy is the people who know the joyful shout (tru'ah)* (Ps. 89:10).
Therefore it is necessary on that day that the one who performs the trumpeting know the essence of the matter and direct his mind in the *tru'ah*[13] and perform the matter with wisdom.
Therefore it is written, *Happy is the people who know the*

joyful shout and not who perform the joyful shout, as has been said.[14]

Rabbi El'azar finds in the verse from Genesis a reference to the state of the divine being in the seventh month of the year, the month *Tishrei*, associated primarily with themes of judgment. The zoharic conception of divinity is, as we have stated, dynamic, and the divine being, or more accurately, the different aspects comprising the divine being, the sefirot, are constantly in flux. The face that God shows to the world is thus dependent on the particular configuration of the various divine grades, which change throughout the day and night, the week, the month, and the year. In this case, the ark, one of the *Zohar*'s symbols for the tenth sefirah, *Malkhut*, sometimes referred to also as the "lesser court" as She is responsible for administering justice below, is presented as primed (arrayed) to fulfill Her task in judging the world. The location of the ark, "on the mountains of Ararat," also contains a kabbalistic secret. No doubt based on the proximity of the word *Ararat* and the Hebrew word for curse, *arur*, Rabbi El'azar reads out of the verse a description of some of the many fantastic celestial creatures found throughout the *Zohar*, in this case, those charged with retribution, here termed frighteningly, "masters of the groan and moan" and "shield-bearing warriors." The verse from Genesis containing minor details about the location of the ark—"what does it matter to us if it rests here or there?! It must have rested somewhere!"—has now been revealed to contain a deep kabbalistic mystery pertaining to the resting of *Malkhut* (the ark) on the forces of judgment and retribution (the mountains of Ararat) in the seventh month of the year, corresponding to the month of Tishrei, the time of the High Holidays when the forces of judgment reign.

Having demonstrated a reading of Torah according to the sefirot, our passage now resumes its narrative thread, before launching into an illustration of yet another mode of zoharic Torah study, in this case geared toward influencing the divine being (theurgy) and attaining ecstasy. As we noted previously, the study of Torah contains an important experiential component, affecting both the divine itself as well as the mystics below:

They walked on that entire day.

When night fell they ascended to a certain place and found a cave.

Rabbi El'azar said: Let someone enter the cave if perchance he may find a site that is more fittingly arrayed.

Rabbi Yose entered and saw another cave within, the light of a candle glowing inside.

He heard a voice saying: *Be-ha'alotekha, When you light the lamps, the seven lamps will give light at the front of the lamp stand* (Num. 8:2).

Here the Assembly of Israel receives the light and the Supernal Mother is crowned and all the lights radiate from Her.

In Her two small glowing marshals fly,[15] wedding attendants, linking all upward and from there below.

Rabbi Yose heard and rejoiced and approached Rabbi El'azar.

Rabbi El'azar said to him: Let us enter for the Blessed Holy One has appointed for us this day that miracles befall us.

They entered.

When they entered they saw two people plying Torah.

Rabbi El'azar said: *How precious is your loving-kindness O God, human beings shelter in the shadow of Your wings* (Ps. 36:8).

They [the two people] arose and they all sat down and rejoiced.

Rabbi El'azar said: *How precious is Your loving-kindness O God*—that I found you.

The Blessed Holy One has shown us loving-kindness in this place.

Now light the lamps!

As happens frequently in the *Zohar*, the Companions find their way to a cave. As we shall observe repeatedly, caves occupy an important place in zoharic narratives, their mysterious ambience providing a wondrous backdrop for the Companions' expositions. Their cavernous or womb-like quality also recalls *Malkhut*, the divine female, and in entering the cave, the Companions, as it were, enter *Malkhut* whom they will now array and illuminate with their Torah innovations. The cave motif, so ubiquitous throughout the *Zohar*, is also derived from the famous Talmudic account (BT *Shabbat* 33b–34a; PT *Sheviit* 9:1) of Rabbi Shimon bar Yoḥai and his son El'azar, who while fleeing the Romans, hid in a cave for thirteen years, during which time, according to tradition, they engaged in mystical Torah study. To these considerations, we might also add the prevalence of caves in Spanish legends and literature throughout the medieval period, no doubt influenced by the many caves found across the Spanish landscape.[16]

In this cave narrative, the Companions enter within where they hear the voice of two anonymous men reciting the opening verse from the Torah portion *Be-ha'alotekha* that contains the divine injunction to light the lamps of the menorah, the lamp stand that stood in the courtyard of the Tabernacle and later the Temple of Solomon. The glowing candle adds a deft touch to the scene that is about the lighting of the menorah. While the verse they quote is simple enough, layers of rabbinic interpretation inform the mysterious cave dweller's enigmatic statements. The following comment is characteristic of a number of rabbinic treatments of this verse:

> *When you light the lamps . . .* (Num. 8:2) . . . This bears on the text, *The Lord desired for His righteousness' sake to make the Torah great and glorious* (Isa. 42:21).
>
> The Blessed Holy One said to Moses: It is not because I require lamps that I have reminded you about them, but only in order that Israel might acquire merit.
>
> For it says, *The light dwells with him* (Dan. 2:22), and it is written, *Even the darkness is not too dark for You, but the night shines as the day; the darkness is even as the light* (Ps. 139:12). All this serves to teach you that He does not need the lamps of mortals . . .
>
> Why then did He command you to kindle lamps?
>
> In order to enable you to acquire merit. This is why it says, *be-ha'alotekha, when you light the lamps.*
>
> —*Numbers Rabbah* 15:2, *Be-ha'alotekha*
> (Soncino, modified)

Another midrash that follows soon after restates the same point. Focusing on the opening word of the verse, *be-ha'alotekha*, which means when you light or ignite, although more literally might be rendered, when you elevate, the rabbis have God remark: "I only told you to kindle lamps in order to elevate you" (15:7). Where the rabbis insist that God has no need for humans to provide Him with light, and that the entire ritual is aimed at facilitating human spiritual elevation, the *Zohar* adopts a different view entirely. Not only does God need to be ignited, as it were, by human beings, but the elevation referred to in the verse is of a more "real" nature than that intimated by the rabbis. As we have seen, one of the central innovations of kabbalistic thought is the remarkable inversion that sees the fate of God placed in human hands. According to the kabbalistic conception of divinity, the divine being is dependent on humanity for its perfection and actualization, and in sharp contrast with the rabbinic text from *Numbers Rabbah*, the Blessed Holy One is indeed in need of human beings for illumination:

> *Command the children of Israel to bring you pure oil of beaten olives for lighting, for kindling the lamp continually* (Lev. 24:2)
> . . .
>
> Come and see: If a person says that there is no need for deeds at all, or to utter words, or make them audible—may his spirit deflate!
> This portion on kindling the lamps and offering incense proves otherwise, as it is written, *Oil and incense rejoice the heart* (Prov. 27:9), and by this deed, kindling and joy abide above and below, and there is union as one, as is fitting.
>
> —*Zohar* 3:105a

The idea that what we do below impacts and influences the divine realm above (theurgy) lies at the heart of the zoharic worldview, and here the mysterious cave dwellers find in the verse from Numbers a description of the illumination of the various divine grades and the flow of the divine plenty into the last sefirah, *Malkhut*. The seven-pronged candelabra, whose biblical origins are most probably as a stylized Tree of Life, and whose Near Eastern antecedents might even include an image of the divine mother,[17] appears here in the *Zohar* in full mythological force as a symbol for the divine being itself, requiring illumination from those below who, through their Torah study, take the place of the biblical high priest.

The inversion that sees the fate of divinity in human hands is dramatically, if somewhat enigmatically, conveyed through the second statement uttered by the cave dwellers: "In Her two small glowing marshals (*tufsirin*) fly, wedding attendants (*shushbinin*), linking all upward and from there below." Not only do the two anonymous men enjoy an ascent into the divine, but through their Torah study they fulfill the central theurgic task of unifying the sefirot, in particular, bringing the male and female aspects of divinity into a state of harmony and union. The term *shushbinin* is of particular significance and takes us to the heart of the zoharic view of humanity. As we have already noted, the chief task of the Companions of the *Zohar* is to facilitate the union of the divine couple, the Blessed Holy One, the male grade of divinity, and *Malkhut*, the *Shekhinah*, the female aspect of the divine. According to the zoharic myth, it is the mystics below who, through their Torah study and performance of the commandments, must prepare the divine couple for sexual union. In this capacity, the Companions are sometimes referred to as "the maidens of the bride," the female attendants of the *Shekhinah*, whose task it is to beautify and adorn the female prior to Her union with Her lover:

> For behold, the *Matronita* (great lady / consort) is not fit to come to Her husband, except with those young women, Her maidens, who come with Her and escort Her until She reaches Her husband, as is written, *Maidens in her train, her companions* (Ps. 45:15). And what need is there for this? To bring Her to unite with Her husband.
>
> —*Zohar* 2:197b[18]

In our narrative, the mysterious cave dwellers refer to themselves as wedding attendants, *shushbinin*, and it is their exposition of the lighting of the menorah that serves to enable the sacred union (*hieros gamos*) between *Tiferet* and *Malkhut*. The significance of the term *shushbinin*, used quite frequently in the *Zohar* to describe the theurgic task of the Companions,[19] is brought into sharp relief when we compare the zoharic deployment of this term against its rabbinic uses. In *Avot de-Rabbi Natan*, a rabbinic midrash, we read that God fulfilled the task of *shushbin* for Adam and Eve:

> Once as Rabbi Judah bar Il'ai sat teaching his disciples, a bride passed by. So he took myrtle twigs in his hand and cheered her until the bride passed out of his sight.
>
> Another time as Rabbi Judah bar Il'ai sat teaching his disciples, a bride passed by. "What was that?" he asked them. "A bride passing by," they replied.
>
> "My sons," he said to them, "get up and attend upon the bride. For thus we find concerning the Holy One, blessed be He, that He attended upon a bride, as it is said, *And the Lord God built the rib* (Gen. 2:22). If He attended upon a bride, how much more so we!"
>
> And where do we find that the Holy One, blessed be He, attended upon a bride? For it is said, *And the Lord God built (va-yiven) the rib*. Now, in the sea towns they call plaiting *binyata*. Hence we learn that the Holy One, blessed be He, fixed Eve's hair and outfitted her as a bride and brought her to Adam, as it is said, *And He brought her unto the man* (ibid.).
>
> —*Avot de'Rabbi Natan* 4[20]

Where the rabbis imagine God in the role of wedding attendant for Adam and Eve, in the *Zohar*, it is the mystics who play the role of wedding attendants entrusted to bring the divine male and female together.

After encountering this unexpected scene, Rabbi Yose informs Rabbi El'azar, who, as the most senior of the assembled companions, now suggests they all enter the cave. Upon seeing the two men plying Torah, Rabbi El'azar recites a verse from Psalms, "How precious is your loving-kindness (*ḥasdekha*) O God, human beings shelter in the shadow of Your wings." Not only is the verse particularly apt as the Companions now shelter in a cave, the reference to loving-kindness, *ḥesed*, serves as a counterpoint to Rabbi El'azar's opening comment about divine judgment (*din*) with which the unit opened. To use a later Hasidic formulation, the Companions' Torah study has indeed "sweetened the judgments." As is often the case in the *Zohar*, the broader landscape from which the verse is taken is also significant, and the verses surrounding the sentence extracted by Rabbi El'azar resonate with numerous aspects of our narrative:

> O YHVH, Your faithfulness reaches to heaven;
> Your steadfastness to the sky;
> Your beneficence is like the high mountains;
> Your justice like the great deep;
> Man and beast You deliver, O YHVH.
> How precious is Your faithful care O Elohim!
> Mankind shelters in the shadow of Your wings.
> They feast on the rich fare of Your house;
> You let them drink at Your refreshing/edenic stream.
> With you is the fountain of life;
> by Your light do we see light.
>
> —Psalms 36:6–10

As we have seen, mountains and light have been key themes in the narrative so far, while the motif of the edenic stream will appear shortly. As we shall see in greater detail in chapter 9, it is the *Zohar*'s ability to integrate biblical verses with narrative that accounts for much of its literary wonder.

Following Rabbi El'azar's invitation to "light the lamps," to illuminate and adorn the divine being through words of Torah, Rabbi Yose begins his exposition. The homilies that follow take us to the experiential and theurgic heart of the *Zohar*. For the Companions, reading Torah is not only (perhaps not even primarily) about knowing or dis-

covering the secrets of divinity; nor is it only about acting for the sake
of God. Reading the Torah according to "the mystery of faith," *raza de-
mehemenuta*, involves an active participation in the world of divinity
and the Companions, through their Torah interpretations alone, step
into this flowing dimension of being. Expressed differently, the realities
they explicate become realities they experience. The lights and oil of the
menorah, no longer frozen words from the biblical landscape, are transformed into qualities of God and experiences open to the mystic here
and now.

Rabbi Yose opened, saying:
*Be-ha'alotekha, When you light the lamps—be-ha'alotekha,
when you elevate*, literally, [that is] when you light.
For behold the priest performs two services as one, a single
bond.
And what are they?
Oil and incense, as it is written, *Oil and incense rejoice the
heart* (Prov. 27:9).[21]
It is written, *Aaron shall burn upon it aromatic incense,
morning after morning, when he dresses (be-heitivo) the lamps
he shall burn it* (Exod. 30:7) and it is written, *And when Aaron
lights (be-ha'alot) the lamps at twilight he shall burn it* (ibid.
30:8).[22]
What is the difference between what is written here *when
he dresses (be-heitivo)* and what is written there *when he lights
(be-ha'alot)*?
Rabbi Yehudah said: It is all one.
Rabbi Yose said: *Be-heitivo, when he dresses*—as it is said,
For your loving is better (tovim) than wine (Song of Songs 1:2).
Tovim—saturated with wine, as it is said, *For we were satiated and were good (tovim)* (Jer. 44:17).[23]
Rabbi Yehudah said: *Hatavah, dressing/making good*, literally, as it is said, *a good-hearted person is a continuous feast*
(Prov. 15:15).[24]
When he lights (be-ha'alot)—when they are watered and
saturated from the waters of the river, then the supernal beings
elevate (*ilain iluya*) and blessings are found in all of them and
joy in all, and therefore it is written, *be-ha'alot—when he elevates*.
Rabbi Aha said: When the Depth of All illuminates it irradiates the river, and the river flows on in a straight path to
water all.

Then it is written, *be-ha'alot, when he elevates* (alt., *be-heitivo*, when he dresses), for from the Depth of All they issue forth;

be-ha'alot, when he elevates, which comes from the supernal facet of the Depth of All which is called Thought.

It is all one matter.

Then the Assembly of Israel is blessed and blessings are found in all the worlds.

Rabbi Yose begins his exposition, as we expect he will, with a literal reading of the opening word of the verse expounded by the cave dwellers—*be-ha'alotekha*. While in its biblical context the word is taken to mean "lighting," its literal meaning of elevation calls out for zoharic exegesis. "*Be-ha'alotekha mamash*, when you elevate, literally," the *Zohar* says, making clear the idea that the lighting of the menorah is in fact an elevation of the supernal lights, the various grades of divinity. The commandments of the Torah are no empty ritual, but penetrate to the very heart and life of divinity: "oil and incense rejoice the heart." Where incense binds bonds in the upper realms, igniting or raising the flame of the menorah elevates the lights of the divine being. In classical midrashic style, Rabbi Yose then asks why the Torah uses two different words to describe the lighting of the menorah—first *be-heitivo*, when he tends or dresses, and then *be-ha'alot*, when he elevates. Whereas Rabbi Yehudah understands both words to refer to the same thing—"it is all one"—with both words signifying the lighting of the menorah, Rabbi Yose takes a different view, connecting the word *be-heitivo* with the verse from the Song of Songs, "For your loving is better (*tovim*) than wine." Through this equation (*be-heitivo/tovim*), Rabbi Yose reads out of the verse from Exodus a description of the saturation of the sefirot with the divine flow prior to the state of union and illumination. Before the divine being can be ignited, the various divine grades must be infused with the divine plenty, frequently symbolized in the *Zohar* through the flow of wine, oil, and water (see chapters 5 and 7). Rabbi Yehudah, for his part, understands the word *be-heitivo* as designating illumination itself (*hatavah mamash*), based both on Maimonides equation of tending and lighting in the *Mishneh Torah*[25]and pre-zoharic kabbalistic exegesis of the same verse.[26] His proof text, "a good-hearted person is a continuous feast," would seem to refer to the *Shekhinah*, the last of the sefirot (sometimes referred to as heart) in a state of sexual union with the male grade of divinity, *Yesod* in particular, the divine phallus, symbolized through the word *good*.[27] Although rather techni-

cal Rabbi Yose and Rabbi Yehudah's dispute does reveal the great precision with which the *Zohar* reads the verses of the Torah and its ability
to find subtle processes in the divine world encoded within her words.
Above and beyond the specific details of their homilies, though, lies
their quest to find in the verses of scripture the flowing dimension of
divinity, and it is this dimension that Rabbi Yose calls forth in response
to Rabbi El'azar's invitation to "light the lamps."

The final homily in our narrative takes us to the heart of the
zoharic quest. As we shall see in greater detail in succeeding chapters,
the Companions deepest desire is to enable and then bathe in the river
of divinity, the river that flows from Eden, a quest they accomplish
through their innovations in Torah. *Be-ha'alotekha* is at once the lighting of the menorah, the elevation of the supernal worlds as well as the
act of raising the flow of divinity, drawing it out from the innermost
depths of the divine, Thought/*Hokhmah*, the primal point of all being,
on to those below:

> Rabbi Ḥizkiyah opened: *A Song of Ascents (shir ha-ma'alot).*
> *Out of the depths I have called You O YHVH* (Ps. 130:1) . . .
>
> Whoever desires to petition the King should direct his
> thought and his will to the depth of all depths, in order to draw
> blessings from the depth of the well, so that it might pour out
> blessings from the source of all.
>
> And what is [the depth of the well]? It is the place from
> which the river begins to flow, as it is written, *A river issues*
> *from Eden* (Gen. 2:10), and it is also written, *There is a river*
> *whose streams gladden the city of Elohim* (Ps. 46:5). And this is
> the meaning of *out of the depths*—the depth of all, the depth of
> the well, from which sources flow to shower blessings upon all.
> —Zohar 2:63a–b (Tishby and Goldstein modified)

Like the biblical high priest who prepares the oil and raises the flame of
the menorah, the mystics of the *Zohar* saturate and elevate the divine
being, drawing it out of its own hiddenness to flow into our reality that
blessings might be found in all the worlds.

The *Zohar* passage elucidated here is one of the more extended
zoharic reflections on the Torah. In the space of one and half folio
pages, the *Zohar* combines narrative, a theoretical statement about the
Torah, an illustration of the sefirotic mode of interpreting scripture, followed by an act of reading geared at influencing the divine being. Our
passage might even be thought of as a demonstration of the mystical

encounter with the Torah in its varied modes. The "loving doe," "the maiden without eyes," "the Torah of truth" is the embodiment of divinity and he who knows how to read her verses with "the mystery of faith" gains access to a world without peer.

• ◆ •

CHAPTER THREE

In the Image of God

Zohar 3:159a–b

Rabbi Yehudah was walking on the way with Rabbi Abba.

He asked him and said: I wish to ask you a certain matter.

Since the Blessed Holy One knew that man was destined to sin before Him and that He would decree upon him death, why then did He create him?

For behold, the Torah preceded the creation of the world by two thousand years and it is written therein, *When a person dies in a tent* (Num. 19:14), *If a man dies* (ibid. 27:8), *then Adam died, and so and so lived and then he died* (Gen. 5).

What does the Blessed Holy One want from man in this world, for even if he engages Torah day and night he will die, and if he does not engage Torah he will also die!? All travel the one path, aside from the distinction of that world, as it is said, *as for the good, so for the sinner* (Eccles. 9:2).

He said to him:

What concern have you with the ways and decrees of your master?!

What you have permission to know and contemplate, ask, and as for that which you do not have permission to know, it is written, *Do not let your mouth cause your flesh to sin* (Eccles. 5:6). For regarding the ways and mysteries of the Blessed Holy One, supernal secrets, which He has hidden and concealed, we may not ask.

He said to him: If that is the case then the entire Torah is hidden and concealed, for it is the supernal holy name, and whoever engages Torah is as though he engages in the holy name. If that is so, then there is nothing for us to ask or contemplate!

He said to him: The entire Torah is both concealed and revealed and His holy name is both concealed and revealed, as it is written, *The hidden things are for YHVH our God, but the revealed things are for us and for our children* (Deut. 29:28).

The revealed things are for us—for we have permission to ask, to probe and to contemplate them and to know them.

But *the hidden things are for YHVH our God*—they are His and are fitting for Him.

For who can know and attain His hidden thought, let alone ask?!

Come and see:

The people of the world do not have permission to utter concealed things and expound them, aside from the Holy Luminary, Rabbi Shimon, for the Blessed Holy One consented [that mysteries be revealed] through him and because his generation is inscribed above and below.

Therefore matters are uttered openly by him.

There will not be a generation like this generation in which he abides until King Messiah comes.

But come and see:

It is written, *And God created the human in His image, in the image of God He created him* (Gen. 1:27).

The mystery of the matter:

The Blessed Holy One has three worlds and He is concealed within them.

The first world, supernal, hidden from all, unseen and unknown except by He who is hidden within.

The second world, connected to the one above, is the one from which the Blessed Holy One is known, as it is written, *Open for me the gates of righteousness* (Ps. 118:19), *This is the gate of YHVH* (Ps. 118:20). And this is the second world.

The third world is the world below them, where separation is found, and this is the world in which the supernal angels abide, and the Blessed Holy One is present and not present there.

He is present there now—but when they wish to contemplate and to know Him, He departs from them and cannot be seen, so that they all ask, *Where is the place of His glory?*[1] [and answer] *Blessed be the glory*

of YHVH from His place (Ezek. 3:12).
This is the world where He is not continuously present.

Similarly, *in the image of God He made humankind* (Gen. 9:6) and
therefore he has three worlds.
The first world, the world called the world of separation, in which man
is both present and not present. When they wish to look upon him, he
departs from them and cannot be seen.
The second world, a world linked to the supernal world, and this is the
earthly Garden of Eden, linked to another supernal world, from which
this other world is grasped and known.
The third world, a supernal world, mysterious, concealed, and hidden;
no one can comprehend it, as it is written, *No eye has seen O YHVH
but You, what He will do for those who trust Him* (Isa. 64:3).
All is as above, as it is written, *in the image of God He made
humankind* (Gen. 9:6).

Therefore it is written, *You are children of YHVH your God* (Deut.
14:1).
It is as they have established.
And these are in the image of God and these inherit a supernal inheritance, like His.
Therefore He warned in the Torah, *You shall not gash yourselves or
shave the front of your heads [because of the dead]* (ibid.), for he is not
annihilated, but is found in good, supernal, and precious worlds.
And [therefore] they should rejoice when the righteous depart from this
world.

Come and see:
Had man not sinned, he would not have tasted the taste of death in this
world when he entered the other worlds.
But since he sinned, he tastes the taste of death before he enters those
worlds.
The spirit (*ruaḥ*) divests itself of the body and leaves it behind in this
world, and the spirit bathes in the river of fire (*nahar di-nur*) to receive
its punishment.
Afterward, it enters the earthly Garden of Eden, where another garment
of light awaits, just like the semblance of the body of this world, in
which it adorns and arrays itself.
And there is its abode forever.
On New Moons and Sabbaths it joins with the soul (*neshamah*),
ascends, and is crowned above and beyond, as it is written, *And new*

*moon after new moon, and Sabbath after Sabbath, all flesh shall come
to worship Me* (Isa. 66:23).

Why *new moon after new moon?*
The mystery of the matter:
Because of the renewal of the moon that is adorned at that time to radi-
ate from the sun.
And so, *Sabbath after Sabbath* (*shabbat be shabto*).
Shabbat—this is the moon.
Be-shabto—this is the sun, for Her light comes to Her from there, and
therefore it is all one.
And this is the explanation of the matter, apart from the wicked about
whom is written death in all the worlds, excision from all the worlds,
annihilation from all, if they do not enter repentance.

Rabbi Yehudah said: Blessed is the Merciful One that I asked this question, acquired these words and understood them!

Commentary on *Zohar* 3:159a–b

Rabbi Akiva used to say: Beloved is man for he was created in the image; still greater was this love in that it was made known to him that he was created in the image, as it is written, In the image of God He made humankind (Gen. 9:6).

Beloved are Israel for they are called children of God; still greater was this love in that it was known to them that they are called children of God, as it is written, You are children of YHVH your God (Deut. 14:1).

—*Avot* 3:14

Thus said God, YHVH, who created the heavens and stretched them out, who spread out the earth and what it brings forth, who gave neshamah to the people upon it, and ruaḥ to those who walk thereon: I YHVH, have called you in righteousness, and I have grasped you by the hand.

—Isaiah 42:5–6

What does it mean to be created in the image of God? The concept of *Imago Dei* or *Tzelem Elohim* is surely one of the foundations of Jewish thought. Associated with the fundamental dignity of humanity, human individuality, as well as our creative and in particular our procreative capacities, the idea of *Tzelem Elohim* received new and diverse interpretations at the hands of medieval philosophers and mystics.[2] Maimonides, for example, the most famous and important of the medieval Jewish rationalists, identified our being created in the divine image with humanity's unique capacity for intellectual apprehension.[3] The *Zohar* too contributed new understandings to this central idea, but unlike Maimonides, who recoiled from anthropomorphisms and corporeal understandings of the divine, the *Zohar* saw in our very bodies, both physically and psychologically, a microcosm of the divine macrocosm. The structure of the divine being, the sefirot, is commonly depicted through the ideogram of *Adam Kadmon*, with the different aspects of divinity mapped onto the human body.[4] Our very physicality, rather than being something that we need to overcome or transcend, is actually a reflection of the deepest mysteries of God, and on many occasions the *Zohar* directs the reader to contemplate our own being—body and soul—as a gateway into knowledge of the divine.

The text in this chapter offers one particular zoharic reflection on the meaning of this foundational idea. Unlike the majority of passages examined in this book, the composition before us contains only a sparse narrative. No adventures or twists befall the Companions and the unit is driven entirely by the conversation and questions of the two traveling mystics. The text can perhaps be thought of as a zoharic version of a platonic dialogue between a master, Rabbi Abba, and a more junior member of the mystic fraternity, Rabbi Yehudah, although as we shall see, aside from his original question, Rabbi Yehudah plays only a minor role in the expositions that follow. The dialogue form is not unknown in Jewish literature. In the *Kuzari*,[5] Yehuda Halevi employed this literary device to great effect in his grand "apology" of Judaism, while in the generation preceding the writing of the *Zohar*, Rabbi Azriel of Gerona used the dialogue format in his "Explanation of the Ten Sefirot."[6] The *Zohar* of course is not a conventional dialogue, although it is most definitely dialogical. The spiritual-mystical world of the *Zohar* is always generated by and transpires through encounters between two or more people. Mystical experience and insight are always the patrimony of an encounter with an other.[7]

> Rabbi Yehudah was walking on the way with Rabbi Abba.
> He asked him and said: I wish to ask you a certain matter.
> Since the Blessed Holy One knew that man was destined to sin before Him and that He would decree upon him death, why then did He create him?
> For behold the Torah preceded the creation of the world by two thousand years and it is written therein, *When a person dies in a tent* (Numbers 19:14), *If a man dies* (ibid. 27:8), *then Adam died, and so and so lived and then he died* (Genesis 5).
> What does the Blessed Holy One want from man in this world, for even if he engages Torah day and night he will die, and if he does not engage Torah he will also die!? All travel the one path, aside from the distinction of that world, as it is said, *as for the good, so for the sinner* (Eccles. 9:2).

Our text begins with a question, perhaps the question of all questions. Rabbi Yehudah, the more junior of the companions, asks Rabbi Abba why God created the first man given that He knew that he would sin before Him and that he would therefore die. This question, which is stark in its directness even for the *Zohar*, is more complex than would first appear. On first view the question is one that we can all understand. Why create a being who will die? What is the purpose of human life in light of mortality? Elsewhere in the *Zohar*, Rabbi El'azar, the son of the grand master, Rabbi Shimon, asks his father a similar question: "Since it is revealed before the Blessed Holy One that human beings will die, why does He bring souls down into the world? Why does He need this?" (*Zohar* 1:235a). If the souls enjoy a beatified existence in the celestial realms, why bring them into this world? What is gained by their descent into corporeal, finite existence? In his commentary on our passage in his voluminous work *Or Yakar*, Rabbi Moses Cordovero, the leading kabbalist in Safed in the generation prior to Isaac Luria, succinctly captures the problem: "It would have been better if from the outset he would abide in that world and not come to this world . . . and not sin and not depart from it. For it emerges, that his coming and going are in vain . . . and he has gained nothing other than sin."[8] As important as this question is, Rabbi Yehudah's query is yet more multi-tiered and as we soon learn opens to a horizon of numerous theological difficulties. Rabbi Yehudah does not "prove" that God knew that Adam would sin by appealing to God's omniscience, but rather through citing a proof from the Torah itself that, according to a rabbinic teaching, preceded the creation of the world by two thousand years.[9] If it was already written in the preexistent Torah that we were destined to die, what then was the meaning of the commandment not to eat from the Tree of Knowledge of Good and Evil? Was not this commandment the ultimate test of human free will? Did humans bring death into the world or was mortality already assigned to them from the very outset?[10] As if these questions were not troubling enough, Rabbi Yehudah's final query opens yet another theological difficulty. No matter how we behave in this world death awaits us all. The Torah, the elixir of life, is seemingly helpless in the face of death. What did God want from humanity? What does He want?

The rabbis of the Talmudic era had already explored many of these difficulties. In *Midrash Tanḥuma*, a classical midrashic collection, we find the following daring exposition:

> *Come and see the works of God, He is terrible in His doing toward the children of men* (Ps. 66:5) . . . Rabbi Yehoshua ben Korha said: Come and see. When the Blessed Holy One created the world, He created the angel of death already on the first day. How do we know this? Rabbi Berahya said: Because scripture states, *And darkness was upon the face of the deep* (Gen. 1:2)—this is the angel of death who darkens the face of mankind, whereas man was created on the sixth day, yet he was blamed for having brought death into the world, as it is said, *For on the day you eat of it, you shall surely die* (Gen. 2:17).
>
> To what can the matter be compared?
>
> To a man who wished to divorce his wife. When he decided to go home, he wrote a bill of divorce; then he entered his

house with the divorce in his possession seeking a pretext for giving it to her. He said to her: Mix me a cup (of wine) to drink. She mixed his cup. When he took the cup from her hand, he said to her: Here is your divorce. She said to him: What sin have I committed? He replied: Go from my house, for you have mixed me a lukewarm cup of wine. She retorted: You already knew beforehand that I should mix you a tepid cup of wine, for your wrote the divorce and brought it with you!

Even so did Adam argue before the Blessed Holy One: Master of the Universe, two thousand years before you created the world, the Torah was with you as a confidant, as it is written, *I was with Him as a confidant, a source of delight every day* (Prov. 8:30), for two thousand years, and it is written therein, *This is the law: when a man dies in a tent* (Num. 19:14). If you had not prepared death for mankind, would you have written thus? Only You have come to put the blame on me. This is the meaning of the verse, *He is terrible in His doing toward the children of men.*

—*Tanḥuma Vayeshev* 4[11]

Rabbi Yehudah's opening question is more than a zoharic paraphrase of this surprising rabbinic passage. Where the text from *Tanḥuma* merely criticizes God (He is terrible in His doing toward the children of men) for blaming death on humanity when in fact God had always intended that mankind be mortal, Rabbi Yehudah goes a step further, asking why create a being who will know the pain of death in the first place, as well as raising the thorny question of human free will and predestination. Rabbi Abba, the more senior of the two, senses that in asking these questions, questions that pertain to the inscrutable divine will, Rabbi Yehudah has perhaps exceeded the limits of human inquiry.

He said to him:
What concern have you with the ways and decrees of your master?!

What you have permission to know and contemplate, ask, and as for that which you do not have permission to know, it is written, *Do not let your mouth cause your flesh to sin* (Eccles. 5:6). For regarding the ways and mysteries of the Blessed Holy One, supernal secrets, which He has hidden and concealed, we may not ask.

He said to him: If that is the case then the entire Torah is hidden and concealed, for it is the supernal, holy name, and whoever engages Torah is as though he engages in the holy name. If that is so, then there is nothing for us to ask or contemplate!

He said to him: The entire Torah is both concealed and revealed and His holy name is both concealed and revealed, as it is written, *The hidden things are for YHVH our God, but the revealed things are for us and for our children* (Deut. 29:28).

The revealed things are for us—for we have permission to ask, to probe and to contemplate them and to know them.

But *the hidden things are for YHVH our God*—they are His and are fitting for Him.

For who can know and attain His hidden thought, let alone ask?

Rabbi Abba responds tersely, "What concern have you with the ways and decrees of your master?!" and berates his colleague for asking that which one may not ask. Paraphrasing Ben Sirah in *Genesis Rabbah* (8:2), "About what is too great for you do not inquire; what is too hard for you do not investigate; what is too wonderful for you know not; of what is hidden from you do not ask; contemplate what was permitted to you: you have no business with hidden things," Rabbi Abba sets a limit to Rabbi Yehudah's inquiry.[12] There are things we cannot know. Indeed, there are things one cannot even ask, "for regarding the ways and mysteries of the Blessed Holy One, supernal secrets, which He has hidden and concealed, we may not ask." (In his gloss to this passage, Moses Cordovero notes, "He is the knowledge, He is the knower and He is the known, and it is not proper to inquire about His knowledge at all.")[13] Despite his insistence that Rabbi Yehudah's question is off-limits, it is difficult to imagine that this is really Rabbi Abba's opinion. The *Zohar* delights in revealing secrets, and we cannot help but feel that Rabbi Abba is merely testing his colleague, to determine whether he is worthy of receiving the mysteries of Torah. In any event Rabbi Yehudah is not intimidated and insists on his right to inquire. After all, the entire Torah is full of secrets and mysteries ("it is the supernal, holy name")[14] and should we say that these are off-limits, then there would be nothing at all left to do; Torah study would be forfeit. It is at this point that Rabbi Abba presents an intermediate view. The Torah is both concealed and revealed, an expression that appears frequently throughout the *Zohar*, and the correct approach is one that maintains the tension between disclosure and concealment.[15]

Before returning to Rabbi Yehudah's opening question and beginning his exposition, Rabbi Abba offers one final declaration:

Come and see:

The people of the world do not have permission to utter concealed things and expound them, aside from the Holy Luminary, Rabbi Shimon, for the Blessed Holy One consented [that mysteries be revealed] through him and because his generation is inscribed above and below.

Therefore matters are uttered openly by him;

There will not be a generation like this generation in which he abides until King Messiah comes.

We are about to be drawn into a world of secrets, a world that ought to remain concealed. These are privileged times. The generation of Rabbi Shimon, or peeling off the pseudo-epigraphical veneer of the composition, the generation of the *Zohar*, is a unique generation in the annals of Jewish history where mysteries can be disclosed.[16] This refrain about the unique status of "the generation of Rabbi Shimon" appears frequently in zoharic narratives and serves an important performative function, tantalizing and seducing the reader. It is as though the *Zohar* is saying: "You are about to hear that which cannot be said, that which ought not be said, and that which will never be said again."

But come and see:

It is written, *And God created the human in His image, in the image of God He created him* (Gen. 1:27).

The mystery of the matter:

The Blessed Holy One has three worlds and He is concealed within them.

The first world, supernal, hidden from all, unseen and unknown except by He who is hidden within.

The second world, connected to the one above, is the one from which the Blessed Holy One is known, as it is written, *Open for me the gates of righteousness* (Ps. 118:19), *This is the gate of YHVH* (Ps. 118:20).

And this is the second world.

The third world is the world below them, where separation is found, and this is the world in which the supernal angels abide, and the Blessed Holy One is present and not present there.

He is present there now—but when they wish to contemplate and to know Him, He departs from them and cannot be seen, so that they all ask, *Where is the place of His glory?* [and answer] *Blessed be the glory of YHVH from His place* (Ezek. 3:12).

This is the world where He is not continuously present.

Rabbi Abba now begins his exposition. Citing the verse from Genesis, "And God created the human being in His image, in the image of God He created him," he proceeds to outline an "image" of the divine. The Blessed Holy One, in this case used to designate divinity as a whole, has three worlds, three different modes or domains of being. The first supernal world, indicating the upper realms of divinity, the realm of *Ein Sof* and *Keter*, the hidden and unknowable aspect of God as well as the inscrutable divine will and primordial nothingness, is totally beyond the horizons of human cognition and experience. Like Maimonides, the *Zohar* too has its own mode of "negative theology," namely, a God beyond God, pure undifferentiated infinity, who cannot be named or described in language.[17] This is the domain of the "concealed of the concealed," the "mystery of mysteries," the divine being prior to its first stirrings, before bursting forth outside of itself to create knowable reality. Here "silence is praise before Thee" (Psalms 65:2). Here thought and language reach their limits. The second world is the world of knowable divinity, the dynamic and complex world of the sefirot, from *Ḥokhmah*, the primal seed of being, to *Malkhut*, the ruler of our world. While there are aspects of the divine that must remain concealed, the divine also seeks to reveal itself, to penetrate beyond its own mysterious concealment, to be known, seen, and experienced. "Open for me the gates of righteousness that I may enter them and praise Yah. This is the gate of YHVH, the righteous shall enter it" (Psalms 118:19–20). These verses function as a kind of code and mantra throughout the *Zohar*. Divinity is not totally concealed, and the mystic is invited to enter within through the gates of righteousness (a zoharic symbol for *Malkhut*, the feminine aspect of the divine, the tenth sefirah) to explore the variegated qualities of the divine. God is both beyond and unattainable while simultaneously open to experience and intimacy. It is this dialectic between the concealed and the revealed that is so central to the zoharic conception of divinity. To paraphrase one particularly beautiful teaching, *Elohim*/ אלהים is both *Eleh*/אלה/these— the knowable aspects of divinity and therefore designated by the demonstrative, and *Mi*/מי/Who—the uppermost mysterious face of God designated only by a question. Only together, when *Mi* is with *Eleh*, when the abiding mystery is combined with knowable aspects of God, is the divine reality, *Elohim*, complete.[18]

The third world is the world outside the divine realm, evocatively called "the world of separation," *alma de-peruda*, a world where God is "present and not present." This term, which plays an important role in later kabbalistic thought, especially in Hasidism, originated among medieval philosophers who referred to the angels as "separated intelligences" because they were understood as pure spiritual forms totally separate from matter. However, among the first generations of kabbalists, this term came to signify something very different and was used to designate existence outside of and separate from the pure divinity of the sefirot, the world of unification.[19] The *Zohar* frequently cites the verse "A river issues from Eden to water the garden and from there it divides and becomes four branches" (Gen. 2:10) to describe the river of divine plenty, the flow of divinity from its innermost depths in Eden, the sefirah *Ḥokhmah*, into the garden, the last of the emanations, the sefirah *Malkhut*. According to one passage, "From here below [i.e., beneath the sefirot] are called mountains of separation, as it is written, *From there it divides* (Gen. 2:10), mountains of division" (*Zohar* 1:158a). It is in this realm of division that we abide. Separation among things, among people, and above all, from God, are the hallmarks of our reality. To be sure, God is not absent from this realm, yet the manner of His manifestation is that of being "not continuously present." Expressed differently, although our world is brimming with divinity, God is far from "obvious." In this domain of being, knowledge of the divine is elusive and enigmatic: "when they wish to contemplate and to know Him, He departs from them and cannot be seen, so that they all ask, "Where is the place of His glory?"[20]

This division of reality into three domains is not a kabbalistic innovation. Similar systems can be found among medieval Neoplatonic and Aristotelian philosophers. Plotinus, for example, speaks of the world of the intellect, the world of the soul, and the world of nature, while Aristotelian philosophers spoke of an upper world, a middle world, and a lower world. Later kabbalists developed yet another system, the four worlds—emanation, creation, formation, and making. In any event, the hierarchy outlined in our text is religiously compelling, at once allowing for mystery and unknowability (the first world), knowledge and intimacy with the divine (the second world, the world of the sefirot), as well as distance, separation, and division (the third world, *alma de-peruda*).

Similarly, *in the image of God He made humankind* (Gen. 9:6) and therefore he has three worlds.

The first world, the world called the world of separation (*alma de-peruda*), in which man is both present and not present.

When they wish to look upon him, he departs from them and cannot be seen.

The second world, a world linked to the supernal world, and this is the earthly Garden of Eden, linked to another supernal world, from which this other world is grasped and known.

The third world, a supernal world, mysterious, concealed, and hidden; no one can comprehend it, as it is written, *No eye has seen O YHVH but You, what He will do for those who trust Him* (Isa. 64:3).

All is as above, as it is written, *in the image of God He made humankind* (Gen. 9:6).

Rabbi Abba draws a comparison between the structure of divinity and the human being. Just as God has three worlds, so too the human being. Significantly, in outlining the threefold nature of humanity that corresponds with the threefold nature of the divine, Rabbi Abba begins with the lower world, *alma de-peruda*, the primary locus of human life, and only then proceeds to outline our higher domains of being. In the preceding paragraph, when outlining the threefold structure of divinity, Rabbi Abba began with the highest and most inscrutable aspect of the divine. The directionality of the divine flow is one of unfolding from hiddenness and oneness to knowability and onto division and separation. The path of human life, however, runs in the opposite direction, from division and multiplicity to unity and integration. The zoharic world is one of overflowing Eros; God flows to us and we to Him, and in moments of grace we meet one another in the middle.

The human being's first world is the world of separation, where "man is both present and not present." This is the domain of finitude, where division but also death prevails: "when they wish to look upon him, he departs from them and cannot be seen." In this dimension of reality, human life is transient and our knowledge fleeting and partial.[21] Human beings, however, like God are multidimensional. We inhabit or have the capacity to inhabit other dimensions of being. The second world—the earthly Garden of Eden—is simultaneously a training ground for the soul in its descent into the world, the destination of the soul after death, as well as a domain inhabited by the righteous during life. In fact, as we shall see further on (see chapter 7) the Companions of the *Zohar* ascend to this realm every night in their nocturnal study vigil, the *shaashua*, the nocturnal delight. The earthly Garden of Eden is where the souls receive their instruction prior to their descent to earthly reality where they are given a taste of corporeality in a luminescent body. The garden is filled with images of things that exist in the physical world, but they are all imbued with a heavenly light, almost like a zoharic version of the Platonic world of forms: "The images and forms of this world are all depicted there and they are all engraved and inscribed there on the pattern of this world" (*Zohar* 2:150a).[22] From this realm, the righteous—in death and in life—grasp the third world, divinity itself, "a supernal world, mysterious, concealed and hidden," itself beyond the limits of human experience. While Rabbi Abba is, as we shall see later, describing the different stations of the human being in life and in death (we move from the world of separation to the earthly Garden of Eden and into the divine realm itself), he is simultaneously describing the different dimensions of reality inhabitable here and now. We simultaneously inhabit the world of separation as well as the higher worlds. In *The Enneads*, a philosophical-mystical masterpiece of great importance for *Zohar* study and a work to which we shall return numerous times, Plotinus describes something similar: "even our human soul has not sunk entire; something of it is continuously in the Intellectual Realm, though if that part which is in the sphere of sense hold the mastery . . . it keeps us blind to what the upper phase holds in contemplation."[23] Divinity, then, has three worlds, three domains or modes of being, and humanity too, created in the divine image, inhabits or participates in three different realms of existence.

> Therefore it is written, *You are children of YHVH your God* (Deut. 14:1).[24]
>
> It is as they have established.
>
> And these are in the image of God and these inherit a supernal inheritance, like His.
>
> Therefore He warned in the Torah, *You shall not gash yourselves or shave the front of your heads [because of the dead]* (ibid.), for he is not annihilated, but is found in good, supernal, and precious worlds.
>
> And [therefore] they should rejoice when the righteous depart from this world.

If we are, as the *Zohar* says, multidimensional beings, then death is not really death. Physical, bodily death pertains only to the world of separation. Death is merely the passage, bitter though it may be, from one world into others, "supernal and precious." In citing the verses

"You are children of YHVH your God" and "You shall not gash your-selves," Rabbi Abba's exposition sends us to another well-known pas-sage in the *Zohar* where we learn that death ought to be greeted with rejoicing:

> This may be compared to a king to whom a son was born. He sent him to a village to be raised until he came of age and could be taught the ways of the royal palace. The king heard that his son had grown up and come of age. What did he do? Out of love for his son, he sent the matron, his mother, and brought him into his palace and rejoiced with him every day.
>
> Similarly, the Blessed Holy One had a son by the *Matron-ita*.[25] And who is that?
>
> The supernal holy soul. He sent him to a village—to this world—so that he could grow up there and be taught the ways of the royal palace. When the King knows that His son has grown up in the village, and that the time has arrived to come to His palace, what does He do? Out of His love, He sends the *Matronita* for him and brings him into His palace. For the soul does not ascend from this world until the *Matronita* comes for it, escorting it into the palace of the King, where it dwells for-ever.
>
> Despite all this, it is the way of the world that those vil-lagers cried over the departure of the king's son. One wise man was there; he said to them: Why are you crying?
>
> Isn't he the son of a king? It is not fitting for him to dwell any longer among you, but rather in his father's palace!
>
> Similarly, Moses, who was wise, saw the villagers crying over this. He said, *You are children of YHVH your God! Do not gash yourselves* . . . (Deut. 14:1).
>
> —*Zohar* 1:245b (Matt, *The Zohar*)[26]

We will return to the question of the origin of the soul and its descent into terrestrial existence in greater detail in the following chapter. For our purposes, it is sufficient to highlight the idea that the soul originates in the divine realm (it is a child of YHVH and *Elohim*, the Blessed Holy One and *Malkhut*) from whence it is sent forth to the world to learn the ways of the King's palace. The soul is "exiled" from its divine abode and therefore death ought to be understood as a form of homecoming. The idea of death as a celebration, or *hillula* in Aramaic, is widespread in the *Zohar* (though the *Zohar* also knows how to lament the pain of separation—see 1:4a) and in the *Idra Zuta*, the section of the *Zohar*

that recounts the death of Rabbi Shimon, we are given a glimpse of the
ecstatic and blissful death of the grand master. Rabbi Abba, who is
given the task of recording Rabbi Shimon's final revelations of Torah,
describes his passing as follows:

> All day long, the fire in the house did not go out. No one
> reached him, no one could: light and fire surrounded him! All
> day long, I lay on the ground and wailed. After the fire disap-
> peared I saw the Holy Spark, Holy of Holies leaving the world,
> enwrapped, lying on his right side, his face smiling.
> —*Zohar* 3:296b, *Idra Zuta* (Matt, *Book of*
> *Enlightenment*; see also *Zohar* 1:218b)

Where the Companions experience terror and great sadness with the
passing of their master, Rabbi Shimon, like the wise man from the parable, knows that death is merely the passage into true life—the last word
on his lips is "life"—and therefore is able to greet death with rejoicing.

It is at this point that Rabbi Abba finally returns to the question
posed by Rabbi Yehudah at the beginning of our story:

> Come and see:
>   Had man not sinned, he would not have tasted the taste of
> death in this world when he entered the other worlds.
>   But since he sinned, he tastes the taste of death before he
> enters those worlds.

It is true that we were always intended to be mortal. Yet the death
envisaged for us was of a very different kind. "Had man not sinned, he
would not have tasted the taste of death in this world when he entered
the other worlds." Unlike Nahmanides, for example, who understood
death as a fall from our original eternal nature,[27] in this passage, death
is presented as part of God's design from the outset. The sin of the First
Man did not bring death into the world, only the pain, "the taste of
death." While the preexistent Torah does mention human mortality, the
mortality envisaged was one of peaceful and painless transition from
one mode of reality to another. Like Rabbi Shimon in the *Idra Zuta* and
the wise man in the parable, our entry into the other dimensions of
being was not intended to be accompanied by the sense of loss and
annihilation that now characterizes our experience of death. The *Zohar*
frequently discusses the dramatic change in human nature brought
about by Adam's sin, for example, the loss of our originary radiance,

the loss of our unmediated connection with the Tree of Life, as well as the contamination of our bodies.[28] In this text, the great transformation wrought by Adam's sin was not the fact of death, but our experience of it. Though death is now accompanied by its bitter taste, the prospect of returning to an Edenic state, where we might pass joyfully and painlessly from one dimension to another, like Enoch and Elijah, remains the patrimony of the righteous, the mystics, who understand that we are "children of YHVH" and that death is but a homecoming.

In the continuation of his homily, Rabbi Abba outlines the fate of the different parts of the soul, which neatly articulates with the three-fold structure employed earlier in his homily:

> The spirit (*ruaḥ*) divests itself of the body and leaves it behind in this world, and the spirit bathes in the river of fire (*nahar dinur*) to receive its punishment.
>
> Afterward, it enters the earthly Garden of Eden, where another garment of light awaits, just like the semblance of the body of this world, in which it adorns and arrays itself.
>
> And there is its abode forever.
>
> On New Moons and Sabbaths it joins with the super-soul (*neshamah*), ascends, and is crowned above and beyond, as it is written, *And new moon after new moon, and Sabbath after Sabbath, all flesh shall come to worship Me* (Isa. 66:23).

Like Plato and Aristotle, the *Zohar* adopts a tripartite notion of the soul. In place of Plato's desire, power, and intellect or Aristotle's vegetative faculty, animal faculty, and intellectual faculty, the *Zohar* employs the nomenclature of *nefesh, ruaḥ,* and *neshamah*.[29] While in the Bible and Talmud these terms are used synonymously, the *Zohar* reads them as signifying different parts in the totality of the human being. Like modern psychology that has developed a varied scheme for describing the different components of human personality (unconscious, id, ego, etc.), the *Zohar* also has its own language for describing our complex inner reality:

> *Nefesh*, soul, is lower arousal—supporting the body, nourishing it. The body fastens on her; she is fastened to the body. Afterward she is arrayed, becoming a throne on which settles *ruaḥ*, spirit, through the arousal of *nefesh* fastened to the body . . . Once both have been arrayed, they are ready to receive *neshamah*, for *ruaḥ* becomes a throne for *neshamah* . . .

> Come and see: *Nefesh*, lower arousal, cleaving to the body like the light of a candle. The lower light which is black, cleaves to the wick, never parting from it, arrayed by it alone. Once arrayed by the wick, it becomes a throne for the white light settling upon the black light. When both are arrayed, the white light becomes a throne for a concealed light—invisible, unknowable—settling upon the white light. Then the light is perfect.
>
> —*Zohar* 1:83b (Matt, *The Zohar*)

Nefesh is intimately associated with the body, *ruaḥ* serves a mediating function between the lower and higher aspects, while *neshamah*, the super-soul is associated with mystical and spiritual attainment. The *neshamah*, like the higher more recondite aspects of divinity, is a concealed light, invisible and unknowable.

The origin of the different parts of the soul is a complex matter with many contradictory statements found throughout the *Zohar*. In the main, though, while there is debate about the precise origin of the *nefesh* and the *ruaḥ*, namely, whether they have their origin in the divine or extra-divine world, there is no doubt that the *neshamah*, the super-soul, the highest faculty of the human being, has its origin in the world of the sefirot, in divinity itself. According to one zoharic statement with particular resonance for our passage, the *nefesh* and *ruaḥ* unite with the *neshamah* outside the realm of divinity among the "mountains of separation."

> Come and see: The *neshamah* emerges, navigating the mountains of separation, and *ruaḥ* is joined to soul. As it descends, *nefesh* joins spirit, all of them descending, joining one another.
>
> —*Zohar* 1:62a (Matt, *The Zohar*)

The different parts of the soul also meet with very different fates:

> The human soul is called by three names: *nefesh*, *ruaḥ*, and *neshamah*.
>
> They are all comprised one with the other and in three abodes their power is found.
>
> *Nefesh* is found in the grave while the body decomposes in the earth and flits about in the world, going here and there among the living, to know their sorrows, seeking mercy for them in their hour of need.

Ruah enters the earthly garden [of Eden], and is drawn there in the semblance of the body of this world, in a garment that it adorns there.

There it enjoys the pleasures and desires of the splendor of the garden.

On Sabbaths, New Moons, and festivals it ascends aloft, delights there, and returns to its place. About this it is written, *And the ruah returns to Elohim who bestowed it* (Eccles. 12:7)
. . .

Neshamah ascends directly to her place, to that domain from which she came forth, and it is on her account that the light is kindled, to shine above.

She never again descends below.

In her is comprised the One who embraces all sides, above and below.

Until she [*neshamah*] ascends to join with the throne, *ruah* is unable to be crowned in the earthly garden, and *nefesh* cannot rest in her place.

When she ascends, they all have rest.

—*Zohar* 2:141b[30]

Our text too outlines a similar destiny. The body (and presumably the *nefesh*) is left behind in this world, the world of separation, while the *ruah*, after being cleansed in the river of fire/light (see Daniel 7:10), takes up its abode in the earthly Garden of Eden. There it receives a garment of light, "just like the semblance of the body in this world," and enjoys a beatified existence. Elsewhere in the *Zohar*, this garment is described as woven from the good deeds performed on earth: "Happy are the righteous! Their days are all stored up with the Holy King, woven into radiant garments to be worn in the world that is coming" (*Zohar* 1:224a–b). The *neshamah*, the highest human faculty and that aspect of the soul with real propinquity to the divine, returns to the divine realm proper, above and beyond. Significantly, while the *ruah* must undergo purification before passing from this world to the next, the *neshamah* escapes all judgment. In one of his Hebrew works, *Sefer Nefesh ha-Hakhamah*, Moses de Leon comments on the logic of this arrangement. "If the *neshamah* is in the image of God and is derived from Him, how can He possibly judge Himself, His own essential being, since it is actually He Himself?"[31]

Interestingly, in the zoharic conception of the afterlife, time, or more specifically, Jewish time, is still operative. Every new month and every Sabbath, the *ruah* ascends into the realm of divinity where it unites with the *neshamah*. The sacred days are part of a mythological drama where the male and the female grades of divinity join together and enjoy union and harmony. This sacred drama impacts not only upon life in our world but also upon the soul's eternal existence.

> Why *new moon after new moon (hodesh be-hodsho)*?
>   The mystery of the matter:
>   Because of the renewal of the moon that is adorned at that time to illuminate from the sun.
>   And so *Sabbath after Sabbath (shabbat be-shabto).*
>   *Shabbat*—this is the moon.
>   *Be-shabto*—this is the sun, for Her light comes to Her from there, and therefore it is all one.

The *Zohar* finds in the last verses of Isaiah a description of the mythological union of the moon and the sun, *Malkhut* and *Tiferet*. The expression *hodesh be-hodsho*, which is usually rendered as new moon after new moon, is understood by the *Zohar* as symbolizing the renewal of the moon, the illumination of the last grade of divinity when it unites with *Tiferet*, the male aspect of the divine (the word *hodesh* is close to the word *hidush*, meaning renewal). The expression *shabbat be-shabto* is interpreted similarly. Shabbat, the seventh day, is a frequent symbol for *Malkhut*, the last of the sefirot and the seventh of the children of *Hokhmah* and *Binah*, while the word *shabto* is read as a symbol for the sun, the male aspect of the divine, perhaps because of the final *vav*, which is often taken as a marker of male divinity (*vav* has the numerical value of six and the male aspect of divinity is comprised of six different sefirot). *Shabbat be-shabto*, Sabbath after Sabbath, is thus read here as signifying the union of the male and female—*shabbat*, the female, *be-shabto*, with or in the male. To this densely encoded structure we might also add Rabbi Moses Cordovero's understanding of the verse where *be-shabto* is read as *be-shivto*, meaning "in his sitting," referring to the male aspect of divinity seated on the throne of *Malkhut*. Intricate exegesis aside, the zoharic world is dynamic to the core and even in the next world the soul's eternal life is characterized by movement and change, part of the never-ending divine story.

> And this is the explanation of the matter, apart from the wicked about whom is written death in all the worlds, excision from all the worlds, annihilation from all, if they do not enter repentance.

Rabbi Yehudah said: Blessed is the Merciful One that I asked this question, acquired these words and understood them!

As we shall see throughout this book, many zoharic narratives end with pathos-filled emotional responses—the Companions weep, kiss, express their great joy in hearing new words of Torah, and generally reflect on all that had befallen them. In our case, Rabbi Yehudah is not only delighted that he has acquired wisdom, but significantly blesses the Merciful One that he asked his question in the first place. Rabbi Yehudah's affirmation of his question is all the more significant in light of Rabbi Abba's earlier rebuke for having inquired after that which ought to remain concealed.

Having examined in detail the various parts of our unit, we can return now to Rabbi Yehudah's original questions: Why create a finite being who will know death? If it was already written in the preexistent Torah that we were fated to die, what of human free will? And, why does the Torah not save one from death in this world? Rabbi Abba's solution to Rabbi Yehudah's various questions turns on his fascinating understanding of the divine image. The divine reality is multidimensional, comprising hiddenness and unknowability, extension and revelation, as well as diminution of a kind, as the divine enters the world of separation. The human being is similarly constructed and to be in the divine image one must exist in three different modes—our world, the world of separation where death prevails; the earthly Garden of Eden, our luminescent or astral self; and divinity itself, the abode of our souls. Moses Cordovero explains as follows:

> The answer [to Rabbi Yehudah's question] is that it is impossible that a human being be in the upper world and not descend, for behold the essence of his perfection is to exist in all the worlds, to be like his father, namely, the mystery of the divine image . . . and if he did not exist in the lower world, then he is not in the image, for the essence is his being in three worlds which are like the three upper [worlds] . . .[32]

It is only in our descent to this realm, where we experience separation and death, that we complete our divine *imago*. We are spiritual beings, but spiritual beings who must experience physical existence and all that is associated with it to complete our divine nature. Death is not a fall from an ideal state and not the consequence of sin. Sin has only brought about the pain of death, which, as we have seen, can still be overcome.

The Torah, the Tree of Life, doesn't save us from death in this world because, according to our text, we need to die to complete our *imago*. Like God, we need to experience being present and not present. This we accomplish through the experience of finitude and transience in the world of separation. As we shall see in the following chapter, the question of the soul's descent into corporeality occupies a central place in zoharic speculation. In contrast to Gnostic and even Neoplatonic thought, corporeal life has great value. Indeed according to our text, death itself, the greatest of all human terrors and the ultimate consequence of corporeal existence, is given mystical meaning. Far from being the end, death merely signifies the completion of our divine nature.

Rabbi Yehudah came to his more senior colleague with the most difficult question of all—why create a being who will know the pain of death. When Rabbi Yehudah exclaims, "Blessed is the Merciful One that I asked this question, acquired these words, and understood them," we hear his joy and relief, and sense his consolation. We do not know what prompted Rabbi Yehudah to ask his question. The author does not tell us. We can assume that he was gripped by a dark, nihilistic moment. Perhaps he had lost someone dear to him or perhaps he was contemplating his own terrifying mortality. Whatever the case, between his opening question and his closing reflection, Rabbi Yehudah, and along with him we the readers, have been consoled through words of Torah. Walking and talking, the Companions have expanded our view of death and removed its bitter taste.

CHAPTER FOUR

•—•

The Magical Book
in the Cave of Souls

Zohar 3:303a *Tosafot* and *Zohar Ḥadash* 53 c–d

Rabbi Abba said: One day Rabbi Yehudah of Akko and I were walking
in the desert when we entered a certain cave and found there an ancient
book from primeval times. We opened it and found written at the beginning of its words: *The former things have come and new things I now
say* (Isa. 42:9), and [the book] explained the verse as referring to the
souls of the righteous.

> From the day that it arose in Thought to create the world, but
> before the world was created, all the spirits of the righteous
> were concealed in Thought before Him, each and every one in
> its own image.
>
> When He fashioned the world, they were all revealed and
> they stood in their image before Him in the Great Heights.
>
> Afterward He placed them in a certain treasury in the
> upper Garden of Eden. This treasury is never full and calls out
> continuously, *The former things have come and new things I
> now say.* What are the *things I now say*? All of them by their
> names. And this treasury's only desire and yearning is to draw
> down souls continuously, just as the only desire and yearning of
> *Gehinnom* is to receive souls, to be purified there, and everyday
> calls out: *Hav, Hav,* Give, Give! What is *hav, hav*? Burn, burn!

This treasury keeps all those souls until the time comes to robe them when they descend to this world. And because of the sin of the First Man, who darkened the world and drew down the evil other side to the world, these souls need to be robed in this garment, for behold, the Blessed Holy One desired to adorn these souls in another garment.

The book spoke: Till here. Be silent!
I saw further—erased letters, impossible to decipher, and afterward I saw them in a dream and they said: Be silent! Do not reveal to anyone except the Mighty Rock.
And so I did.
And I found in the book:

Should you say: Since the Blessed Holy One is destined to enrobe those souls in another garment in the future to come, why did He not prepare that garment for the dead restored by Ezekiel?

Well, it is because the time had not yet arrived to blow through the world that pure air that makes garments, and because of this He enrobed them just as they were. And so it will be at the resurrection of the dead except that the primal slime will not be found there.

When a human being departs this world, everyone—including the righteous, the pious, the wholehearted, the sinners, and the evildoers—everyone travels through the air to see the First Man of all the people of the world, and from there take the path either to the Garden of Eden or to *Gehinnom*. All those whose path is to the Garden of Eden approach the outer wall of the three walls there. Then a guardian comes out, rouses before them, calls out and says: Blessed are you O righteous in all the worlds. That guardian—Ye'azrael is his name—teaches them the way and they go before him until [they reach] one of the gates of *Gehinnom*. The guardian calls out loudly and says: Cool the smoke, cool the fires! In haste they cool them. Everyone enters, immerses, and passes through, and all the guilty are handed over to *Dumah* and enter *Gehinnom*. All the righteous are not handed over to him, but to the guardian, and after they immerse and pass, that guardian goes before them until they reach the wall of the Garden of Eden. The guardian calls out to the opening and says: *Open the gates, let a righteous nation enter, the nation that keeps faith* (Isa. 26:2). Then they open the opening and he brings them in, and so in every opening. Once they have entered within the site of the righteous, other righteous arise. How much delight upon delight for the righteous?! All the members of the academy rejoice! After three days concealed in known chambers they emerge. Air currents blow and they are all are drawn in their image. From here on they inherit an inheritance as is fitting for each and every one. The sight beheld in the Garden of Eden, from the glorious appearance of the image of all images, the spectrum of all spectrums of the Holy King, is not revealed in the hall and not in any single place. Rather, the embroidered firmament above the garden expands in four directions and is filled with the glorious, holy splendor and all the righteous shine. Who has seen the delight and yearning of this delightfulness of YHVH?!

Until this point I had permission to look in that book.
While I was turning around seeking to read more it flew out of my hands and I could not see it. I remained sad and wept.
I fell asleep there in that cave and saw him who is Clothed in Garments. He said to me: Why should you cry? Do not be saddened.
For it flew to the one whose book it was and he took it. For before he left this world he concealed it in this desert cave. Now that it was revealed to the living here, it flew in the air and he took it.
Now, go forth on your way!
Ever since that day it has not been revealed to me and I have not merited to hear whose book it was and whenever I remember this I am saddened.
Rabbi El'azar said: Perhaps the Blessed Holy One seeks His glory in desiring that it not be revealed in the world?
While they were sitting and engaging in other supernal and precious matters, day broke. They arose and walked on.
Rabbi El'azar said: Now is a time of favor before the Holy King. Let us say words of Torah and engage her and join with the *Shekhinah*.
He opened, saying: *Hear my voice O YHVH at daybreak; at daybreak I plead before you and wait* (Ps. 5:4).

Commentary on *Zohar* 3:303a *Tosafot* and *Zohar Ḥadash* 53 c–d

> *Man cannot live without a permanent trust in something inde-*
> *structible in himself, though both the indestructible element and*
> *the trust may remain permanently hidden from him.*
> —Franz Kafka, The Blue Octavo Notebooks

> *God—we read—is outside of none, present unperceived to all;*
> *we break away from Him, or rather from ourselves; what we*
> *turn from we cannot reach; astray ourselves, we cannot go in*
> *search of another . . . to find ourselves is to know our source.*
> —Plotinus, The Enneads

In *Pirke Avot* (The Sayings of the Fathers), the great collection of rabbinic aphorisms, a sage from the first century of the Common Era called Akavya ben Mahalalel directs us to consider three things as a result of which we will not fall into the hands of sin: "Know whence you came and where you are going and before whom you will have to give account and reckoning."[1] According to Akavya ben Mahalalel, knowledge and contemplation of our ultimate origin and destination provide the key to a life of humility and responsibility before God. Although quite different in religious orientation, Akavya's statement recalls a famous Gnostic riddle from antiquity that similarly views knowledge of our origin and destination as the key to attaining salvation: "What liberates is the knowledge of who we were, what we have become, where we were, whereinto we have been thrown, and whereto we speed . . . "[2] As is now well known, Gnostic salvation is predicated on the knowledge, the gnosis, of our celestial origins—origins that lie far indeed from our present earthly reality. According to the Gnostic myth, the human predicament is inextricably bound with the forgetting of our ultimate origins, our true nature and self, and salvation constitutes an act of remembering and return.[3] That the *Zohar* displays many Gnostic features and sensibilities is well established. In fact, Gershom Scholem, the pioneer of the modern academic study of Jewish mysticism, understood the emergence of the Kabbalah as a Gnostic explosion in the heart of Rabbinic Judaism.[4] Like the Gnostics, the *Zohar* too is particularly concerned with the question of our ultimate origins, and frequently tells the "story" of the soul's origin, descent, and then reintegration into the world of divinity. In fact, the *Zohar* describes such knowledge as a "secret and mystery divulged to the wise" (*Zohar* 2:11a), and refers to the Companions as "those who know the secrets of the spirits of the righteous" (*Zohar* 2:13a). In the previous chapter we touched upon the mystery of the soul's descent from its celestial abode into the world of separation. Many questions and issues, however, were left unexplored. Where precisely does the soul come from? What is the nature of its celestial existence? Why does it descend? How does it descend? How does it fare in the body on earth? And finally, what happens to soul upon death? It is to these questions that we now turn.

The passage before us, while itself a self-contained narrative, is actually part of a much longer zoharic unit (see *Zohar* 3:193b) and is found in two slightly different versions in *Zohar Ḥadash* and the *Tosafot* (additions) to the third volume of the *Zohar*. Our narrative begins with Rabbi Abba recounting to Rabbi El'azar a journey he once embarked upon through the desert with his companion Rabbi Yehudah from Akko.[5]

> Rabbi Abba said: One day, Rabbi Yehudah of Akko and I were walking in the desert when we entered a certain cave and found there an ancient book from primeval times. We opened it and found written at the beginning of its words: *The former things have come and new things I now say* (Isa. 42:9), and [the book] explained the verse as referring to the souls of the righteous.

As happens frequently in the *Zohar*, the traveling Companions first chance upon a cave, a key locus for many zoharic stories, and then find a mysterious book from primeval times containing the mysteries of the peregrinations of the soul. We shall return to this motif of mysterious books in greater detail further on. For now, it is sufficient to note that our story is woven through three different planes of reality—the first, the adventures of Rabbi Abba and Rabbi El'azar and all that befalls them on the way; the second, the side narrative featuring Rabbi Abba and Rabbi Yehudah recounted by Rabbi Abba to Rabbi El'azar; and the third, the contents of the ancient book they discover. The *Zohar* often plays with different levels of narration to great effect, and the story within a story is one of the zoharic authors' favored literary devices. In addition to adding depth to the narration, the impact upon the reader of being granted a glimpse of a book from primeval times is most pronounced. As we shall see, these primeval books contain the promise of a wisdom from the very dawn of humanity, and in presenting its teaching through the guise of an ancient book, it is as though the *Zohar* is taking us to a time before time, before history and before religion. Elsewhere in the *Zohar*, Rabbi Abba, who on many occasions appears as the great expert on these mysterious books, explains their origin and transmission. Especially significant in his account is the fact that "the wise of the

generation" (presumably the Companions themselves) have knowledge
of such works through which they discover higher wisdom:

> Rabbi Abba said: An actual book was brought down to Adam,
> from which he discovered supernal wisdom. This book reached
> the sons of Elohim, the wise of the generation, and whoever are
> privileged to contemplate it discover higher wisdom . . .
> Hanokh had a book—a book from the site of the book of the
> generations of Adam, mystery of wisdom . . . Happy are the
> devout of the world, to whom supernal wisdom is revealed,
> never to be forgotten, as it is said, *The secret of YHVH is for*
> *those in awe of Him; to them He reveals His covenant* (Ps.
> 25:14).
>   —*Zohar* 1:37b (Matt, *The Zohar*)[6]

In the inner recesses of a cave, Rabbi Abba and Rabbi Yehudah
begin reading from the mysterious work and find a verse from Isaiah
(42:9), "The former things have come and new things I now say" at the
top of the page. In its biblical context, the verse itself is quite straightforward and merely refers to God having fulfilled all that He predicted.[7]
Rabbi Abba, however, informs us that the book explained the verse as
referring to the souls of the righteous. What follows is, as it were, a
direct quote from the primeval book:

> From the day that it arose in Thought to create the world, but
> before the world was created, all the spirits of the righteous
> were concealed in Thought before Him, each and every one in
> its own image.
>   When He fashioned the world, they were all revealed and
> they stood in their image before Him in the Great Heights.
>   Afterward He placed them in a certain treasury in the upper
> Garden of Eden. This treasury is never full and calls out contin-
> uously, *The former things have come and new things I now say.*
> What are the *things I now say*? All of them by their names. And
> this treasury's only desire and yearning is to draw down souls
> continuously, just as the only desire and yearning of *Gehinnom*[8]
> is to receive souls, to be purified there, and everyday calls out:
> *Hav, Hav*, Give, Give! What is *hav, hav*? Burn, burn![9]
>   This treasury keeps all those souls until the time comes to
> robe them when they descend to this world. And because of the
> sin of the First Man, who darkened the world and drew down
> the evil other side to the world, these souls need to be robed in

this garment, for behold, the Blessed Holy One desired to adorn these souls in another garment.

The primeval book transports us to a primeval time, before the creation of the world, into the divine Thought itself, and proceeds to tell the story of the soul's descent, from the innermost recesses of the divine, through the sefirot, into the storehouse in the upper Garden of Eden, and finally into the world. We shall presently explain all the details of this important and complex zoharic passage. Before doing so, however, we need to outline the contours of one of the *Zohar*'s grand mythic structures—the origin and descent of the soul.

Although the *Zohar* contributes original understandings of the nature of the soul and its descent into corporeal existence, this "story" is already familiar to us, in its broad outline, both from the world of the Sages, and from Neoplatonic literature. Already in Talmudic times we encounter the idea of the preexistence of the soul. An enigmatic statement by Rav Yose in tractate *Yevamot* (62a) from the Babylonian Talmud with direct relevance for our text notes:

> The son of David will not come until all the souls in *Guf* (lit., body) have come to an end, for it is said: *For the spirit enwraps itself before Me and the souls that I have made* (Isa. 57:16).

The great medieval exegete Rabbi Shimon ben Isaac, better known by the acronym Rashi, wrote in his gloss to this passage: "There is a treasure house called *Guf*, and at the time of creation all the souls destined to be born were formed and placed there."[10] While the question of the sages' varied beliefs concerning the preexistence of the soul is a complex matter,[11] there seems little doubt that already in the Talmudic era, the Platonic idea of the soul's preexistence was widespread. Without doubt, the most important text in this regard is the passage found in Midrash *Tanḥuma* (*Pekudei* 3), known as *Seder Yetsirat ha-Valad* (The Order of the Formation of the Child):

> Rabbi Yoḥanan said: What is the meaning of the verse, *Who performs great deeds that cannot be fathomed, and wondrous things without number* (Job 9:10)?
>
> Know that all the souls, those that existed since Adam and those that will still come into being until the end of the whole world, were created in the six days of creation, and all are in the Garden of Eden, and all were present at the giving of the Torah . . .

When a man has sexual relations with his wife, the Blessed Holy One beckons the angel in charge of pregnancy, whose name is Layla, and says: Know that this night a person has been formed from the seed of so and so . . .

Immediately, the Blessed Holy One beckons the angel in charge of spirits and says to him: Bring Me such and such a spirit, which is in the Garden of Eden, is called so and so and whose appearance is thus and so.

At once the angel goes and brings the spirit to the Blessed Holy One.

When the spirit arrives it bows and prostrates itself before the King who is King of Kings, the Blessed Holy One.

In that instant the Blessed Holy One says to the spirit: Enter the drop that is in such and such an angel's hands.

The spirit opens its mouth and declares before Him: Master of the Universe, it is enough for me the world in which I have dwelt since I was created. Why is Your will to inject me into this putrid drop, for I am holy and pure, and I am hewn from the substance of Your glory?!

The Blessed Holy One immediately answers the soul: The world into which I will bring you will be better for you than that in which you dwelt; moreover, when I formed you, I did so only for this drop.

Immediately the Blessed Holy One compels it to enter therein.[12]

This text, only part of which has been quoted here and which deserves much greater attention, contains the key features of the rabbi's myth of the descent of the soul. Laid bare before us is the soul's preexistence in the Garden of Eden, its semi-divine or celestial status, and perhaps most importantly, the soul's reluctance to descend into this world, content as she is in the celestial realm. Indeed this antagonism between the soul, born of another realm, and our world is one of the key features of both the rabbinic and Neoplatonic myth.[13]

The *Zohar* explicitly references this text in a well-known passage that outlines the zoharic version of the soul's descent:

At the time that the Holy One, be blessed, was about to create the world, He decided to fashion all the souls that would in due course be dealt to the children of men, and each soul was formed into the exact outline of the body she was destined to tenant . . .

Each one in due time the Holy One, be blessed, bade come to Him, and then said:

Go now, descend into this place and into this body.

Yet often enough the soul would reply: Lord of the world, I am content to remain in this realm, and have no wish to depart to some other, where I shall be in thraldom and become stained.

Whereupon the Holy One, be blessed, would reply: Thy destiny is, and has been from the day of thy forming, to go into that world.

Then the soul, realizing it could not disobey, would unwillingly descend and come into this world.

The Torah, counsel of the entire world, saw this, and cried to mankind: Behold, see how the Holy One, be blessed, takes pity on you! Without cost, He has sent to you His costly pearl that you may use it in this world, and it is the holy soul.

And if a man sell his daughter to be a maid servant (Exod. 21:7)—that is, when the Holy One, be blessed, gives over to you His daughter the holy soul for your maid servant, to be held in bondage by you, I adjure you, in her due time, *she shall not go out as the men servants do* (ibid.), that is, stained with sin, but in freedom, in light, in purity, so that her Master may rejoice in her, and in rewarding her exceedingly with the glories of Paradise, as it stands written, *And the Lord will satisfy thy soul with brightness* (Isa. 58:11), that is, when she shall have ascended back to that sphere, bright and pure . . .

This is the significance of the words: *And if he espouses her unto his son, he shall deal with her after the manner of daughters.* What mean the words *after the manner of daughters?*

It is a secret held solely in the trust of the wise: A palace that is known as the Palace of Love sits amid a vast rock, a most secret firmament. Here in this place the treasures of the King are kept, and all His kisses of love. Every soul loved by the Holy One, be blessed, enters into that palace. And when the King makes His appearance, *Jacob kisses Rachel* (Gen. 29:11), which is to say, the Lord discerns each holy soul, and taking each in turn to himself, embraces and caresses her, *dealing with her after the manner of daughters*, even as a father acts toward his beloved daughter, embracing and caressing her, and presenting her with gifts.

—*Zohar* 2:96b[14]

Leaving aside some of the complex exegesis in this passage, we find here an account of the soul's descent and then reintegration into the divine realm. Our soul, the "costly pearl,"[15] "the daughter of the Blessed Holy One," hails from another realm and we are, as it were, sent forth against our will from the celestial domain into this world. As a part of divinity "exiled" from the divine self, the soul longs for its source, "the soul has only one longing: for the place from which it was taken" (*Zohar Ḥadash*, *Bereshit*, 18b), and the soul's journey is only complete upon returning home, so poetically depicted here through the tender and intimate image of the "Palace of Love."

As in both Gnostic and Neoplatonic versions of the soul's descent, the zoharic myth presents a view of the human being (or part of the human being) as at once divine yet also estranged from this world. As soul, we properly pertain to the celestial realm, yet find ourselves thrust into a very different reality.[16] We have already touched upon some of the reasons for the soul's descent, this "failing of the wings,"[17] and we will return to this important question again later. What is important for our purposes at present is the religious-spiritual sensibility underwriting this myth. Plotinus, the preeminent Neoplatonic philosopher, whose writings and thought were so important for Jewish, Christian, and Islamic mysticism, beautifully expresses this sensibility:

> But we . . . Who are "we"? Are "we" only the Spirit, or are we those who have added themselves on to the Spirit, and who came into being within time? We were other people before our birth, in that other world . . . As pure souls, we were Spirit . . . we were a part of the spiritual world, neither circumscribed nor cut off from it. Even now, we are still not cut off it. Now, however, another person, who wanted to exist and has found us . . . has added himself on to the original person . . . He joined himself on to the person we were then . . . Then we became both: now we are no longer only the one we were, and at times, when the spiritual person is idle and in a certain sense stops being present, we are only the person we have added on to ourselves.[18]

We need not subscribe to either Plotinus's or the *Zohar*'s ontology to appreciate the spiritual view outlined in this myth. Our true self is often hidden from us, and the return to our source is actually a return to our deepest self. Knowledge of the divine is simultaneously knowledge of our inner being. The rabbis, Plotinus, and the *Zohar* each understand our yearning for divinity as stemming not only from the fact of our primal soulfulness, but more specifically from our having once enjoyed celestial existence: "You would not seek Me if you had not already found Me," as Pascal observed.[19] The rabbis, for their part, express this same sentiment through the well-known account of the foetus studying Torah in utero,[20] while the *Zohar* achieves the same effect through the powerful image of each soul being granted a personal audience with the Blessed Holy One just prior to its descent:

> [The soul] is presented to the Holy King so that it might gain knowledge in this world and study the Blessed Holy One through the mystery of faith. This is the meaning of, *You have been presented so that you might know [that the Lord, He is God]* (Deut. 4:35)—you have been presented by the officer to the Blessed Holy One, *so that you might know*—so that you might gain a knowledge and understanding in this world of the mystery of faith, of the mystery of the Torah.
>   —*Zohar* 2:161b (Tishby and Goldstein, see also 2:13b)

Before descending into the world the soul is imprinted with the divine, and it is this memory that triggers and enables the human being to acquire knowledge of divinity in this world. We desire to and in fact can know God in this world, not only because part of us hails from the divine—as Plotinus writes, "Soul, a divine being and a dweller in the loftier realms, has entered body: it is a god, a later phase of the divine"[21]—but also because we have already known God.

But why does the soul descend? If the soul enjoys such a beatified existence in the celestial realm, why does God send her forth to be in "thraldom" in this world? In one of his Hebrew works, Moses de Leon provides a classical Neoplatonic answer:

> The purpose of the soul entering this body is to display her powers and actions in this world, for she needs an instrument. By descending to this world, she increases the flow of her power to guide the human being through the world. Thereby she perfects herself above and below, attaining a higher state by being fulfilled in all dimensions. If she is not fulfilled both above and below, she is not complete.
>
> Before descending to this world, the soul is emanated from the mystery of the highest level. While in this world, she is completed and fulfilled by this lower world. Departing this world, she is filled with the fullness of all the worlds, the world above and the world below.

At first, before descending to this world, the soul is imperfect; she is lacking something. By descending to this world, she is perfected in every dimension.[22]

While the soul faces great perils and dangers in this world, she is able to accomplish here, in our realm, what she cannot in the divine abode.[23]

Before returning to the account found by Rabbi Yehudah and Rabbi Abba in the mysterious primeval book, it is important to stress that unlike various Gnostic traditions that view the soul's descent as a great tragedy—"I am a Mana of the great Life. Who had made me live in the *Tibil*, who has thrown me into the body stump?"; "Grief and woe I suffer in the body garment into which they transported me and cast me"[24]—the *Zohar*, like Plotinus, is much more relaxed in its soul/world or soul/body dualism. While it is true that on occasion the *Zohar*, like Plato, views corporeal existence as a prison for the soul,[25] in general the *Zohar* adopts a favorable and optimistic view of corporeal life. The world is full of delights and the path to the divine is not beyond this world, but through this world, itself a reflection or extension of divinity.[26]

Back to our book in the desert cave:

From the day that it arose in Thought to create the world, but before the world was created, all the spirits of the righteous were concealed in Thought before Him, each and every one in its own image.

When He fashioned the world, they were all revealed and they stood in their image before Him in the Great Heights.

Afterward He placed them in a certain treasury in the upper Garden of Eden.

The descent of the soul is described here in three stages.[27] Before the creation of the world, the souls are described as abiding concealed in the divine Thought, an allusion to the second sefirah *Hokhmah*, the primal seed of being. At this stage, it seems, the souls exist in potential only, yet significantly are already described as being "each and every one in its own image." These potential souls are not merely amorphous, generalized entities, but already here, in the inner recesses of the divine, display individuality. Our individuality then is no accident of history or chance, but is inscribed in the divine mind at the beginning of time. We are who we are because we were already so in the divine thought. The second stage of the descent is somewhat unclear, yet seems to suggest the progressive actualization of the souls at the time of the creation of

the world from mere potential in the divine thought to a more actualized existence in the world of the sefirot (the Great Heights). From here
the souls are placed in a treasury in the upper Garden of Eden from
whence they are poured forth into the world, their birth or delivery
beautifully portrayed as a personal speech act by the divine realm—"all
of them by their names." As the celestial realm speaks our name we
flow into being and become ourselves.

The souls abide in the upper Garden of Eden enjoying celestial bliss
until the time comes for their descent to the world. Elsewhere the *Zohar*
writes that thirty days prior to their descent into the earthly realm, the
souls descend into the lower Garden of Eden, where they are given a
taste of corporeal life and adorned with their luminescent body.[28] In our
text, however, this stage is not outlined, and we are told instead that it
is only because of Adam's sin that souls are required to be garbed in
bodies of flesh and blood. God, it seems, had something else in mind,
"for behold the Blessed Holy One desired to adorn those souls in
another garment." Following a well-known rabbinic midrash where we
learn that human beings were originally to have been garbed in coats of
light rather than coats of skin,[29] the *Zohar* attributes the loss of our
originary supernal radiance to the sin of the First Man (see *Zohar*
1:36b). We are then beings who hail from the divine thought as well as
beings of light, even if only in intention.

It is worth pausing momentarily and reflecting on this rich zoharic
myth. As we have seen, the *Zohar* frequently recounts the "story" of
the soul's descent, and the Companions often discuss our celestial origins deep in the inner recesses of divinity. Above and beyond the doctrinal content such accounts relay, these stories are perhaps best thought
of as zoharic meditations on our primal soulfulness.[30] By telling the
story of our soul's origin in the depths of the divine realm, we are
reminded or perhaps we might say awakened to our deepest nature, a
nature that has its origin in the primal seed of being. These stories, then,
play an important performative function and serve to evoke in the
reader a consciousness of our higher selves. In his wonderful book on
the thought of Plotinus, Pierre Hadot explains what he terms Plotinus's
central intuition, which we might easily apply to the *Zohar*:

> . . . the human self is not irrevocably separated from its eternal
> model, as the latter exists within divine Thought. The true
> self—the self in God—is within ourselves. During certain privi-
> leged experiences, which raise the level of our inner tension, we
> can identify ourselves with it. We then become this eternal self;
> we are moved by its unutterable beauty, and when we identify

ourselves with this self, we identify ourselves with divine Thought itself, within which it is contained.[31]

The zoharic passage we have just read and others like it aim at something similar and seek to evoke in us, the readers, an image of ourselves as we exist in the divine mind and deep within ourselves.

Having been granted a glimpse of the teachings from the mysterious book and having learned the stages of the soul's descent, we are surprised to find the book itself, till now, an ordinary book, distinguished only by its great age and wondrous content, suddenly come to life and address our protagonist.

> The book spoke: Till here. Be silent!
> I saw further—erased letters, impossible to decipher, and afterward I saw them in a dream and they said: Be silent! Do not reveal to anyone except the Mighty Rock.
> And so I did.

Like a scene from a child's fairytale or from one of Tolkien's adventures in Middle Earth, the book now reveals its magical qualities, speaking to Rabbi Abba, abruptly setting a limit to his inquiries. The book, like the *Zohar*, is protective of its secrets. The letters on the page then begin to disappear, only to appear once again, this time in a dream. Now it is the letters themselves that address Rabbi Abba, granting him permission to see more, as long he agrees not to divulge the mysteries contained in its pages to anyone, save Rabbi Shimon, the Mighty Rock. While Rabbi Abba informs Rabbi El'azar that he indeed fulfilled his pledge—"and so I did"—as readers we can only smile as we, like Rabbi El'azar, have been brought into a secret domain.

If the first encounter with the mysterious book focused on the soul's descent, the second encounter, whether in a dream or in waking we cannot be certain, takes as its focus the soul's ascent and reintegration into the divine. In contrast to medieval Jewish philosophers who tended to downplay or allegorize some of the mythical and fantastic attitudes to the afterlife found in the rabbinic corpus, the *Zohar* freely adopts and expands these mythical horizons. Maimonides, for example, famously ignored hell in his conception of the afterlife, and reinterpreted rabbinic expressions of celestial bliss to fit his Aristotelian conception of the eternity of the intellect. Commenting on a well-known Talmudic passage, "In the world to come there is no eating, no drinking, no sexual intercourse, no commerce, no envy, no hatred and no rivalry; but the righteous sit with their crowns on their heads enjoying the radiance of the Divine Presence" (BT *Berakhot* 17a), Maimonides writes:

> In this passage the expression "with their crowns on their heads" signifies the immortality of the soul being in firm possession of the Idea which is God the creator. The crown is precisely the Idea which great philosophers have explicated at length. The expression, "they delight in the radiance of the Divine Presence" means that souls enjoy blissful delight in their attainment of knowledge of the truly essential nature of God the creator . . . [32]

As we shall now see, the zoharic conception of the afterlife is far indeed from such rational treatments, and prefers instead a hyper-imaginative approach to our postmortem fate.

While the *Zohar* contains many rich descriptions about the moment of death itself, even detailing on occasion the violent and painful separation of the soul from the body (see *Zohar* 3:126a–127a), our text begins with a journey we all must take once we have left our bodies behind in this world:

> When a human being departs this world, everyone—including the righteous, the pious, the wholehearted, the sinners, and the evildoers—everyone travels through the air to see the First Man of all the people of the world, and from there take the path either to the Garden of Eden or to *Gehinnom*.

All human beings begin their postmortem existence with a private encounter with our great ancestor, Adam, the First Man of all. Here, the *Zohar* is borrowing an idea already found in rabbinic literature. In *Numbers Rabbah* (19:18) we read that human beings "do not depart this life without gazing upon the face of the *Shekhinah* and reproving Adam, saying: You inflicted death upon us!" Adam, we read, responds by saying, "As for me, I possess only one sin, while in your case, every single one of you possesses more than four."[33] Beyond conveying the rabbinic idea that there is no death without sin, this audience with Adam marks the first stage in our return to our origins.

The souls then continue on their journey:

> All those whose path is to the Garden of Eden approach the outer wall of the three walls there. Then a guardian comes out, rouses before them, calls out and says: Blessed are you O right-

eous in all the worlds. That guardian—Ye'azrael is his name[34]—teaches them the way and they go before him until [they reach] one of the gates of *Gehinnom*. The guardian calls out loudly and says: Cool the smoke, cool the fires! In haste they cool them. Everyone enters, immerses and passes through, and all the guilty are handed over to *Dumah*[35] and enter *Gehinnom*. All the righteous are not handed over to him, but to the guardian, and after they immerse and pass, that guardian goes before them until they reach the wall of the Garden of Eden. The guardian calls out to the opening and says: *Open the gates, let a righteous nation enter, the nation that keeps faith* (Isa. 26:2).[36]

Led by a celestial guardian, all the souls are escorted into *Gehinnom*. The passage into the celestial realm requires that even the righteous immerse themselves in the *nahar di-nur*, the river of fire/light, and before returning to its divine abode, the soul must be purged of the dross of corporeality.[37] The scene, while ceremonial and formal, is also humorous, (the *Zohar* as we shall see is often quite comic), as the guardian requests that the furnaces of hell be turned down a few degrees so as not to frighten the tender souls of the righteous.

In response to the guardian's invocation, the celestial realm opens and we are granted a glimpse of soul's homecoming:

Then they open the opening and he brings them in, and so in every opening. Once they have entered within the site of the righteous, other righteous arise. How much delight upon delight for the righteous?! All the members of the academy rejoice! After three days concealed in known chambers they emerge. Air currents blow and they are all are drawn in their image. From here on they inherit an inheritance as is fitting for each and every one. The sight beheld in the Garden of Eden, from the glorious appearance of the image of all images, the spectrum of all spectrums of the Holy King, is not revealed in the hall and not in any single place. Rather, the embroidered firmament above the garden expands in four directions, and is filled with the glorious, holy splendor and all the righteous shine. Who has seen the delight and yearning of this delightfulness of YHVH (*noam YHVH*)?!

As in rabbinic literature, the celestial realm is imagined as a heavenly academy and the souls are joyously greeted by other righteous souls already resident there. Then begins the process of the soul's transformation. Like a caterpillar in a cocoon undergoing its metamorphosis into a butterfly, the souls spend three days in "known chambers." The air currents of the garden then blow and the souls regain their astral image, the preexistent heavenly garment worn by the soul in its paradisiacal existence prior to entering the body. Every realm has its garment and even in the celestial domain souls require a garment in order to behold the divine glory.[38]

Drawn in their heavenly garb, the souls enjoy a beatific vision, "the image of all images, the spectrum of all spectrums." It is not that souls see God Himself, but rather that the reality or dimension that they now inhabit is filled entirely with "glorious holy splendor," termed by the *Zohar* the "delight of YHVH." The firmament of the Garden of Eden, whose wondrous properties are frequently expounded by the *Zohar*,[39] expands and pours forth a delicate and subtle substance in which the souls bathe and bask:

> Twenty-two letters are inscribed and engraved upon that firmament. Each and every letter drips dew from the dew above the garden. From the dew of these letters the souls are bathed and healed after immersing in the river of fire to be purified. The dew descends only from within the letters that are inscribed and engraved upon that firmament, because these letters are the entirety of the Torah.
>
> —*Zohar* 2:210a

In *Seder Gan Eden*, a Hebrew work with many parallels to our own passage, and most likely written by Rabbi Moses de Leon, the firmament of the garden is depicted in a most dynamic fashion. The firmament revolves emitting a sweet melody, reminiscent, as Moshe Idel has pointed out, of the Pythagorean music of the spheres:

> The voice of the melody of the firmament . . . travels by the hand of the Man Clothed in Garments, and he moves away and the firmament stands and the pillar sings, it ascends and descends, so that the light of splendor, the light of the pleasantness, is drawn from above within that pillar, and the righteous stand vis-à-vis that light and enjoy it until midnight. It is at midnight that God comes with the righteous to listen to the voice of the turn of the firmament, and the pillar sings and the soil of the garden is elevating, and the righteous are ascending from their mansions toward their Creator, and the entire garden is filled by His glory.[40]

Both in this passage and in our text the culmination of the soul's celestial vision is the infusion of the "delight of YHVH" into the garden.

This delight of YHVH, the "*noam YHVH*," appears frequently in the *Zohar* as the pinnacle of mystical experience, both in this world and in the next.[41] The term itself is derived from a verse in Psalms, "One thing I ask of YHVH, that alone do I seek: to dwell in the house of YHVH all the days of my life, to gaze upon the delight (*noam*) of YHVH, and to frequent His palace" (Ps. 27:4). In the *Zohar*, this delight is understood as a liquid quality that originates within the depths of divinity, sometimes associated with the sefirah *Binah*, termed by the *Zohar* "the world that is coming," and sometimes with the most recondite aspect of divinity, *Atika Kadisha*, the sefirah *Keter*, the most primal and undifferentiated aspect of the divine.

> This delightfulness is the delight issuing from the world that is coming . . . Alternatively, the world that is coming is called delightfulness.
> —*Zohar* 1:197b (Matt, *The Zohar*)

> But the secret of the matter is in that which is written, *to gaze upon the delight of YHVH, to frequent His temple* (Ps. 27:4) . . .
> The delight of YHVH—that which comes from *Atika Kadisha*, and in which the Blessed Holy One delights, for that delight flows from *Atika*.
> —*Zohar* 3:267b

The experience of bathing in the *noam YHVH* is one of nourishment, satiety, and fullness produced as a result of abiding in the presence of God and being satiated by the vision of divinity.[42] With this satiety and fullness, the soul's journey is now complete and the Psalmist's desire to "dwell in the house of YHVH all the days of my life" attained.

Having first outlined the soul's descent and then, in the second encounter with Rabbi Abba, recounted the soul's reintegration into the divine abode, the book has completed its account of the soul. Its story now complete, the book once again displays its magical qualities:

> Until this point I had permission to look in that book.
> While I was turning around seeking to read more it flew out of my hands and I could not see it. I remained sad and wept.

I fell asleep there in that cave and saw him who is Clothed in Garments.[43]

He said to me: Why should you cry? Do not be saddened.

For it flew to the one whose book it was and he took it. For before he left this world he concealed it in this desert cave.[44] Now that it was revealed to the living here, it flew in the air and he took it.

Now, go forth on your way!

Ever since that day it has not been revealed to me and I have not merited to hear whose book it was and whenever I remember this I am saddened.

Rabbi El'azar said: Perhaps the Blessed Holy One seeks His glory in desiring that it not be revealed in the world?

While they were sitting and engaging in other supernal and precious matters, day broke. They arose and walked on.

Rabbi El'azar said: Now is a time of favor before the Holy King. Let us say words of Torah and engage her and join with the *Shekhinah*.

He opened, saying: *Hear my voice O YHVH at daybreak; at daybreak I plead before you and wait* (Ps. 5:4).[45]

As happens in many zoharic narratives figuring such mysterious books, the book flies out of Rabbi Abba's hands. In *Zohar* 2:13b, in a story with many similarities to our own, we find yet another account about the soul's descent accompanied by the motif of a disappearing book. In this story, it is Rabbi El'azar who is given a mysterious written parchment by an anonymous wandering Jew, who in turn obtained it in a paradisiacal cave from a "man with a scepter." When Rabbi El'azar takes the bundle of writings and opens them, "a tongue of flame emerged and surrounded him. He examined it and then it flew out of his hands." Aryeh Wineman has artfully explored the significance of this zoharic literary motif. Commenting on the book of Adam, a book given by Raziel (the angel of mysteries) to Adam while in the Garden of Eden, and through which Adam was able to "daily wield treasures of his Lord, discovering supernal mysteries of which supernal ministers are unaware" (*Zohar* 1:55b),[46] Wineman suggests that these ancient books function as a virtual mirror of the *Zohar* and enable the *Zohar* to speak of itself and its own kind of wisdom. Like the book of Adam, the *Zohar* contains mysteries of the higher realms and wisdom hailing from the onset of human history, and like the book of Adam, these mysteries must be guarded and concealed from those not worthy.[47] In our story, the book from primeval times flies out of Rabbi Abba's hands, leaving him depressed and eager to peruse more pages of its ancient wisdom. The frequent disappearance of these books and the ensuing frustration of their would-be readers is perhaps also a zoharic reflection on the nature of mystical knowledge and insight. While the mystical path is full of moments of insight and illumination, such moments are elusive and enigmatic, and although they can be experienced, they cannot be firmly grasped. In the introduction to *The Guide of the Perplexed*, a work dedicated to exploring philosophical truth rather than mystical truth, Maimonides neatly expresses this quality of intellectual attainment:

> You should not think that these great secrets are fully and completely known to anyone among us. They are not. But sometimes truth flashes to us so that we think that it is day, and then matter and habit in their various forms conceal it so that we find ourselves again in an obscure night, almost as we were at first. We are like someone in a very dark night over whom lightning flashes time and time again.[48]

The *Zohar*'s disappearing books, often accompanied by flames of fire, function as a narrative expression of this same idea. Like the book discovered by Rabbi Abba, mystical knowledge and spiritual attainment are fleeting. Books, like knowledge, appear, come to life and disclose, only to disappear again, leaving us changed but still uncertain: "Now that it was revealed to the living here, it flew in the air and he took it!"

As Rabbi Abba finishes recounting his subterranean desert adventure, day breaks and Rabbi Abba and Rabbi El'azar continue on their journey, engaging in words of Torah so as to unite with the *Shekhinah*. Our passage with all its complexity is merely one side story, itself containing multiple levels of narration, in a much larger narrative. The Argentinean writer Jorge Luis Borges, whose short stories have much in common with zoharic narratives, once remarked that all fantasy literature relies on four fundamental techniques: the story within a story, the dream, the voyage in time, and the character double or doppelganger.[49] As we have seen in this chapter and as we shall see throughout this book, zoharic narrative freely and artfully plays with these techniques, and the *Zohar*, in addition to being the great medieval repository of kabbalistic teaching, is also a masterpiece of fantasy literature.

•◆•

CHAPTER FIVE

"Feast Friends and Drink, Drink Deeply O Lovers"

Rabbi Yeisa the Younger on Wine and the Divine Flow

Zohar 3:39a–41a

Rabbi Yehudah and Rabbi Yitzhak were walking on the way from Beit Meron to Sepphoris, and with them was a child with a donkey carrying wine spiced with honey.

Rabbi Yehudah said: Let us say a word of Torah while we walk.

Rabbi Yitzhak opened, saying: *Your mouth like choicest wine, flowing smoothly to my beloved* (Song of Songs 7:10).

Your mouth like choicest wine—this is the wine of Torah that is good, for there is another wine that is not good, but the wine of Torah is good for all, good for this world and good for the world that is coming. And this is the wine that pleases the Blessed Holy One more than all. And by virtue of this, he who is saturated with the wine of Torah will awaken to the world that is coming and will merit to arise to life when the Blessed Holy One shall raise the righteous.

Rabbi Yehudah said: *Rousing (dovev) the lips of sleepers* (ibid. 7:10)— for we have learned that even in that world he will merit to ply Torah, as it is written, *causing the lips of sleepers to move.*[1]

The child said: Were it written, *Your mouth* **from** *choicest wine*, I would agree. But it is written, **like** *choicest wine* and not **from** choicest wine. They looked at him.
Rabbi Yehudah said: Say your word, my son, for you have spoken well.

He said: I have heard that he who engages Torah and cleaves to her, and that word of Torah is heard in his mouth, not whispered in a whisper, but rather he raises his voice—for Torah requires that one's voice be raised, as it is written, *At the head of busy streets she calls; [at the entrance of the gates, in the city, she speaks out]* (Prov. 1:21), to raise the song of Torah, not in a whisper—[such a person] is *like choicest wine*, like choice wine that is not silent, and is destined to raise his voice when he shall depart this world.
Flowing smoothly (meisharim, lit., straight) to my beloved—he will not stray to the right or the left with no one to delay him.
Rousing the lips of sleepers—even in that world his lips will murmur Torah.

I have further heard:
Your mouth like choicest wine—this verse was addressed to the Assembly of Israel and was said in Her praise.
If so, who is it that praises Her thus? If it is the Blessed Holy One why does it say, *flowing to my beloved*? It should have said, *flowing to me*!
Rather, for certain the Blessed Holy One praises the Assembly of Israel, just as She praises Him, as it is written, *his mouth is delicious* (Song of Songs 5:16), so the Blessed Holy One praises the Assembly of Israel, *your mouth like choicest wine*, the choice wine that is the preserved wine.
Flows to my beloved—this is Isaac who is called "beloved from the womb."
Meisharim, straight—as it is said, *You established equity (meisharim)* (Ps. 99:4), to contain the left in the right, and this is *meisharim*. On account of the joy of that choice wine, the left is contained in the right and all rejoice.
Rousing the lips of sleepers—for all are aroused with joy and blessings, and all the worlds rejoice and are aroused to pour forth blessings below.

Rabbi Yehudah and Rabbi Yitzhak came and kissed him on the head and rejoiced with him. They said to him: What is your name?
He said to them: Yeisa.
They said: You shall be Rabbi Yeisa and you will live longer than Rabbi Yeisa our companion who has departed from us.

They said to him: And who is your father?

He said to them: He has passed from the world. Every day he used to teach me three matters of Torah, and every evening three matters of wisdom of Aggadah. These words I learned from father. Now my abode is with a man who separates me from the Torah and every day I attend to his work. Every day I repeat those matters I learned from father.

They said to him: This man, does he know any Torah?

He said to them: No. He is an old man and doesn't even know how to bless the Blessed Holy One, and he has sons and he does not send them to school.

Rabbi Yehudah said: Were it not so I would enter the village to speak on your behalf. Now, however, we are forbidden from even seeing his face! Leave your donkey and you will come with us.

They said to him: Who was your father?

He said to them: Rabbi Zeira from the village of Ramin.

Rabbi Yehudah heard and wept. He said: I was in his house and I learned from him three matters pertaining to the cup of blessing, and two regarding the work of creation (*maaseh bereshit*).

Rabbi Yitzḥak said: If from this child his son we have learned, how much more so from him!?

They walked on holding his hand.

They saw a field and sat there.

They said to him: Recite one word of those your father taught you about the work of creation . . .

Rabbi Yehudah said: It really is not fitting for this child to know so much! Yet I see in him that he will ascend to a supernal site . . .

They arose and walked on.

Rabbi Yehudah said: Let us join this youth with us and every one shall say a word of Torah.

Rabbi Yehudah opened, saying: *Prop me up with raisins, refresh me with apples, for I am faint with love* (Song of Songs 2:5). This verse has already been expounded and it is well.

But the Assembly of Israel says this in exile.

Prop me up (samkhuni)—what is meant by *prop me up*? The one who falls is in need of support, as it is written, *YHVH supports (somekh) all who stumble and makes all who are bent stand straight* (Ps. 145:14). And therefore the Assembly of Israel who has fallen, as it is written, *fallen, not to rise again [is Maiden Israel]* (Amos 5:2), requires support, and says, *prop me up*.

To whom does She speak? To Israel Her children, for they are in exile with Her.

With what [shall they support Her]? With *raisins*. These are the patriarchs who are the first to be filled with that good, preserved wine, and when they are filled blessings are found for Her through a certain grade, the Righteous One.

He who knows how to unify the holy name, even though blessings are not found in the world, provides succour and support for the Assembly of Israel in exile.

Refresh me with apples—it is all one as we have said.

But this is the mystery:

Raisins intoxicate, apples detoxicate and harness desire.

Therefore raisins and apples. Raisins to saturate with wine and apples to harness desire so that the wine not cause harm.

Why all of this? *For I am faint with love*—in exile.

He who unifies the holy name must unite judgment in mercy, comprising them fittingly, perfuming and arraying all as is proper.

This is what supports the Assembly of Israel in exile.

Rabbi Yitzḥak opened: *Who ate the fat of their offerings and drank their libation wine?* (Deut. 32:38). Happy are Israel for they are holy and the Blessed Holy One desires to sanctify them.

Come and see: Israel are holy. All the eternal life they inherit depends entirely on the world that is coming, for it is the life of all, above and below, the site where the preserved wine is stored, from where life and sanctity go out to all.

The wine of Israel is on account of the wine of another Israel, one depending on the other. For Israel above draws into itself life and therefore is called the Tree of Life, the tree from the site called Life, from where life flows forth. Therefore [Israel] bless the Blessed Holy One with wine . . .

The child opened, saying . . .

Come and see:

Oil for the priests and wine for the Levites.

Not because they need wine, but rather because some of the preserved wine flows to their side, to unite all as one, bringing joy to all the worlds, so that all will be found in them, the right and the left contained this one in that, in them the amiability of all, and the love of the sons of faith.

Whoever attaches his will to this is perfect in this world and in the world that is coming, and all his days cleaves to *Teshuvah*, Return, the place where wine and oil are found.

Then he will not cleave to this world, neither to its riches nor to its delights.

About this did King Solomon cry out, saying, *He who loves wine and oil does not grow rich* (Prov. 21:17), for other riches await him, for him to partake, that he might have a portion in the world that is coming, the place where wine and oil are stored, in this world and in the world that is coming.

Whoever loves this place does not require wealth and does not pursue it.

Happy are the righteous who everyday engage in the supernal wealth, as it is written, *Gold or glass cannot match its value, nor vessels of fine gold be exchanged for it* (Job 28:17), this is in this world, and afterward [in the world to come], *to endow those who love me with substance (yesh), I will fill their treasuries* (Prov. 8:21) . . .

Rabbi Yehudah and Rabbi Yitzḥak came and kissed his head.

From that day on he never left Rabbi Yehudah's house, and when he would enter the *beit midrash*, Rabbi Yehudah would rise before him, saying: I have learned something from him and it is fitting that I should treat him with respect.

Afterward, he ascended to the rank of the Companions and they would call him Rabbi Yeisa, the hammerhead who smashes rocks and makes sparks fly in all directions, and Rabbi El'azar used to apply to him the verse, *Before I created you in the womb, I knew you* (Jer. 1:4).

Commentary on *Zohar* 3:39a–41a

Wisdom has built her house, she has hewn her seven pillars. She
has prepared the feast, mixed the wine, and also set the table.
She has sent out her maids to announce on the heights of the
town: "Let the simple enter here." To those devoid of sense she
says: "Come, eat my food, and drink the wine that I have
mixed. Give up simpleness and live, walk in the way of under-
standing (binah)."

—Proverbs 9:1–6

The Lover is ever drunk with love;
he is free, he is mad, he dances with ecstasy and delight.
Caught by our own thoughts, we worry about every little thing.
But once we get drunk on that love, whatever will be will be.

—Rumi

Of the many literary productions and innovations to emerge from
the quills of the Jews of Spain, one of the most endearing, and perhaps surprising, is wine poetry. The Golden Age of Spanish Jewry has
bequeathed to us a formidable collection of poems that take as their
focus the "fruit of the grape," as well as detailed and evocative descriptions of elaborate wine parties, held between midnight and dawn. It is
to the Jews of Spain that we owe the Jewish rediscovery of poetry as a
literary form, a form they learned and adapted from the Muslims of
Andalusia.[2] Although somewhat strange to the modern ear, Arabic wine
poetry occupied an important place in the cultural life of the aristocracy
and upper classes, and was, to say the least, a lavish affair. From the
poetry itself, as well as from contemporary accounts, we are able to
glean a picture of this fascinating cultural practice, where men would
assemble under the night sky, in gardens, in courtyards, and by the river,
attended by servants and entertained by musicians, to drink wine, recite
poetry, and play improvisational poetic games. Like their Islamic coun-
terparts, the Jewish aristocracy also composed wine poetry and, presumably, although we possess no accounts to confirm this, engaged in
the same kind of wine parties and poetic play evidenced in the Islamic
sources. Shmuel Ha-Nagid (993–1055), the vizier of the ruler of
Granada, is without doubt the greatest exponent of this genre. His
poems are rich, nuanced, ironic, and playful, as the following short
poem demonstrates:

Your debt to God is righteously to live,
And His to you, your recompense to give.

Do not wear out your days in serving God;
Some time devote to Him, some to yourself.
To Him give half your day, to work the rest;
But give the jug no rest throughout the night.
Put out your lamps! Use crystal cups for light.
Away with singers! Bottles are better than lutes.
No song, nor wine, nor friend beneath the sward—
These three, O fools, are all of life's reward.[3]

In addition to the irreverent tone—take God seriously, but not too seriously, after all, life must be enjoyed—we are struck by the closing lines of the poem, which celebrate fraternity, poetry, and wine as the greatest goods of life. The poem transports us to a scene more familiar from ancient Greece, as in Plato's *Symposium*, for example, where men would drink and eat, enjoying one another's company, while engaging in philosophical conversation. In perhaps his most famous wine poem, Shmuel Ha-Nagid cautions us not to speculate on hidden things, but instead, to fill the cup with coral drink and keep Ecclesiastes' rule, a reference no doubt to Ecclesiastes' philosophy of carpe diem, as found throughout the book: "Go, eat your bread in gladness and drink your wine in joy; for your action was long ago approved by God" (Eccles. 9:7).

My friend, we pass our lives as if in sleep;
Our pleasures and our pains are merely dreams.
But stop your ears to all such things, and shut
Your eyes—may Heaven grant your strength!—
Don't speculate on hidden things; leave that
To God, the Hidden One, whose eye sees all.

But send the lass who plays the lute
To fill the cup with coral drink,
Put up in kegs in Adam's time,
Or else just after Noah's flood,
A pungent wine, like frankincense,
A glittering wine, like gold and gems,
Such wine as concubines and queens
Would bring King David long ago.

The day they poured that wine into the drum,
King David's singer Jerimoth would strum
And sing: "May such a wine as this be kept

Preserved and stored in sealed-up kegs and saved
For all who crave the water of the grape.
For every man who holds the cup with skill,
Who keep the rule Ecclesiastes gave,
Revels, and fears the tortures of the grave."[4]

In this wonderful poem, full of rich descriptions and subtle allusions, the poet takes up one of the key themes of Arabic wine poetry, namely, the age and vintage of the water of the grape, "put up in kegs in Adam's time," a theme with strong resonances both in rabbinic literature and our *Zohar* passage.

The Jews of Spain, of course, were not the first Jews to celebrate, describe, and lament the wonders of wine, for both the Bible and rabbinic literature are replete with references to both the positive and negative effects of the fruit of the vine. The Torah portion *Shemini* contains a stern warning to the priests not to consume wine in their divine service: "And YHVH spoke to Aaron, saying: Drink no wine or other intoxicant, you or your sons, when you enter the Tent of Meeting, that you may not die. This is a law for all time throughout the generations" (Lev. 10:10). While "wine rejoices the hearts of men" (Ps. 104:15), it also seduces and impairs judgment: "Do not ogle that red wine, as it lends its color to the cup, as it flows on smoothly; in the end, it bites like a snake; it spits like a basilisk" (Prov. 23:31–32; see also Prov. 7). It is in the Song of Songs, however, so beloved to the *Zohar*, that wine receives it most lavish treatment. Here, in the garden of Eros, the fertile landscape of the two lovers, wine is ever present, used both to describe the flowing and dynamic love of the young couple, as well as the sexual act itself:

Kiss me, make me drunk with your kisses!
Your sweet loving is better than wine.
You are fragrant, you are myrrh and aloes.
All the young women want you.
Take me by the hand, let us run together!
My lover, my king, has brought me into his chambers.
We will laugh, you and I, and count each kiss, better than
    wine.
                                        —Song of Songs 1:2–4

I have come into my garden, my sister, my bride.
I have gathered my myrrh and my spices,
I have eaten from the honeycomb,

I have drunk the milk and the wine.
Feast, friends and drink, till you are drunk with love.
                                    —Song of Songs 5:1[5]

While the Andalusian milieu and the tradition of Jewish wine poetry are indispensable references, it is the Song of Song's depiction of wine—flowing, arousing, erotic, and delightful—that above all informs the *Zohar*'s creative use of this literary motif.

As noted, rabbinic literature is also filled with references to the multivalent nature of wine. Wine is simultaneously the root of all evil, "We have been taught that Rabbi Meir said: The tree whose fruit Adam ate was a vine, for nothing brings as much woe to man as wine" (BT *Sanhedrin* 70a), as well as the ultimate good awaiting the righteous in the world to come: "*No eye has seen O God but You* (Isa. 64:3)—What does *no eye has seen* refer to? Rabbi Yehoshua the son of Levi said: To the wine that has been preserved in its grapes since the six days of creation" (BT *Sanhedrin* 99a; see also BT *Berakhot* 34b). A felicitous *gematria* (numerology) establishes the connection between wine and *sod*, secrets or mysteries (both have the numerical value of seventy; BT *Eruvin* 65a), and repeatedly, the Torah is compared to wine:

> *Your sweet loving is better than wine*—The words of the Torah are compared to water, to wine, to oil, to honey, and to milk . . . Shall I say that just as water after being drunk is imperceptible in the body, so are the words of Torah? Not so, since it is compared with wine: just as wine leaves its mark when drunk, so words of Torah leave their mark and people point with the finger and say, that is a scholar. Shall I say that just as water does not gladden the heart, so the words of Torah? Not so, since it is compared with wine: just as wine rejoices the heart, as it is written, *wine that rejoices the heart of men* (Ps. 104:15), so words of Torah rejoice the heart, as it says, *The precepts of the Lord are just, rejoicing the heart* (Ps. 19:9).
> —*Song of Songs Rabbah* 1.2.3 (trans. Soncino modified)

The sensual-erotic nature of wine, so apparent in the Song of Songs, is also employed by the Rabbis to describe the giving of the Torah, often compared to the marriage between the Children of Israel and God. Commenting on the verse "Now he has brought me to the house of wine, and his flag over me is love" (Song of Songs 2:4), the rabbis remark:

> *Now he has brought me to the house of wine*—Rabbi Meir and
> Rabbi Yehudah gave different explanations of this. Rabbi Meir
> said: The Assembly of Israel said: The evil inclination obtained
> mastery over me like wine and I said to the calf, *These are your
> gods O Israel* (Exod. 32:4). When wine goes into a man it con-
> fuses his mind.
>
> Rabbi Yehudah said to him: Enough of that, Meir. We do
> not expound the Song of Songs in a bad sense but only in a
> good one, since the Song of Songs was composed only for the
> praise of Israel.
>
> What then is meant by, *Now he has brought me into the
> house of wine*? The Assembly of Israel said: The Blessed Holy
> One brought me to a great wine cellar, namely Sinai . . .
> —*Song of Songs Rabbah* 2.4.1 (trans. Soncino modified)

The joy, the influence, and the flow of wine are thus central metaphors
for the intoxication of Torah. It is with this rich store of imagery and
associations that the *Zohar* begins its exploration of wine.

··•··

Let us now return to our passage that appears in the *Zohar*'s commentary to the Torah portion *Shemini*, which as we have already seen contains the warning to the priests not to consume any alcohol in their
divine service. While it is not always easy to understand why a particular zoharic narrative is placed where it is, in this case, the logic behind
the location of our narrative, with wine as its focus, is readily apparent.
Our unit begins, as is the *Zohar*'s custom, with two of the Companions
walking on a journey, in this case from Beit Meron to Sepphoris, two
locales of particular significance in the *Zohar*,[6] and displays the now
familiar format of the classical zoharic narrative—the invocation to
learn Torah while walking on the way, as well as the anonymous fellow
traveler looming in the background, who as we have come to expect
will soon enter the story:

> Rabbi Yehudah and Rabbi Yitzhak were walking on the way
> from Beit Meron to Sepphoris, and with them was a child with
> a donkey carrying wine spiced with honey.
>
> Rabbi Yehudah said: Let us say a word of Torah while we
> walk.

The narrative detail about the child and his cargo, wine spiced with
honey, immediately raises our expectation that this child, like so many

of the wunderkinder encountered throughout the *Zohar*'s pages, is no ordinary youth. As we have already noted, the Torah is repeatedly compared to both wine and honey, their juxtaposition here also recalling their erotic combination in the Song of Songs (5:1): "I have eaten from the honeycomb, I have drunk the milk and the wine."

The associative method of the *Zohar*, whereby the protagonists respond to all that befalls them on the way, allowing the external "real" world to generate their interpretations of Torah, leads Rabbi Yitzḥak to expound a verse about wine.

> Rabbi Yitzḥak opened, saying: *Your mouth like choicest wine, flowing smoothly to my beloved* (Song of Songs 7:10).
>
> *Your mouth like choicest wine*—this is the wine of Torah that is good, for there is another wine that is not good,[7] but the wine of Torah is good for all, good for this world and good for the world that is coming. And this is the wine that pleases the Blessed Holy One more than all. And by virtue of this, he who is saturated with the wine of Torah will awaken to the world that is coming and will merit to arise to life when the Blessed Holy One shall raise the righteous.
>
> Rabbi Yehudah said: *Rousing (dovev) the lips of sleepers* (ibid. 7:10)—for we have learned that even in that world he will merit to ply Torah, as it is written, *causing the lips of sleepers to move.*[8]

Rabbi Yitzḥak's opening verse takes us immediately to the erotic heart of the Song of Songs. The verse he cites is in fact part of a short dialogue between the two young lovers. The young man, the lover, voices his deepest erotic desires: "I said in my heart, let me climb into that palm tree and take hold of its branches. And oh, may your breasts be like clusters of grapes on a vine, the scent of your breath like apricots, your mouth like choicest wine," at which point the young woman, the beloved, playfully interrupts her lover, completing his sentence, "flowing smoothly to my beloved, rousing the lips of sleepers." Following earlier rabbinic interpretation equating Torah and wine, Rabbi Yitzḥak expounds the verse as referring to the ingestion of the wine of Torah, which in turn rouses the imbiber from a state of slumber. The quest here is to be saturated with the wine of Torah, filled with the divine plenty, the flow of divinity, through learning or, more literally, imbibing and internalizing words of Torah.[9] As wine arouses the senses, so too the Torah, "rouses the lips of sleepers." While the *Zohar* here seemingly follows an older rabbinic interpretation of the verse suggesting that even in the next world the righteous continue to learn Torah (see BT *Sanhedrin* 90b; *Song of Songs Rabbah* 7.10.1), it may also be referring to the Torah's ability to affect a transformation in the consciousness of the learner, leading one from a state of slumber, unaware of the divine dimensions of reality, to a state of mystical awareness, the knowledge of the world that is coming, the sefirah *Binah*, the source of the flow of divinity into the world. The motif of the passage from slumber to wakefulness, as well as the idea of the Torah as the active agent capable of leading the adept to a state of mystical awareness, is found repeatedly in the *Zohar*,[10] and it is precisely this kind of arousal that lies at the heart of the entire zoharic quest. Returning to the verses from the dialogue in the Song of Songs, we now understand the full erotic import of the lover's desire—"to climb into that palm tree and take hold of its branches"—to cleave to the Torah, the " tree of life to those who cling to her," and in so doing, to experience her flowing love.

Following this opening homily, the narrative unfolds in classical zoharic fashion. The young child, till now silent, raises an objection to the rabbis' interpretations:

> The child said: Were it written, *Your mouth **from** choicest wine*, I would agree. But it is written, ***like** choicest wine* and not **from** choicest wine.
>
> They looked at him.
>
> Rabbi Yehudah said: Say your word, my son, for you have spoken well.
>
> He said: I have heard that he who engages Torah and cleaves to her, and that word of Torah is heard in his mouth, not whispered in a whisper, but rather he raises his voice—for Torah requires that one's voice be raised, as it is written, *At the head of busy streets she calls; [at the entrance of the gates, in the city, she speaks out]* (Prov.1:21), to raise the song of Torah, not in a whisper[11]—[such a person] is *like choicest wine*, like choice wine that is not silent, and is destined to raise his voice when he shall depart this world.
>
> *Flowing smoothly (meisharim, straight) to my beloved*—he will not stray to the right or the left with no one to delay him.
>
> *Rousing the lips of sleepers*—even in that world his lips will murmur Torah.

The child's objection is at once precocious, technical, and brilliant. Insisting on reading the verse absolutely literally, the child points out that the verse in fact reads "your mouth **like** choicest wine," and not "from choicest wine," a reading that has served as the basis for the rabbi's focus on the state of being filled from the wine of Torah. Astounded, the Companions invite the child to speak, at which point he suggests an alternate reading of the verse. Like choice wine that is not silent but generates voice, the student of Torah must sing her song, raising his voice—and not in a whisper. Where the rabbis focused on the process of imbibing and internalizing, the child now focuses on the process of speaking out and pouring forth. While Torah must be imbibed, this alone is insufficient. Zoharic arousal is geared toward creativity and innovation, and mystical arousal only reaches its peak when the mystic verbalizes and externalizes, creates and innovates.

The child continues:

> I have further heard:
> *Your mouth like choicest wine*—this verse was addressed to the Assembly of Israel and was said in Her praise.
> If so, who is it that praises Her thus? If it is the Blessed Holy One why does it say, *flowing to my beloved*? It should have said, *flowing to me*!
> Rather, for certain the Blessed Holy One praises the Assembly of Israel, just as She praises Him, as it is written, *his mouth is delicious* (Song of Songs 5:16), so the Blessed Holy One praises the Assembly of Israel, *your mouth like choicest wine*, the choice wine that is the preserved wine.
> *Flows to my beloved*—this is Isaac who is called "beloved from the womb."[12]
> *Meisharim, straight*—as it is said, *You established equity (meisharim)* (Ps. 99:4), to contain the left in the right, and this is *meisharim*. On account of the joy of that choice wine, the left is contained in the right and all rejoice.
> *Rousing the lips of sleepers*—for all are aroused with joy and blessings, and all the worlds rejoice and are aroused to pour forth blessings below.

In the continuation of his homily, the child finds in the verse from the Song of Songs a description of the erotic play between the male aspect of divinity, the Blessed Holy One, and its female face, the Assembly of Israel. Their love drama constitutes the central axis of the divine story in the *Zohar*. Where the rabbis of the Talmudic era read the song as a dialogue between the People of Israel and God, the *Zohar* finds in this love story the paradigmatic account of the complex love relations— desire, longing, union, and separation—between the male and female

aspects of divinity. Following Rabbi Akiva, who viewed the Song of
Songs as the "holy of holies," the *Zohar* likewise views the song as the
most sublime expression of the divine dynamic. Repeatedly throughout
the *Zohar*, the Companions expound its Eros-laden verses as symbolizing the drama of the flow of divinity, with particular emphasis on the
sexual relations between the Blessed Holy One, the sefirah *Tiferet*, and
the Assembly of Israel, the *Shekhinah*. Drawing on the rabbinic idea of
the preserved wine awaiting the righteous in the world to come, the
child reads the verse "Your mouth (*hekekh*) like choicest wine" as signifying the process of the infilling of the divine female with the flowing
fluids from above, from the higher recesses of divinity. The child here is
perhaps playing on the word *hekh*, "mouth," which is quite close to the
word *hek*, meaning "lap" or even "womb," and thus finds in the verse
an erotic account of the fertilization and impregnation of the *Shekhinah*
whose mouth/womb is filled with the wine/semen of divinity. This wine,
whose origins we will soon learn are in the sefirah *Binah*, "the world
that is coming," flows through the divine being, into the sefirah *Gevurah*, the left side associated with the demonic, after which it is "contained in the right," the sefirah *Hesed*, and brought into a state of
balance in *Tiferet*, symbolized here by the term *meisharim*, equity. Its
harsher aspects softened through this act of mediation (see further on),
the wine of divinity then flows into the divine female who, once filled, is
able in turn to pour forth her bounty to the mystics below, "rousing the
lips of sleepers" to generate mystical arousal.

As we shall see in greater detail in chapter 7, the *Zohar* frequently
conceptualizes divinity as a flowing river, seeking to burst forth out of
itself and bathe the world, especially human consciousness, with its
diverse qualities. While water and light are the most important symbols in the *Zohar*'s description of this dynamic aspect of the divine,
wine too plays a key role in the *Zohar*'s account of the flow of the
divine plenty. In one of the more complex and developed narratives in
the *Zohar*, which begins during the day beneath some trees on the
plain of Ginnosar, and continues on to the house of Rabbi Shimon at
midnight,[13] we find the culminating mystical experience of the Companions described as the flow of the preserved wine throughout the
divine being and onto the assembled mystics. After a day full of Torah
innovations Rabbi Yose, who until this point in the narrative has not
expounded Torah, is invited to speak by Rabbi Shimon. Following a
series of expositions focusing on the Song of Songs, he takes up the
theme of the preserved wine. Beginning once again with a verse from
the Song of Songs, "Let him kiss me with the kisses of the mouth, for
your love is better than wine," Rabbi Yose uncovers the grand story of

the descent of the divine flow through the various grades of the sefirot and onto those below:

> *Let him kiss me with the kisses of his mouth, for your love is better than wine* (Song of Songs 1:2) . . .
>
> To whom does *Let him kiss me refer*? To the one concealed in supernal concealment . . .
>
> *Let him kiss me*—the concealed one above.
>
> With what? With the supernal chariot, upon which all the hues depend, in which they fuse. This is Jacob,[14] as we have said, the cleaving with which the King cleaves to His son, and therefore it is written, *with the kisses of his mouth.*
>
> *For your love is better than wine (me-yayin)*—[the verse] returns to the sun that illuminates the moon from the light of those supernal kisses; He takes the light from all of them and illuminates the moon.
>
> And these lights that unite in him [Jacob], from which site do they illuminate?
>
> [The verse] resumes and says, *from wine (me-yayin)*—from the preserved wine, the wine that is the joy of all joy.
>
> What is this wine that gives life and joy to all? This is Living God, *Elohim Ḥayyim*, the wine that gives life and joy to all.
>
> —*Zohar* 2:147a (see also *Zohar* 1:70b, 3:4a)

In this delightful homily Rabbi Yose outlines the descent of the pre-served wine, the "kisses of the mouth," from their origins in the con-cealed of the concealed, the most hidden recesses of the divine, through the divine male, termed here Jacob, and onto the divine female, the moon. The wine from which "all are illuminated and rejoice" Rabbi Yose calls, *Elohim Ḥayyim*, Living God, and is at once a reference to the source of the preserved wine in the sefirah of *Binah*, as well as testimony to the state of being filled, here and now, with the divine flow, rendered tenderly and erotically as kisses of the mouth. Rabbi Shimon recognizes that the wine they have been expounding is now present within the Companions themselves, and declares: "Now I know for sure that the High Holy Spirit is vibrating within you."[15] Rabbi Yose's homily then is actually a "real time" description of the descent of the wine of divinity from on high into the innermost parts of the mystics below. While our passage does not contain this heightened ecstatic state, the child's homily shares the same basic structure, celebrating the descent of the divine wine, its ingestion as well as the mystical arousal it engenders.

Returning to our narrative:

Rabbi Yehudah and Rabbi Yitzḥak came and kissed him on the head and rejoiced with him. They said to him: What is your name?

He said to them: Yeisa.

They said: You shall be Rabbi Yeisa and you shall live longer than Rabbi Yeisa our companion who has departed from us.

They said to him: And who is your father?

He said to them: He has passed from the world. Every day he used to teach me three matters of Torah, and every evening three matters of wisdom of Aggadah. These words I learned from father. Now my abode is with a man who separates me from the Torah and every day I attend to his work. Every day I repeat those matters I learned from father.

They said to him: This man, does he know any Torah?

He said to them: No. He is an old man and doesn't even know how to bless the Blessed Holy One,[16] and he has sons and he does not send them to school.

Rabbi Yehudah said: Were it not so I would enter the village to speak on your behalf. Now, however, we are forbidden from even seeing his face. Leave your donkey and you will come with us.

They said to him: Who was your father?

He said to them: Rabbi Zeira from the village of Ramin.

Rabbi Yehudah heard and wept. He said: I was in his house and I learned from him three matters pertaining to the cup of blessing, and two regarding the work of creation (*maaseh bereshit*).[17]

Rabbi Yitzḥak said: If from this child his son we have learned, how much more so from him!?

They walked on holding his hand.

They saw a field and sat there.

They said to him: Recite one word of those your father taught you about the work of creation.

Astounded by his masterful expositions, the companions now inquire of the child, who reveals that he is in fact the child of Rabbi Zeira from the village of Ramin (the Village on High), a fellow mystic master, although apparently from a different mystical fellowship. While the village of Ramin is unknown to us from rabbinic sources, it appears again in the *Zohar*. In the *Zohar*'s commentary to *parashat Noah*, we find a fabulous story featuring Rabbi Ḥiyya and Rabbi Yose in which they encounter a Jew en route to obtain a *lulav* and the four species for Sukkot. In the course of their conversation, the Jew informs them about his town, the village of Ramin: "True, the place we live in is small, but everyone there engages in Torah under the guidance of one inflamed by the rabbis: Rabbi Yitzḥak, son of Yose from Mahoza, who each day tells us new words" (*Zohar* 1:63a, Matt). On numerous occasions the *Zohar* hints at the existence of other mystical groups centered around various leaders. While these may merely be fictional tropes, it is also possible that these alternate mystical fellowships refer to real circles of mystics in Spain, different from, but nevertheless sharing some spiritual kinship with, the circle responsible for the *Zohar*.[18]

The Companions admit the child into their rank, noting that he will now replace their colleague, Rabbi Yeisa the Elder, who died in the great mystical assembly recounted in the *Idra Rabba*, perhaps the pinnacle moment in the entire zoharic corpus. Our narrative, which recounts the ascent of Rabbi Yeisa the Younger, as he comes to be known, represents an interesting development of this same character as he is first found in an earlier stratum of the *Zohar*, *Midrash ha-Ne'elam* (*Zohar Ḥadash* 84d–85c),[19] where he appears as a young man possessing mystical knowledge about the book of Ruth. While we do not know exactly how the *Zohar* was written, whether by one man as Gershom Scholem thought, or by a group of men over numerous generations as scholars have suggested more recently, zoharic narratives demonstrate both a series of subtle and more explicit connections with one another, as well as narrative and character development across the composition's different literary layers. In this case, we find a reworking of an earlier zoharic character, Rabbi Yeisa the Younger, who is now given a "back story" or spiritual biography explaining how he came to be associated with the Companions of Rabbi Shimon.[20] That Rabbi Yeisa the Younger, or Rabbi Yeisa Zeira in Aramaic, is actually the child of a rabbi by the name of Zeira adds a charming element of play to this account. We shall return later to further developments in the life of this zoharic character.

After recounting one of the teachings he learned from his father, where he uncovers in the verses of creation the sefirotic structure of divinity, focusing once again on the flow of divinity throughout its various grades, Rabbi Yehudah returns to the theme of wine and the Song of Songs:

Rabbi Yehudah opened, saying: *Prop me up with raisins, refresh me with apples, for I am faint with love* (Song of Songs 2:5). This verse has already been expounded and it is well.[21]

But the Assembly of Israel says this in exile.

Prop me up (samkhuni)—what is meant by *prop me up*? The one who falls is in need of support, as it is written, *YHVH supports (somekh) all who stumble and makes all who are bent stand straight* (Ps. 145:14). And therefore the Assembly of Israel who has fallen, as it is written, *fallen, not to rise again [is Maiden Israel]* (Amos 5:2), requires support, and says, *prop me up*.

To whom does She speak? To Israel Her children, for they are in exile with Her.

With what [shall they support Her]? With *raisins*. These are the patriarchs[22] who are the first to be filled with that good, preserved wine, and when they are filled blessings are found for Her through a certain grade, the Righteous One.[23]

He who knows how to unify the holy name, even though blessings are not found in the world, provides succour and support for the Assembly of Israel in exile.

Refresh me with apples—it is all one as we have said.

But this is the mystery:

Raisins intoxicate, apples detoxicate and harness desire. Therefore raisins and apples. Raisins to saturate with wine and apples to harness desire so that the wine not cause harm.

Why all of this? *For I am faint with love*—in exile.

He who unifies the holy name must unite judgment in mercy, comprising them fittingly, perfuming and arraying all as is proper.

This is what supports the Assembly of Israel in exile.

Rabbi Yehudah reads out of the verse in the song a description of the existential situation of the *Shekhinah*, the divine female, the last of the sefirot, as well as Her relationship with the children of Israel. In exile with Her children, separated from Her divine lover, the Blessed Holy One, the *Shekhinah* calls on the children of Israel to support Her. As we have noted, one of the central innovations of kabbalistic thought in general, and the *Zohar* in particular, is the idea that the fate of God, in this case, the divine feminine, is in the hands of humanity below. For the *Zohar*, God's perfection and healing depend on the actions of human beings, who through their worship and Torah study, cause the divine plenty to flow throughout the divine organism, enabling the union of the two lovers. In exile, the *Shekhinah* is lovesick, desperate for Her lover, the Blessed Holy One, and it is the children of Israel who must support Her with raisins, the flow of the preserved wine.

The verse, however, contains yet another zoharic mystery, of supreme importance both for the *Shekhinah* and the mystics below. While the two parts of the verse "Prop me up with raisins / refresh me with apples" refer to the same idea—"it is all one as we have said"— there is, nevertheless, a secret in the combination of two different foods with which the children of Israel must sustain the *Shekhinah*. Although arousing, wine, as we all know, can also be harmful, and its raw rousing power requires tempering and mediation. Saturation with wine, both for the *Shekhinah* and the mystic, requires the combination of the intoxicating quality of the wine, balanced by the harnessing quality of the apples, the forces of judgment tempered by the forces of mercy, the left contained in the right. As Elliot Wolfson has pointed out, this idea of perfection, both human and divine, as contingent on the balancing of opposing forces, lies at the heart of zoharic anthropology and theosophy:

> Come and see: From the right hand of God all light, blessings, and happiness are aroused. Within the right the left is contained, just as there is in a human being a right and left hand, and the left is contained in the right . . . When the right is aroused the left is aroused with it, for the left is held and contained within the right . . . When the right hand is found, the left is found with it, and acts of judgment do not dominate in the world . . . But if the right is removed and the left is summoned, then acts of judgment are stirred up in the world and judgment rests upon all.
>
> —*Zohar* 2:57a

Beyond the union of the male and female, the mystics of the *Zohar*, like God, must cultivate the correct balance between love and justice, and it is this advice that Rabbi Yehudah finds in the verse from the song. Religious-spiritual life does not require that the left, the darker, more dangerous and seductive aspects of ourselves be eliminated; the task, rather, is to incorporate them into the right:

> The perfect state is not one in which evil is entirely obliterated, but rather one in which it is contained within the good. Only the sick soul must eliminate all traces of the left; the healthy soul by contrast, can re-appropriate the left and thereby unite it

with the right. Indeed the essence of divine worship is to worship God with both hearts, i.e., to contain the evil inclination
within the good, the left within the right.[24]

The child's closing homily on wine, like Rabbi Yitzhak's before him,
functions as a kind of conclusion to all that has preceded, insofar as it
offers an explicit statement regarding the correct orientation of religious
life. Following the Hermetic adage, "as above, so below," Rabbi
Yitzhak expounds the significance of earthly wine as a symbol for the
divine wine—"the wine of Israel is on account of the wine of another
Israel," namely, the Blessed Holy One, who draws wine from the world
that is coming, the sefirah *Binah*. Israel below bless God with wine,
both to theurgically draw down the divine wine into their reality, and
simultaneously to evoke their contemplative goal, "the site called Life,
from where life flows forth." The child' s exposition leaves no doubt as
to the ultimate goal of mystical activity:

Come and see:
   Oil for the priests and wine for the Levites.
   Not because they need wine, but rather because some of
the preserved wine flows to their side, to unite all as one, bringing joy to all the worlds, so that all will be found in them, the
right and the left contained this one in that, in them the amiability of all, and the love of the sons of faith.[25]
   Whoever attaches his will to this is perfect in this world
and in the world that is coming, and all his days cleaves to
Teshuvah, Return, the place where wine and oil are found.
   Then he will not cleave to this world, neither to its riches
nor to its delights.
   About this did King Solomon cry out, saying, *He who loves
wine and oil does not grow rich* (Prov. 21:17), for other riches
await him, for him to partake, that he might have a portion in
the world that is coming, the place where wine and oil are
stored, in this world and in the world that is coming.
   Whoever loves this place does not require wealth and does
not pursue it.
   Happy are the righteous who everyday engage in the supernal wealth, as it is written, *Gold or glass cannot match its
value, nor vessels of fine gold be exchanged for it* (Job 28:17),
this is in this world, and afterward [in the world to come], *to
endow those who love me with substance (yesh), I will fill their
treasuries* (Prov. 8:21) . . . [26]

As we have seen throughout this chapter, and as we find repeatedly throughout the *Zohar*, the mystic is instructed to direct his thoughts, attention, and contemplative focus to "the world that is coming," the sefirah *Binah*, the source of the river of divine plenty that flows through the varied layers of reality. This, in short, is the mystical quest—to attain the river of emanation and through its flow, connect with its and all of reality's origin, evocatively called "*Teshuvah*," the site to which we seek to return. Attuned to this level of being, the mystic has no interest in the riches of this world, which as the verse from the Hymn to Wisdom in Job suggests, pale in comparison to the attainment of knowledge of the divine. "He who loves wine and oil does not grow rich" (Prov. 21:17). Where the proverb cautions against a life of hedonism warning that "he who loves pleasure comes to want," the *Zohar* finds in this verse a description of mystical life. Focused on the wine and oil of divinity, the mystic turns from the riches of this world to the supernal wealth of live contact with God. Cleaving to *Teshuvah*, "the place where wine and oil are found," the mystic bathes in the saturation of the divine flow, endowed with *yesh*, the sefirah *Ḥokhmah*, ultimate divine reality, the primal point of divine being, and is filled with the variegated qualities of divinity.

.◆.

Our narrative, as already noted, is a form of spiritual biography, of which we find many throughout the *Zohar*,[27] and concludes with a brief account of Yeisa' s initiation into the fellowship of the Companions:

> Rabbi Yehudah and Rabbi Yitzḥak came and kissed his head.
>
> From that day on he never left Rabbi Yehudah's house, and when he would enter the *beit midrash*, Rabbi Yehudah would rise before him, saying: I have learned something from him and it is fitting that I should treat him with respect.[28]
>
> Afterward, he ascended to the rank of the Companions and they would call him Rabbi Yeisa, the hammerhead who smashes rocks and makes sparks fly in all directions,[29] and Rabbi El'azar used to apply to him the verse, *Before I created you in the womb, I knew you* (Jer. 1:4).[30]

Although now a member of the mystical fraternity centered around Rabbi Shimon, Rabbi Yeisa the Younger's status as a junior member of the fellowship returns on numerous occasions (see *Zohar* 2:153a). One of the charming features of the *Zohar*, which is not organized according to any linear or chronological logic, is the often surprising discovery of narrative and character threads that weave across the composition's many layers. Of particular significance in this regard is a touching tale of yet another step in Rabbi Yeisa's mystical initiation. Evidently nervous in the presence of the great master, Rabbi Shimon, Rabbi Yeisa is unable to concentrate his memory on the lesson of the day. As the *Zohar* tells it:

> Rabbi Yeisa could not remember and became distressed; he went home and went to sleep. They showed him in his dream a book of Agaddah in which was written, "wisdom (*Hokhmah*) and glory (*Tiferet*) are in His sanctuary."
>
> He awoke and went to Rabbi Shimon.
>
> He kissed his hands and said: Thus I saw in my dream . . . they showed me a book of Agaddah in which was written, "wisdom (*Hokhmah*) and glory (*Tiferet*) are in His sanctuary. *Hokhmah* above, *Tiferet* below, *His sanctuary* with them." Thus did I once see in my dream, and thus was found on my lips (lit., in my mouth).
>
> Rabbi Shimon said to him: Until now you have been too young to ascend among the reapers of the field. Now they have shown you everything, and this is [indeed the meaning of] what is written, *What is his name and what is his son's name, if you know it?* (Prov. 30:4). *His name* is Hokhmah, *his son* is Tiferet.
>
> —*Zohar* 2:79a–b

In this tender portrayal of a young initiate before his master, we read of Rabbi Yeisa's full acceptance as a member of the zoharic fellowship. While the theosophical content imparted by Rabbi Shimon to Rabbi Yeisa is itself unremarkable, detailing the well-known sefirotic relationship between *Tiferet*, the son, and the primal father, *Hokhmah*, this brief narrative is, at once, humorous, delicate, and profound. Only after forgetting, relearning, forgetting again, and then, through a form of prophecy, regaining the knowledge he once possessed, does Rabbi Shimon consider him worthy of joining the "reapers of the field," one of the more delightful epithets for the Companions themselves.[31] Although zoharic narratives may be entirely fictional, one cannot help but feel, on occasion, that they are infused with the real-life encounters between disciple and master. No doubt, it is this "real" quality that has so captured the hearts of the *Zohar*'s readers across the generations.

·•·

We began our exploration of zoharic wine with a brief glimpse at the Hebrew Andalusian tradition of wine poetry. How different is this

zoharic treatment?! Although the precise influence of Spanish Jewish
poetry on the *Zohar* remains unclear, there can be little doubt that the
author of our text was familiar with the corpus of Hebrew Andalusian
poetry. Our passage, although not a direct polemic against this venera-
ble literary tradition, might nevertheless be thought of as a commentary
on it. If Shmuel Ha-Nagid urged us to taste the real wine and not
overindulge in spiritual matters, the *Zohar* turns the tables—the real
ancient wine to be celebrated and sought after is the wine of *Atika*, the
wine of the Ancient One, which flows through the divine being, through
the Torah and on to those below. In the words of the Prince, it is the
Companions who "crave the water of the grape" and who "hold the
cup with skill." They are the ultimate wine connoisseurs. They know
how to expound it, how to consume it, and how to appreciate it:

> *Drink no wine or other intoxicant, you or your sons, when you*
> *enter the Tent of Meeting that you may not die* (Lev. 10:9).
> Rabbi Yehudah said: From this portion we hear that Nadav
> and Avihu were drunk with wine, in that the priests were cau-
> tioned about this.
>
> Rabbi Ḥiyya opened: *Wine that rejoices the hearts of men,*
> *oil that makes the face shine* (Ps. 104:15). If the priest is
> required to rejoice and to be more resplendent than everyone,
> why then is wine prohibited to him, for behold, joy and splen-
> dor are found within it?
>
> Well, the beginning of wine is joy, its end sadness.
>
> Furthermore, wine derives from the side of the Levites,
> from the site where the wine abides . . .
>
> Rabbi Abba said: Wine, oil, and water issue from the one
> site. Water and oil [that flow] to the right are taken by the
> priests, inherited by them; oil above all, for it is joy, beginning
> and end, as it is written, *It is like fine oil on the head, running*
> *down onto the beard, the beard of Aaron* (Ps. 133:2). Wine
> [that flows] to the left is inherited by the Levites, to raise voice
> and sing, and not to be silent, for behold, wine is never silent,
> while oil is always quiet.
>
> What is the difference between this and that?
>
> Well, oil that is always quiet and in a whisper, comes from
> the side of Thought, which is always in a whisper and unheard
> . . . and wine that is for raising the voice and that is never silent
> comes from the side of Mother, and the Levites inherit from the
> left side, and stand to sing and raise voice . . . therefore, when
> the priest enters the sanctuary to perform the service, it is

forbidden to him to drink wine for his service is performed in silence.

—Zohar 3:39a

Mystical intoxication, or in the language of the *Zohar*, the state of being *ravui ḥamra*, "saturated with wine," is not the same as drunkenness. Mystical intoxication is a heightened state of consciousness, at once the goal of the zoharic quest as well as the precondition for mystical exegesis. The Companions know how to walk the fine line between sobriety, lacking inspiration, and the drunkenness of Nadav and Avihu, knowing no distinctions. Like the Levites, they imbibe wine—the wine of Torah and the wine of God—and in so doing, they sing and raise their voice through the homilies they create. Indeed it is these very homilies that are also in turn the very source of their intoxication! Zoharic mysticism is not a mysticism of "silence is praise before Thee." In response to contact with the Ancient One the Companions are not silent. Like choice wine that is not silent and like the Levites in the Temple, the Companions raise their voice and sing the song of Torah. Their homilies, no doubt created in states of mystical intoxication, are among the sweetest songs ever heard.

May we all merit such saturation!

•◆•

CHAPTER SIX

Pearls in a Beggar's Wallet

The Zohar *Reads* Kohelet

Zohar 3:157a–b

Rabbi Ḥizkiyah and Rabbi Yeisa were walking on the way.

Rabbi Yeisa said to Rabbi Ḥizkiyah: I see by your face that some thought is stirring within you.

He said to him: Most certainly, I have been contemplating this verse that Solomon said, *For in respect of the fate of human beings and the fate of beasts, they have one and the same fate [as the one dies so dies the other, and both have the same life-breath; the preeminence of human beings over beasts is naught, for all is futility]* (Eccles. 3:19).

We have learned that all the words of King Solomon are all concealed levels of wisdom.

If so, this verse requires contemplation, for it contains an opening for those who are not of the sons of faith.

He said to him: Most certainly this is so and indeed it requires contemplation and reflection.

In the meantime, they saw a man approaching.

He asked them for water as he was thirsty and weary from the intensity of the sun.

They said to him: Who are you?

He said to them: I am a Jew and I am weary and thirsty.

They said: Have you plied Torah?

113

He said to them: Instead of talking with you I will ascend this mountain and find water there and drink.

Rabbi Yeisa took out a flask full of water and gave it to him.

After he drank, he [Rabbi Yeisa] said: Let us ascend with you to the water.

They ascended the mountain and found a trickling stream and filled a container.

They sat down.

The man said to them: Now ask, for I have engaged Torah through a son of mine who I have sent to the rabbi's house, and through him I have acquired Torah.

Rabbi Ḥizkiyah said: If through your son, well and good, but as for the matter that occupies us, I see that we need to ascend to another place.

The man said: Say your word, for sometimes in a beggar's wallet you may find pearls.

He quoted him the verse of Solomon and told him [his question].

He said to him: How are you different from other people who do not know?

They said to him: How then?

He said to them: This is the way Solomon meant the verse. He was not speaking about himself, as in the rest of his words, but rather was repeating the words of the foolish of the world who speak thus.

And what do they say?

For in respect of the fate (mikre) of human beings and the fate of beasts, they have one and the same fate (Eccles. 3:19).

The fools who do not know and who do not contemplate with wisdom say that this world proceeds by chance (*mikre*), and that the Blessed Holy One does not watch over them, but rather that *in respect of the fate of human beings and the fate of beasts, they have one and the same fate* (Eccles. 3:19).

When Solomon gazed at those fools who spoke thus, he called them beasts, for they make themselves truly beasts, in saying those words.

From where [do we know this]?

The preceding verse proves it, as it is written, *I said in my heart regarding human beings (al divrat bnei ha-adam) to dissociate them from the divine beings (levaram ha-elohim) and to see that they are beasts, they themselves (behema hema la-hem)* (Eccles. 3:18).

I said in my heart—I thought to observe. To observe what?

The speech of human beings, divrat bnei ha-adam—the foolish word they utter.

God has set them aside, levaram ha-elohim—by themselves, that they will not join with other people who have faith.

To see that they are beasts, behema hema la-hem—that those who have faith will see that they are truly beasts and that their opinions are like animals.

They themselves, hema la-hem—[they are] by themselves and shall not bring this foolish opinion to the sons of faith.

Therefore, *hema la-hem*, they are for themselves and not for others. And what is their opinion?

For in respect of the fate of human beings and the fate of beasts, they have one and the same fate.

May the spirit of those beasts deflate, those fools, those who lack faith! Woe to them, woe to their souls! It would be better for them if they had not come into the world!

And how did Solomon answer them about this?

With the verse that follows. He said, *Who knows if a human's life-breath does rise upward and if a beast's breath does sink down into the earth?* (Eccles. 3:21).

Who knows—who of those fools, who do not know of the glory of the Supernal King, who do not contemplate the Torah, *know that a human's life-breath does rise upward*, to a supernal site, a precious site, a holy site, to be nourished by the supernal light, from the light of the Holy King, to be bound in the bundle of life, to be present before the Holy King as a complete burnt offering (*olah temimah*)—and this is *does rise (olah) upward*—

and that *a beast's breath does sink down into the earth*, and not to the site where all human beings were, about whom it is written, *In the image of God He made man* (Gen. 9:6), and *The soul of man is the lamp of YHVH* (Prov. 20:27).

How could those fools, those who are not of the sons of faith, say that *both have the same life-breath?* (Eccles. 3:19).

May their spirit deflate! About them it is written, *Let them be as chaff in the wind, the angel of YHVH driving them out* (Ps. 35:5). These will remain in Gehinnom, in those lower levels, and will not ascend from there for all generations. About them it is written, *May sinners disappear from the earth, and the wicked be no more. Bless YHVH O my soul, Hallelujah* (Ps. 104:35).

Rabbi Ḥizkiyah and Rabbi Yeisa approached and kissed his head. They said: So much is with you and yet we did not know! Blessed is this hour when we met and were aroused by you! He [the Jew] said further: Did Solomon wonder about this alone?

Behold in another place he said something similar.
He opened, saying: *This is the evil (ze ra) in all that is done under the sun: [that there is one fate for all]* (Eccles. 9:3).
This is the evil, ze ra, indeed!
What is *this is the evil, ze ra*?
This refers to the one who spills seed (*zera*) in vain and destroys his path, for this one does not reside with the Blessed Holy One and will not have a portion in the world that is coming, as it is written, *For you are not a God who desires wickedness, evil (ra) cannot abide with You* (Ps. 5:5).
About this he said, *This is the evil, ze ra*, for he will have no dwelling above.
That there is one fate for all. So too, men's hearts are full of evil and their hearts of madness while they live (Eccles. 9:3)—foolishness is embedded in their hearts. They lack faith and have no portion in the Blessed Holy One or in the sons of faith, not in this world and not in the world that is coming, as is it written, *and then—to the dead* (ibid.).

Come and see:
The Blessed Holy One warns the people of the world and says: *Choose life that you might live* (Deut. 30:19) and this is the life of that world.
And these wicked, who lack faith, what do they say?
For he that is joined to all the living there is certitude (Eccles. 9:4)— even though a person chooses that world, as it is said, it counts for naught.
For we have a tradition, *to all the living there is certitude*, and they have a tradition, *a live dog is better than a dead lion* (ibid.). How can they have life in that world?
Therefore, *This is the evil, ze ra*, indeed! They will not abide with the Supernal King, and will not have a portion in Him.
And even though for all these verses you can find supports for the Companions through other words, certainly Solomon came to reveal about those wicked, lacking faith, that they have no portion in the Blessed Holy One, in this world and in the world that is coming.

They said to him: Would you like us to join you and go with us?
He said to them: Should I do this the Torah would call me a fool, and what's more, I would be sinning against my soul.
They said to him: Why so?
He said to them: Because I am a messenger and they have sent me on a mission, and King Solomon said, *He who sends a message by the hand of a fool cuts short his feet and drinks damage* (Prov. 26:6).

Come and see:
The spies, because they were not found to be sons of faith and were not faithful messengers, sinned against their souls, in this world and in the world that is coming.
He kissed them and left.

Rabbi Ḥizkiyah and Rabbi Yeisa walked on.
While they were walking they met some people.
Rabbi Ḥizkiyah and Rabbi Yeisa inquired about him.
They said: What is the name of that man?
They said: He is Rabbi Ḥagai and he is a companion among the Companions. The Companions of Babylon sent him to learn matters from Rabbi Shimon bar Yoḥai and the other Companions.
Rabbi Yeisa said: Certainly this must be the Rabbi Ḥagai who all his days never sought to display what he knew, and therefore he told us that it was through his son that he had merited Torah, as scripture says, *If you see a man who thinks himself wise, there is more hope for a fool than for him* (Prov. 26:12). Certainly he is a faithful messenger, and happy is the one who dispatches his matters by the hand of a faithful messenger!

Commentary on *Zohar* 3:157a–b

Ecclesiastes, or Kohelet in Hebrew, is a surprising work. In the space of twelve short chapters, the author of this most exceptional biblical book challenges just about every "sacred truth" of normative Judaism as it comes to be expressed in rabbinic religion. Starting with his opening thesis that "all is futility," the author proceeds to question the value of human endeavor, the possibility of an afterlife, and perhaps most dramatically, the functioning of divine providence in the world.[1] The sages of the Talmud were not insensitive to these difficulties and even debated whether the book should be included in the biblical canon. We are indeed fortunate "that on the day Rabbi El'azar ben Azariah was appointed to be head of the academy, a decision was made that Song of Songs and Ecclesiastes were deemed to make the hands unclean."[2] The inclusion of this Jewish-Epicurean work into the Bible, however, did not come easily, and the rabbis were forced to bring all their exegetical and literary genius to bear on this work in their interpretative endeavors. *Ecclesiastes Rabbah*, a late compilation of classical rabbinic interpretations of the book, is at once a testament to rabbinic creativity and to rabbinic discomfort with the *peshat* or literal meaning of the work. One of the first interpretations found in this commentary neatly demonstrates the rabbinic project:

> *What profit has man of all his labor wherein he labors under the sun* (Eccles. 1:3)—Rabbi Benjamin said: The Sages sought to suppress the Book of Kohelet because they discovered therein words that savor of heresy. They declared: Behold all the wisdom of Solomon, which he aims at teaching is, *What profit has man of all his labor?* Is it possible that the words may be applied to man's labor in Torah?! On reconsidering the matter, they declared: He did not say "Of all labor," but "Of all *his* labor." In his own labor one should not labor, but one should labor in the labor of Torah.
> —*Ecclesiastes Rabbah* 1:3 (trans. Soncino modified)[3]

The Rabbis were thus forced very far from the message intended by the book's author. Commenting on a verse that gives dramatic expression to Kohelet's philosophy of *carpe diem*, "I know that there is nothing better for them than to rejoice, and to get pleasure so long as they live; but also that every man should eat and drink" (Eccles. 3:12), the rabbis remark: "All the eating and drinking mentioned in this Book refer to Torah and good deeds."[4]

The *Zohar* too delights in letting its imagination and creativity soar whenever its protagonists encounter the heretical statements found throughout the work. Like the rabbis, the *Zohar* assumes that Kohelet was penned by King Solomon, who is held in high esteem by the *Zohar*, and approaches its words with the assumption that they "are cloaked in other words, like words of Torah that are garbed in the stories of the world" (*Zohar* 3:155b). Even Kohelet contains supernal mysteries, yet these mysteries are obscure and concealed, requiring the perceptive gaze of the Companions.

> As has been said in various places, we have contemplated the words of King Solomon and they appear to be obscure. But all those words spoken by Solomon are to be read with wisdom.
> —*Zohar* 1:223a (Matt, *The Zohar*)

> Rabbi Ḥiyya and Rabbi Yose were walking on the way. Rabbi Yose said to Rabbi Ḥiyya: I am astonished at what Solomon said! All his words are concealed words, unknown; for look, in Ecclesiastes he envelops concealed words!
> —*Zohar* 1:195a (Matt, *The Zohar*)

> Rabbi Shimon said: Did I not say that the words of King Solomon are all inside and within the holy sanctuary?
> —*Zohar* 2:175a[5]

In the *Zohar*'s unique historical consciousness, the generation of King Solomon, while blessed and favored, is nevertheless characterized by a degree of concealment or esotericism,[6] and although Solomon's writings (Songs of Songs, Proverbs, and Ecclesiastes) reveal many mysteries, they are obscure and conceal their profundity. Only the sages of all ages, and in particular the Companions of Rabbi Shimon, are able to fathom their words:

> King Solomon realized that it was not the wish of the supreme King that wisdom should be revealed through him to such an extent that the Torah, which was sealed from the very beginning, should be disclosed, even to a generation like his that was more nearly perfect than other generations. He had opened doors in Torah, but they still remained closed, except to those sages who were sufficiently worthy, and they were confused about them and did not know how to speak of them.

But in this generation in which Rabbi Shimon bar Yoḥai abides, it is the will of the Blessed Holy One, for the sake of Rabbi Shimon, that the sealed things should be revealed by him.
—*Zohar* 2:149a (Tishby and Goldstein modified; cf. *Zohar* 3:236a)

The following passage exemplifies the *Zohar*'s method of reading the words of King Solomon "with wisdom." Commenting on one of Kohelet's pessimistic yet hedonistic declarations, "Enjoy life with a woman you love all the fleeting days of life that you have been granted under the sun—all your fleeting days. For that alone is your portion in life and in your labor in which you labor under the sun. Whatever is in your hand to do, do with all your power" (Eccles. 9:9–10), the *Zohar* offers the following interpretation:

Rabbi El'azar was standing before his father, Rabbi Shimon.
He said to him: It is written: *Enjoy life (re-eh ḥayyim) with a woman you love all the fleeting days of your life* (Eccles. 9:9).
He said to him: Come and see. *Enjoy life with a woman you love*—this is a mystery. For a person must contain *life* in this site. This without that does not go. A person must contain the attribute of day with the night, and the attribute of night with the day . . .
Come and see: All of King Solomon's words are concealed within with wisdom, and in these verses it appears as though the strap has been untied,[7] as is written afterward, *Whatever is in your hand to do, do with all your power. For there is no action, no reasoning, no learning, no wisdom in Sheol, where you are going* (Eccles. 9:10).
This verse requires contemplation.
Whatever is in your hand to do, do with all your power. Now should Solomon, who possessed more supernal wisdom than all the people of the world, speak so?
Rather, all of King Solomon's words were said about the mystery of wisdom.
Come and see: *Whatever is in your hand to do, do with all your power*—this is that a person must contain the left within the right. And everything that he does must only be contained in the right.
Whatever is in your hand to do—this is the left.
Do with all your power—this is the right, as it is said, *Your right hand, O YHVH, glorious in power* (Exod. 15:6).

And when a person takes care that all his deeds are for the right side and contains the left in the right, then the Blessed Holy One dwells with him in this world and gathers him to Himself to the world that is coming.

—*Zohar* 3:177b–178a

In these words of Kohelet, the *Zohar* finds the mysteries of mystical life. The woman is none other than the Assembly of Israel, the female aspect of the divine, and the mystic is enjoined to unite Her with the male grade of divinity, designated in the verse by the term "life." "Enjoy life," *re-eh Ḥayyim*, is read here by the *Zohar* as a call to action: *Re-eh*, consider, pay attention, direct your focus and ensure that "life" and "woman" are always together. In the continuation of the passage, "Whatever is in your hand to do, do with all your power," which on the surface seems to call for unrestrained human action, the *Zohar* finds the core mystical teaching of comprising the left within the right, of containing the attribute of judgment (*din*), symbolized by the word *hand*, within the attribute of *love* (*ḥesed*), symbolized by the word *power*.[8] While the *Zohar*'s interpretations of the verses of the Bible are always daring and original, our wonder at the *Zohar*'s interpretative genius is particularly aroused here in light of the heretical source material. Even the seemingly heretical statements of Kohelet contain wisdom and cannot limit the literary creativity of the *Zohar*'s authors.

As noted, one of the most radical and heretical teachings of Kohelet is its doctrine of divine providence. Where the dominant view of the Torah and the overwhelming majority of the Bible is that God scrutinizes the lives of humanity and rewards and punishes in accordance with human action (see, for example, Deut. 11:13–17), Kohelet espouses a different view entirely:

And here is another frustration: the fact that the sentence imposed for evil deeds is not executed swiftly, which is why men are emboldened to do evil—the fact that a sinner may do evil a hundred times and his [punishment] still be delayed. For although I am aware that "it will be well with those who revere God since they revere Him, and it will not be well with the scoundrel, and he will not live long because he does not revere God"[9]—here is a frustration that occurs in the world: sometimes an upright man is requited according to the conduct of the scoundrel; and sometimes the scoundrel is requited according to the conduct of the upright. I say all that is frustration (Eccles. 8:10–14).

Kohelet does not go as far as Job, who claims, "it is all one; therefore I say, 'He destroys the blameless and the guilty'" (Job 9:22), but he does nevertheless cast doubt on the "orthodox" view of divine recompense.

In the Middle Ages, Jewish thinkers, both philosophers and Kabbalists, were deeply concerned with the question of divine providence. Exposed to the thought of Christian, but especially Islamic, philosophers and through them to the works of Plato and Aristotle, Jewish thinkers began to reflect anew upon the nature and manner of God's relationship to human action. Maimonides' treatment of divine providence found in the *Guide of the Perplexed* and Nahmanides' doctrine of hidden miracles found throughout his literary corpus are without doubt the most important contributions in this regard. In fact, Yeshayahu Leibowitz referred to Maimonides' account of providence as a "Copernican revolution" in Jewish thought,[10] so before turning to our passage from the *Zohar* we would do well to outline in brief the central tenets of their views.

Maimonides' discussion of divine providence is scattered throughout the *Guide of the Perplexed* (3:17, 18, 51 and in 3:22–23 where he offers his wonderful interpretation of the book of Job). While Maimonides' theory is complex and in many places ambiguous, the central tenets are nevertheless quite clear and can be stated through two central propositions. First, that individual providence watches over the human species alone, while the other beings are subject only to universal providence through natural causality; and second, that the level of providential concern for a person depends on that person's intellectual achievement. In 3:51, arguably the most important chapter in the *Guide*, we read the following profound words:

> A most extraordinary speculation has occurred to me just now through which doubts may be dispelled and divine secrets revealed. We have already explained in the chapters concerning providence that providence watches over everyone endowed with intellect proportionately to the measure of his intellect. Thus providence always watches over an individual endowed with perfect apprehension, whose intellect never ceases from being occupied with God. On the other hand, an individual endowed with perfect apprehension, whose thought sometimes for a certain time is emptied of God, is watched over by providence only during the time when he thinks of God; providence withdraws from him during the time when he is occupied with something else . . . Hence it seems to me that all the prophets or excellent and perfect men whom one of the evils of this world befell, had this evil happen to them during such a time of dis-

traction, the greatness of the calamity being proportionate to the duration of the period of distraction or to the vileness of the matter with which he was occupied. If this is so, the great doubt that induced the philosophers to deny that providence watches over all human individuals and to assert equality between them and the individuals of the other kinds of animals is dispelled . . . If a man's thought is free from distraction, if he apprehends Him, may He be exalted, in the right way and rejoices in what he apprehends, that individual can never be afflicted with evil of any kind. For he is with God and God is with him. When, however, he abandons Him, may He be exalted, and is thus separated from God and God separated from him, he becomes in consequence of this a target for every evil that may happen to befall him. For the thing that necessarily brings about providence and deliverance from the sea of chance consists in that intellectual overflow.[11]

Maimonides' comments have been variously interpreted by scholars across the generations. There have been those, like Samuel Ibn Tibbon, the first Hebrew translator of the *Guide*, who read Maimonides to be denying the traditional account of providence as divine intervention in human affairs. While an intellectual act of cognition can release a person from the realm of universal providence (natural causality) and bring one into a state of individual providence, this state does not manifest through such a person escaping the arbitrariness of the world. According to this view, providential concern does not manifest through an intervention or act of God, but through that person's awareness of the divine that thereby renders the material world, and hence suffering, meaningless.[12] Yeshayahu Leibowitz, a modern radical-rationalist reader of Maimonides, expresses this view as follows:

Universal providence is the way of the world, implanted in it by its creator, and we comprehend it as the system of the laws of nature. Special providence is not something accorded to man from above; it is an attainment arrived at by man if he directs himself toward God. He is favoured with God's providence inasmuch as he is attached to God in the knowledge he has of Him.[13]

It was this reading of Maimonides, which imagined God as the First Cause, indifferent to the affairs of humanity, that raised the ire of Jewish traditionalists. In fact, in the century following the publication of the *Guide*, Jewish thinkers of various persuasions (for example,

Jacob Anatoli, Isaac Ibn Latif, and Jacob ben Sheshet) attacked this view, "to answer the words of those who dispute the Torah, the philosophers, who say in their perplexity about Providence that 'the Lord has forsaken the land' (Ezek. 8:12, 9:9)."[14]

Nahmanides' views on providence are no less surprising and fascinating, and given his kabbalistic pedigree—he was the most authoritative halakhicist and kabbalist in the generation before the writing of the *Zohar*—deserving of our attention. Derived in part from Maimonides, but fused with subtle kabbalistic ideas, Nahmanides' theory of providence has, until recently, suffered from numerous misunderstandings. Scholars of medieval Jewish thought had long taken Nahmanides' doctrine of hidden miracles to be a denial of nature and natural causality. In place of Maimonides' naturalistic credo, "the world pursues its normal course," Nahmanides was understood to have dispensed with nature all together, positing instead a series of continuous hidden miracles: "A person has no share in the Torah of Moses without believing that all things that happen to us are miracles; they have nothing to do with 'nature' or the 'customary order of the world'" (commentary to Exod. 13:16). It was from comments like these, found repeatedly throughout his Torah commentary, as well as in his commentary on the book of Job and his sermon on Kohelet, that scholars understood Nahmanides to have affirmed the view that everything is always from God and that divine providence functions absolutely. Gershom Scholem, for example, wrote of Nahmanides' tendency

> to turn what we call the laws of nature into a sort of optical illusion since we regard what is really a continuum of miracles as a manifestation of natural law . . . These hidden miracles, which are the foundation of the entire Torah, are miracles which do not appear miraculous to us . . . The world and the behaviour of nature and their relationship to man are not at all in the category of what we call nature; they are, rather, a constant and constantly renewed miracle, a continuous chain of miracles . . . [15]

In the last twenty years, this view of Nahmanides has been substantially revised. David Berger was the first to point out that Nahmanides believed that divine providence, be it through hidden or manifest miracles, only functioned for the perfectly righteous (and perfectly wicked), whereas the overwhelming majority of the world's inhabitants are in fact subject to natural causality.[16] Recently, Moshe Halbertal has shed much new light on Nahmanides' doctrine, illustrating how his kabbalistic teachings lie at the heart of his doctrine.[17] According to Halbertal, the key to understanding Nahmanidean providence is to appreciate that the three providential domains—natural causality, hidden miracles (i.e., miracles disguised as nature), and manifest miracles—are in fact rooted in three different aspects of the divine being. According to this view the wise and the pious are able to lift themselves out of the domain of natural causality, which is blind to man's religious and moral life, and establish a relationship with the divine that is beyond the laws of nature. Those who cleave to the *Shekhinah* are released from the arbitrary hand of the constellations and attain the level of hidden miracles, while those who cleave to the divine name, the sefirah *Tiferet*, are able to attain the level of manifest miracles. Halbertal stresses that the performance of such miracles for the righteous does not necessitate that we think of them as direct, volitional acts by God, but rather as different laws of nature pertaining to different levels of being. The mystic who cleaves to the *Shekhinah* "activates" a different kind of "nature" than that experienced by the majority of humankind, who can never escape the "course of the world." As in Maimonidean thought, providence is a state attained through an intellectual-spiritual act.

If we have strayed into medieval theological minutia, it is only because such arguments and distinctions are of great importance in seeking to understand the *Zohar*'s treatment of this central medieval debate. As we shall see, the *Zohar*'s reading of Kohelet is "fiercely polemical," as Isaiah Tishby observed, even if the contours of this polemic have not always been clear.[18]

⁘

Rabbi Ḥizkiyah and Rabbi Yeisa were walking on the way.

Rabbi Yeisa said to Rabbi Ḥizkiyah: I see by your face that some thought is stirring within you.

He said to him: Most certainly, I have been contemplating this verse that Solomon said, *For in respect of the fate of human beings and the fate of beasts, they have one and the same fate [as the one dies so dies the other, and both have the same life-breath; the preeminence of human beings over beasts is naught, for all is futility]* (Eccles. 3:19).

We have learned that all the words of King Solomon are all concealed levels of wisdom.

If so, this verse requires contemplation, for it contains an opening for those who are not of the sons of faith.

He said to him: Most certainly this is so and indeed it requires contemplation and reflection.

Rabbi Ḥizkiyah's query takes us to the heart of the rabbinic and zoharic confrontation with Kohelet. The verse that perplexes the wandering mystic is stark, even brutal. Human beings and animals share the same fate. Both are mortal, and human beings, for all their sophistication, are no better than beasts. While the literal meaning of the verse is challenging enough, Rabbi Ḥizkiyah no doubt senses another heresy in Kohelet's words. The Hebrew word *mikre*, rendered here as "fate," also conveys the meaning "chance," and Rabbi Ḥizkiyah is confused by Solomon's words, which seem to suggest that human beings and animals enjoy the same providential relationship. Not only are both mortal, but both are subject to the whims of chance and the arbitrariness of nature. Rabbi Moses Cordovero, the sixteenth-century Safedian kabbalist whose voluminous *Zohar* commentary *Or Yakar* is indispensable for explicating complex *Zohar* passages, understood the verse as posing two separate challenges. First, the suggestion "that there is no judgment and reckoning after death, and that the spirit is annihilated with the death of the body," and second, "that all is by chance, and there is no difference regarding the fate of human beings and the fate of beasts."[19]

The *Zohar*, of course, was not the first to observe the difficulties raised by this verse. In *Tanna Debe Eliyyahu*, a late aggadic work, we find the following exposition:

For that which befalls the sons of men, befalls beasts; even one thing befalls them (Eccles. 3:19). In these words what did Solomon have in mind? Nothing other than man's mortality. Mortal man—his beginning, the worm, and his end, the worm, so that in this respect a man is not all superior to an animal. Inferior rather! Touching an animal's carcass makes one ritually unclean for one day, but touching a human corpse makes one ritually unclean for seven days. Moreover, an animal carcass does not make the dwelling ritually unclean, but a human corpse makes the dwelling ritually unclean . . . Of man's mortality Solomon also said: A living dog is better than a dead lion (Eccles. 9:4). For a feeble day-old infant for whose survival one is justifiably apprehensive is better than Og, King of Bashan, who ejaculated his semen a distance of forty parasangs—when either dies, vermin are all over him. Now of Solomon, it is said that he *was wiser than all men* (1 Kings 5:11). Still, if indeed, he was wiser than all men, how could he have declared, Man has no pre-eminence over a beast (Eccles. 3:19)? How indeed? Consider that after a man eats, he says Grace; after he drinks, he says Grace; when he goes to sleep he says a blessing; and when he wakes up he says a blessing. How then is he to be thought of as though he were no better than an animal, which is incapable of such refinements? What Solomon was referring to by his statement, however, was the disposition made of man at the time of his death. For when a man's time to die has come, the disposing of his body is discussed in much the same way as the disposing of a dying animal is discussed.

—*Tanna Debe Eliyyahu, Eliyyahu Zuta* 24[20]

And in Midrash *Tanḥuma*, another late midrashic compilation, we find:

> For *in respect of the fate of the human being and the fate of beast they have one and the same fate* (Eccles. 3:19). Come and see: It is written concerning human beings, *You shall not wear cloth combining wool and linen* (Deut. 22:11), and it is written concerning beasts, *You shall not plow with an ox and an ass together* (ibid. 22:10).
>
> *One and the same fate*—just as a human being receives impurity, so a beast receives impurity. About human beings it is written, *He who touches the corpse of any human being shall be unclean for seven days* (Num. 19:11), and regarding beasts, *If an animal that you may eat has died, any one who touches its carcass shall be unclean until evening* (Lev. 11:39).
>
> *As the one dies so dies the other* (Eccles. 3:19)—about human beings it is written, *you shall kill the woman* (Lev. 20:16), and regarding the beast, *you shall kill the beast* (ibid. 20:15).
>
> *Both have the same life-breath* (Eccles. 3:19). *Who knows if a human's life-breath does rise upward and if a beast's breath does sink down into the earth?* (ibid. 3:21).
>
> *The human's life-breath*—because it was bestowed from above, ascent is written concerning it.
>
> *The beast's*—because it was bestowed from below, descent is written concerning it.
>
> *The preeminence of the human being over the beast is not/nothing (ayin)* (Eccles. 3:19)—what is not/nothing? He speaks and the beast does *not*. Furthermore, the human being possesses knowledge, and the beast does *not* possess knowledge. The human being can distinguish between good and evil, while the beast knows *nothing*. Furthermore, the human being receives reward for his actions while the beast does *not* receive reward for its actions. The human being dies and he is tended to and buried, while the beast is *not* buried, thus *the preeminence of the human being over the beast is not/nothing*.
>
> —*Tanḥuma Emor* 15

Both texts reveal the rabbis' discomfort with Kohelet's statement and both serve to limit, neutralize, or invert the verse's original heretical claim. Although our passage does not draw on these texts directly in its exposition of the verse, they nevertheless hover in the background, resonating and echoing with the *Zohar*'s new interpretation.

Back to our narrative:

> In the meantime, they saw a man approaching.
> He asked them for water as he was thirsty and weary from the intensity of the sun.
> They said to him: Who are you?
> He said to them: I am a Jew and I am weary and thirsty.
> They said: Have you plied Torah?
> He said to them: Instead of talking with you I will ascend this mountain and find water there and drink.
> Rabbi Yeisa took out a flask full of water and gave it to him.
> After he drank, he [Rabbi Yeisa] said: Let us ascend with you to the water.
> They ascended the mountain and found a trickling stream and filled a container.
> They sat down.
> The man said to them: Now ask, for I have engaged Torah through a son of mine who I have sent to the Rabbi's house, and through him I have acquired Torah.
> Rabbi Ḥizkiyah said: If through your son, well and good, but as for the matter that occupies us, I see that we need to ascend to another place.
> The man said: Say your word, for sometimes in a beggar's wallet you may find pearls.

As we have already observed zoharic narratives are frequently punctuated by a carnivalesque switch, whereby the protagonists, the Companions of Rabbi Shimon, stumble upon a fellow traveler, usually anonymous and usually dismissed as unworthy of their time and consideration, who turns the tables on the mystic masters, disclosing wondrous teachings and revealing the traveling mystics as uncertain novices. In our narrative, this switch is marked by a subtle play on words, impossible to convey in translation. Upon first encountering the wanderings mystics, the anonymous traveler announces that he is weary and thirsty, *laei ve-tzaḥina*, but which, with a slight phonetic and semantic shift, might be read as learned and clear or learned and thirsty for Torah.[21] The Aramaic word for thirst, *tzaḥina*, recalls the Hebrew word for clarity or brightness, *tzaḥ*, while the

Aramaic word for weary, *laei* is close to the Aramaic word for learn or ply, *la'ei* (with an *ayin*). In fact, in the very next sentence, the Companions ask the anonymous Jew whether he has plied Torah (*la'it be-oraita*). The Jew is dismissive, yet the Companions ascend the mountain with him to a trickling stream. This "edenic" setting, to which we shall return repeatedly, functions as a narrative analogue to the Companions' mystical endeavors as they enter the orchard (*pardes*) of Torah and mystical exegesis. More specifically, the narrative details of our story—the ascent to the mountain to drink water to escape the heat of the sun—might also be thought of as a playful engagement with the Ecclesiastan problem with which the Companions are occupied. Standing "under the sun" and contemplating "the evil in all that is done under the sun," namely, the place of human beings in the natural order, the *Zohar* intimates that it is only the mystical waters of Torah imbibed on the mount of revelation that will shade them from the arbitrary hand of nature.

Upon hearing the source of the Companions' perplexity, the mysterious traveler begins his interpretation:

> He said to them: This is the way Solomon meant the verse. He was not speaking about himself, as in the rest of his words, but rather was repeating the words of the foolish of the world who speak thus.
>
> And what do they say?
>
> *For in respect of the fate (mikre) of human beings and the fate of beasts, they have one and the same fate* (Eccles. 3:19).
>
> The fools who do not know and who do not contemplate with wisdom say that this world proceeds by chance (*mikre*), and that the Blessed Holy One does not watch over them, but rather that *in respect of the fate of human beings and the fate of beasts, they have one and the same fate* (Eccles. 3:19).

The Jew's interpretation is based on a simple yet ingenious interpretative device. The heretical words found in the verse are, in fact, not the words of King Solomon at all, but rather the words of the foolish of the world. These fools, who it would seem are none other than the radical Jewish rationalists (perhaps the *Zohar* intends Maimonides, but more likely those who interpreted his works in a radical manner), do not "contemplate with wisdom"—they do not know the mysteries of the sefirot, and believe that the world proceeds by chance alone. They deny divine providence for human beings and insist that humans and beasts enjoy the same kind of providential relationship. We are reminded of Maimonides' account of the first of the five opinions concerning providence regnant in his day:

The first opinion is the profession of those that consider that there is no providence at all with regard to anything whatever in all that exists; that everything in it, the heavens and the things other than they, has happened by chance and in accordance with the way things were predisposed; and that there is no one who orders, governs, or is concerned with anything. This is the opinion of Epicurus . . .[22]

There can be little doubt that our passage addresses its harsh critique against exponents of this view. Yet it is also possible that our text is aimed at those who profess the second opinion listed by Maimonides, what he calls the "opinion of Aristotle," which sees providence as operative only in the realm of the spheres (i.e., God watches over the stars and planets) and the species but indifferent to the affairs of individuals. Maimonides, too, as is well known, rejected this view and insisted that human beings can attain a level of individual providence beyond the providence of species afforded to animals:

For I for one believe that in this lowly world—I mean that which is beneath the sphere of the moon—divine providence watches only over the individuals belonging to the human species and that in this species alone all the circumstances of the individuals and the good and evil that befall them are consequent upon the deserts . . . But regarding all the other animals, and all the more, the plants and other things, my opinion is that of Aristotle. For I do not by any means believe that this particular leaf has fallen because of a providence watching over it; nor that this spider has devoured this fly because God has now decreed and willed something concerning individuals; nor that the spittle spat by Zayd has moved till it came down in one particular place upon a gnat and killed it by a divine decree and judgment . . . For all this is in my opinion due to pure chance, just as Aristotle holds.[23]

The fools of our text, who equate human and animal providence, might well be the exponents of the classic Aristotelian view. As Yitzḥak Baer has noted in his monumental *A History of the Jews in Christian Spain*, the *Zohar* needs to be appreciated, in part, as a response to radical Jewish rationalism, or "Jewish Averroism," which viewed the truth of the Torah as entirely reducible to the truth of Plato and Aristotle.[24] Although heavily indebted to Maimonidean thought, the *Zohar* is nevertheless highly critical of radical Jewish philosophers who, in the words of Moses de Leon, "delight in the words of the Greeks and their assistants; they kiss their words."[25] Our narrative surely counts among the more sustained zoharic polemics against this intellectual-cultural trend within thirteenth-century Spanish and Provençal Jewish life.

In the continuation of his homily, the traveling Jew, and through him, the *Zohar*, intensifies its attack on the rationalists of their day. Employing a classical midrashic strategy—breaking the various words of the preceding verse from Ecclesiastes into smaller units that are then amplified and given new content—Kohelet's problematical statement, "I said in my heart regarding human beings to dissociate them from the divine beings and to see that they are beasts, they themselves" (Eccles. 3:18) is now transformed from a statement of heresy into an assessment of the words uttered by the fools and the philosophers:

> When Solomon gazed at those fools who spoke thus, he called them beasts, for they make themselves truly beasts, in saying those words.
>
> From where [do we know this]?
>
> The preceding verse proves it, as it is written, *I said in my heart regarding human beings (al divrat bnei ha-adam) to dissociate them from the divine beings (levaram ha-elohim) and to see that they are beasts, they themselves (behema hema la-hem)* (Eccles. 3:18).[26]
>
> *I said in my heart*—I thought to observe. To observe what?
>
> *The speech of human beings, divrat bnei ha-adam*—the foolish word they utter.
>
> *God has set them aside, levaram ha-elohim*—by themselves, that they will not join with other people who have faith.
>
> *To see that they are beasts, behema hema la-hem*—that those who have faith will see that they are truly beasts and that their opinions are like animals.
>
> *They themselves, hema la-hem*—[they are] by themselves and shall not bring this foolish opinion to the sons of faith.
>
> Therefore, *hema la-hem*, they are for themselves and not for others.
>
> And what is their opinion?
>
> *For in respect of the fate of human beings and the fate of beasts, they have one and the same fate.*
>
> May the spirit of those beasts deflate, those fools, those who lack faith! Woe to them, woe to their souls! It would be better for them if they had not come into the world!

The *Zohar*'s new reading hinges on alternate explanations for three ambiguous terms in the Hebrew text: *al divrat bnei ha-adam*, "regarding human beings," but read by the *Zohar* as signifying "the speech of human beings"; *levaram ha-Elohim*, "to dissociate them from divine beings," but read as "God has set them aside"; and finally the odd phrase *behema hema la-hem*, "they are beasts," which is broken down into its literal component parts, "they are beasts" and "they are for themselves." As is often the case, the *Zohar*'s original and daring interpretation is closely embedded in the literal form of the text (the *sod*, mystery, is hidden within the *peshat*, the literal). Those who hold such beliefs are to be shunned, kept away from the sons of faith, for they are truly beasts and their opinions are like animals. Once again, Maimonides' elaboration of providence is not far from the surface of our text, which deftly alludes to his assessment of the ignorant: "As for the ignorant and disobedient, their state is despicable proportionately to their lack of this overflow, and they have been relegated to the rank of the individuals of all the other species of animals . . ."27 As we have seen, for Maimonides, individual providence is a state attained through an act of cognition. The ignorant and disobedient, however, remove themselves from this state and place themselves in the providential category of animals. Our passage perhaps suggests something similar: "for they make themselves truly beasts, in saying those words." In denying providence and acknowledging only chance, the fools of the world make themselves into beasts, and place themselves in the providential category of beasts, beyond the divine gaze. As in Maimonides, and as found with slight but important differences in Nahmanides, providence is consequent upon a particular state of relation with the divine.28

Having responded to the first challenge posed by the verse from Kohelet, namely, that the world proceeds according to chance alone and that human beings are abandoned to the whims of natural causality, the Jew now turns to the second "heretical" aspect of the verse—the suggestion that with regard to the afterlife, humans and animals share the same ultimate destiny:

> And how did Solomon answer them about this?
>
> With the verse that follows. He said, *Who knows if a human's life-breath does rise upward and if a beast's breath does sink down into the earth?* (Eccles. 3:21).
>
> *Who knows*—who of those fools, who do not know of the glory of the Supernal King, who do not contemplate the Torah, *know that a human's life-breath does rise upward*, to a supernal site, a precious site, a holy site, to be nourished by the supernal

light, from the light of the Holy King, to be bound in the bundle of life, to be present before the Holy King as a complete burnt offering (*olah temimah*)—and this is *does rise (olah) upward*—

and that *a beast's breath does sink down into the earth*, and not to the site where all human beings were, about whom it is written, *In the image of God He made man* (Gen. 9:6), and *The soul of man is the lamp of YHVH* (Prov. 20:27).

How could those fools, those who are not of the sons of faith, say that *both have the same life-breath?* (Eccles. 3:19).

May their spirit deflate! About them it is written, *Let them be as chaff in the wind, the angel of YHVH driving them out* (Ps. 35:5). These will remain in Gehinnom, in those lower levels, and will not ascend from there for all generations. About them it is written, *May sinners disappear from the earth, and the wicked be no more. Bless YHVH O my soul, Hallelujah* (Ps. 104:35).

As noted in previous chapters, the *Zohar* understands the soul to derive from the highest and innermost aspect of divinity, and here the *Zohar* can only scoff at the idea that human beings share the same fate as animals. The human soul, the "lamp of YHVH" and the "image of God" indeed ascends, *olah*, like the smoke from a burnt offering (*olah temimah*), to bathe in the supernal light, and to be bound in the bundle of life, the *Shekhinah*. The *Zohar*, which as we have seen, places the keys of divinity itself in human hands, can thus barely fathom the words of the medieval atheists and skeptics who would deny the unique status of the human being in the cosmic order.

Continuing his polemic, the traveler now focuses on yet another apparently heretical statement in Ecclesiastes:

He said further: Did Solomon wonder about this alone?

Behold in another place he said something similar.

He opened, saying: *This is the evil (ze ra) in all that is done under the sun: [that there is one fate for all]* (Eccles. 9:3).

This is the evil, ze ra, indeed!

What is *this is the evil, ze ra?*

This refers to the one who spills seed (*zera*) in vain and destroys his path, for this one does not reside with the Blessed Holy One and will not have a portion in the world that is coming, as it is written, *You are not a God who desires wickedness, evil (ra) cannot abide with You* (Ps. 5:5).

About this he said, *This is the evil, ze ra*, for he will have
no dwelling above.

*That there is one fate for all. So too, men's hearts are full of
evil and their hearts of madness while they live* (Eccles. 9:3)—
foolishness is embedded in their hearts. They lack faith and
have no portion in the Blessed Holy One or in the sons of faith,
not in this world and not in the world that is coming, as is it
written, *and then—to the dead* (ibid.).

Where chapter 3 of Kohelet bemoans the shared lot of humanity and
the beasts, chapter 9 employs similar language, but this time lamenting
the shared fate of the wicked and the virtuous:

For the same fate is in store for all: for the righteous, and for
the wicked; for the good and pure, and for the impure; for him
who sacrifices, and for him who does not; for him who is pleas-
ing, and for him who is displeasing; and for him who swears,
and for him who shuns oaths. This is the evil in all that is done
under the sun: *that there is one fate for all*. So, too, men's
hearts are full of evil and their hearts of madness while they
live; and then—to the dead (Eccles. 9:2–3, emphasis added).

The anonymous traveler reads the words "this is the evil," *ze ra*, as a
single word, *zera*, seed, thereby drawing a parallel between the sin (and
fate) of those who spill their seed (referring to masturbation) and those
who deny divine providence.[29] (The word *mikre*, "fate," is perhaps read
here as a reference to *mikre laylah*, a nocturnal emission/mishap as in
Deuteronomy 23:11). He then returns to his earlier interpretative strategy,
whereby a single statement by Kohelet is broken down into component
parts, the first referring to the opinion of the fools, "that there is one fate
for all," and the second, containing Solomon's assessment of this view,
"men's hearts are full of evil and their hearts of madness while they live."

The conclusion of his homily is at once complex, creative, and
ingenious. Drawing on the very next verse from Kohelet, "For he that is
joined to/chooses the living there is certitude—a live dog is better than a
dead lion," the still anonymous journeyman delivers the final blow in
his tirade:

Come and see:
The Blessed Holy One warns the people of the world and
says: *Choose life that you might live, [you and your seed]*
(Deut. 30:19) and this is the life of that world.

And these wicked, who lack faith, what do they say?

For he that is joined to all the living there is certitude (Eccles. 9:4)—even though a person chooses that world, as it is said, it counts for naught.

For we have a tradition, *to all the living there is certitude,* and they have a tradition, *a live dog is better than a dead lion* (ibid.). How can they have life in that world?[30]

Therefore, *This is the evil, ze ra,* indeed! They will not abide with the Supernal King, and will not have a portion in Him.

And even though for all these verses you can find supports for the Companions through other words, certainly Solomon came to reveal about those wicked, lacking faith, that they have no portion in the Blessed Holy One, in this world and in the world that is coming.

Playing on the ambiguity between two variants preserved in the text of Kohelet—*yehubar*/joined and *yivhar*/choose[31]and picking up on the word *living* or *life, ḥayyim,* the Jew quotes a verse from Deuteronomy, "Choose life that you might live," presented here as a call to awaken and cleave to the divine. While in our passage "life" functions as a generalized symbol for the upper worlds, elsewhere in the *Zohar* and when expounding Kohelet, the same word is used to designate more specifically the sefirah *Tiferet.* (It will be recalled that in Nahmanides' doctrine of providence, it is in cleaving to *Tiferet* that the mystic is able to release himself entirely from the laws of nature and chance). Once again, the homily proceeds through interrupting the verses from Kohelet that are now read as a polemic between two sects, an "us" and a "them." The wicked who lack faith, like the original sectarians from old, deny the world to come; "for he that is joined to all the living there is certitude," while the righteous, the "we" of our text, believe that to "*all* the living there is certitude," that is, both in this world and the next. That this final passage seeks to establish the radical Jewish rationalists of the *Zohar*'s day as sectarians is made clear from the subtle reference to the most famous rabbinic account dealing with the origins of Jewish sectarianism:

Antigonus of Soko took over from Simon the Righteous. He used to say: Be not like slaves that serve their master for the sake of compensation; be rather like slaves who serve their master with no thought of compensation. And let the fear of heaven be upon you. Antigonus of Soko had two disciples who used to study his words. They taught them to their disciples, and their disciples to their disciples. These proceeded to examine the words closely and demanded: Why did our ancestors see fit to say this thing? Is it possible that a labourer should do his work all day and not take his reward in the evening? If our ancestors, forsooth, had known that there is another world and that there will be a resurrection of the dead, they would not have spoken in this manner. So they arose and withdrew from the Torah and split into two sects, the Sadducees and the Boethusians: Sadducees named after Zadok and Boethusians, after Boethus. And they used silver vessels and gold vessels all their lives—not because they were ostentatious; but the Sadducees said: *It is a tradition* among the Pharisees to afflict themselves in this world; yet in the world to come they will have nothing.

—Avot de-Rabbi Natan 5 (emphasis added)[32]

Although subtle I would suggest that the expression in our text "we have a tradition," "they have a tradition," evokes this well-known passage from *Avot de-Rabbi Natan*, which also locates the origins of sectarianism in an argument about the existence of the world to come.

His homily now complete, and having so eloquently read Kohelet "with wisdom," and having answered the perplexity of the companions, Rabbi Ḥizkiyah and Rabbi Yeisa invite the wandering Jew to join with them:

They said to him: Would you like us to join you and go with us?

He said to them: Should I do this the Torah would call me a fool, and what's more I would be sinning against my soul.

They said to him: Why so?

He said to them: Because I am a messenger and they have sent me on a mission, and King Solomon said, *He who sends a message by the hand of a fool cuts short his feet and drinks damage* (Prov. 26:6).

Come and see:

The spies, because they were not found to be sons of faith and were not faithful messengers, sinned against their souls, in this world and in the world that is coming.[33]

He kissed them and left.

It is only now toward the conclusion of our unit that we understand why this particular zoharic narrative is found embedded in the *Zohar*'s

commentary to the Torah portion *Shlaḥ Lekha,* which recounts the
story about the ill-fated mission of the spies. The Jew, like the spies, is a
messenger (of whom and to where we do not yet know) and he will not
allow himself to be detained, even by such distinguished sages as the
Companions of Rabbi Shimon.

> Rabbi Ḥizkiyah and Rabbi Yeisa walked on.
>   While they were walking they met some people.
>   Rabbi Ḥizkiyah and Rabbi Yeisa inquired about him.
>   They said: What is the name of that man?
>   They said: He is Rabbi Ḥagai and he is a companion
> among the Companions. The Companions of Babylon sent him
> to learn matters from Rabbi Shimon bar Yoḥai and the other
> Companions.
>   Rabbi Yeisa said: Certainly this must be the Rabbi Ḥagai
> who all his days never sought to display what he knew, and
> therefore he told us that it was through his son that he had
> merited Torah, as scripture says, *If you see a man who thinks
> himself wise, there is more hope for a fool than for him* (Prov.
> 26:12). Certainly he is a faithful messenger, and happy is the
> one who dispatches his matters by the hand of a faithful mes-
> senger!

One final surprise awaits the reader. While the wondrous characters
encountered by the Companions on their travels are usually anonymous, on occasion we are given some details about their identity. In this
case we learn, but only after he has long gone, that the wandering Jew
who was weary and thirsty was in fact Rabbi Ḥagai, "a companion
among the Companions" and that he was sent by the Companions of
Babylon to learn Torah from Rabbi Shimon, as well as his disciples in
the Land of Israel.[34] Exactly who these Babylonian Companions are is
unclear. Boaz Huss has suggested that they may represent the circle of
Nahmanides, that is, another circle of mystics with whom the Companions of Rabbi Shimon (themselves a romantic representation of some
late thirteenth-century mystical fraternity) have some spiritual kinship,
but who, as we learn from other stories in the *Zohar,* fear the innovation and disclosure of mysteries.[35] Like the historical Nahmanides who
concealed his kabbalistic teachings in obscure remarks scattered
throughout his Torah commentary, the Babylonians of the *Zohar*
"insert them beneath an impregnable seal of iron, shut tight on all
sides" (*Zohar* 1:224b, Matt). Regardless of who these Babylonians are,
the ironies are multiple. They have sent Rabbi Ḥagai to learn Torah

from Rabbi Shimon and the Companions, for they after all, are the wise of the generation, and yet, it is the messenger, the representative of the "stammerers," "who toil in Torah stammeringly," as the *Zohar* describes the Babylonians, who teaches the Companions the mysteries of Kohelet's heretical statements. Lest this inversion threaten the stability of the entire zoharic order, we also cannot fail to notice that even here, as the Companions' authority is seemingly challenged, the messenger continues on his way to the grand master himself, Rabbi Shimon, whose mere evocation is enough to reinscribe him and his group's position at the head of the *Zohar*'s mystical hierarchy.

Reading a *Zohar* narrative is a bit like detective work. One needs to grasp all the explicit and not so explicit allusions running through the text in order to comprehend its meaning. One needs to have an ear for the *Zohar*'s playful interpretations as well as a sense of the body of literature with which it is in dialogue. As we have seen, the *Zohar* uses the verses from Kohelet as a springboard for its polemical engagement with Jewish rationalists from its day. That it is able to do so in the form of a charming tale is a great testament to the literary genius of its author(s). The *Zohar* is a variegated composition, and among its pages we encounter diverse sensibilities and tones. Not all of the *Zohar* is concerned with dazzling lights, flowing rivers, and overflowing Eros. The *Zohar* also knows moments of castigation, rebuke, and, as we have now seen, dogmatic polemic. Yet, even here, when criticizing its opponents, the *Zohar* is playful and exegetically brilliant. The *Zohar* enters deep within the heretical heart of Ecclesiastes, at once preserving the radical challenge of the *peshat*, the literal meaning, as well as using the verses as a portal into a range of complex theological issues. The "opening for those who are not of the sons of faith" becomes in the hands of the midrashic maestros of the *Zohar* an opening to subtle Maimonidean and Nahmanidean worlds. And even if we do not identify totally with the author's theological vantage, the *Zohar*'s literary and hermeneutical power and prowess never fails to overwhelm us.

CHAPTER SEVEN

•◆•

Midnight in the Garden of Delight

Zohar 3:67b–68b

Rabbi Abba was sitting before Rabbi Shimon. Rabbi Shimon rose at midnight to ply Torah. Rabbi El'azar and Rabbi Abba rose with him.

Rabbi Shimon opened, saying: *Like a hind craving running streams, so my soul craves for You, O Elohim* (Ps. 42:2).

This verse has been established by the Companions.

Happy are Israel of all the nations, for the Blessed Holy One gave them a holy Torah and bequeathed them holy souls from a holy realm in order to perform His commandments and delight in Torah; for whoever delights in Torah does not fear anything, as it is written, *Were not Your Torah my delight, I would have perished in my affliction* (Ps. 119:92).

What is *my delight*? Torah. For the Torah is called delight, as it is written, *a source of delight every day* (Prov. 8:30).

And this is as we have learned: The Blessed Holy One comes to delight with the righteous in the Garden of Eden.

What is meant by *to delight*? In order to rejoice in them.

As we have learned: Happy are the righteous about whom it is written, *Then you will delight in YHVH* (Isa. 58:14), in order to delight from the potion of the stream, as it is said, *He will satisfy your thirst with sparkling flashes* (ibid. 58:11).

The Blessed Holy One, as it were, delights in them, from the potion of the stream in which the righteous delight, and therefore He comes to delight with the righteous.

Whoever engages Torah merits to delight with the righteous from the potion of the stream.

139

It has been taught:
Like a hind (ayal) craving running streams (Ps. 42:2)—this is the Assembly of Israel, as it is said, *My strength (eyaluti) hasten to my aid* (Ps. 22:20).
Craving running streams—indeed. To be watered with potions from the fountains of the stream through the Righteous One (*tzaddik*).
Craving (taarog)—as it is said, *to the beds (arugot) of spices* (Song of Songs 6:2).
So my soul craves for You, O Elohim—to be watered by You in this world and in the world that is coming.
What are the fountains of the stream? There is one fountain above, as it is written, *A river issues from Eden to water the garden* (Gen. 2:10), and from there it issues and flows and waters the garden. All the streams issue and flow and gather in the two fountains called *Nezaḥ* and *Hod* and these are called *running streams*, at the level of the Righteous One, from where they gush and flow, watering the garden . . .

It has been taught:
The voice of YHVH induces hinds (yeḥollel ayalot) (Ps. 29:9).
Ayalot, hinds—it is written *ayelet*, hind, deficient [i.e., missing the *vav*]. This is the hind of the dawn (*ayelet ha-shaḥar*).
It has been taught:
At midnight, when the Blessed Holy One enters the Garden of Eden to delight with the righteous, this voice goes forth and causes pain to all those hinds surrounding the holy throne of glory, as it is written, *encircled by sixty warriors* (Song of Songs 3:7).
Another interpretation:
Induces hinds (yeḥollel ayalot)—as it is said, *His hand brought on (ḥollelah) the elusive serpent* (Job 26:13).
And strips forests (yearot) bare (Ps. 29:9)—as it is said, *into the honeycomb (be-yaarat ha-dvash)* (1 Samuel 14:27), and it is written, *I have eaten my honey and honeycomb* (Song of Songs 5:1), and she suckles them like a mother suckling her children.

Rabbi Abba said to him:
My soul, I desire You (ivitikha) at night, my spirit within me, I seek You at dawn (ashaḥreka) (Isa. 26:9).
Ivitikha, I desire You—it should have said, *desires You (ivtekha)*.
Ashaḥreka, I seek You at dawn—it should have said, *seeks You at dawn*.
He said to him: Behold they have already established [this verse], as it is said, *In His hand is every living soul and the spirit of all humankind*

(Job 12:10).

Come and see:

Soul and spirit are always joined as one.

It has been taught: The consummate worship with which a person should serve the Blessed Holy One is as we have learned: *You shall love YHVH your God with all your heart and with all your soul and with all your might* (Deut. 6:5), that one should love the Blessed Holy One with love of the soul, literally! This is consummate love, the love of his soul and spirit. Just as these cleave to the body and the body loves them, so a person should cleave to love the Blessed Holy One, cleaving to Him with the love of his soul and spirit. This is what is written, *nafshi ivitikha, with my soul I desire You*—with my soul, literally!

My spirit within me, I seek you at dawn—to cleave to You with great love.

At night—For a person must arise every night, out of love for the Blessed Holy One, to engage in His worship until morning rises, and a thread of grace is extended upon him.

It has been taught:

Happy is the portion of the person who loves the Blessed Holy One with such love;

and these truly righteous who love the Blessed Holy One so, the world abides because of them and they have dominion over all harsh decrees, above and below.

It has been taught:

The righteous person who cleaves with his spirit and soul above to the holy King in love as is fitting, rules over the earth below, and all that he decrees for the world endures.

From where do we know this? From Elijah, as it is written, *As YHVH lives, the God of Israel, whom I serve, there will be no dew or rain these years except at my bidding* (1 Kings 17:1) . . .

It has been taught:

Before the world was created, one hundred and twenty five thousand degrees of the souls of the righteous arose in Desire, which the Blessed Holy One designates for this world in every generation. They ascend, soar throughout the world, and join the bundle of life. In the future the Blessed Holy One will renew the world through them. About them it is written, *As the new heaven and new earth [which I will make stand before me, declares YHVH, so shall your seed and your name endure]* (Isa. 66:22).

Commentary on *Zohar* 3:67b–68b

We are stardust, we are golden, and we've got to get ourselves
back to the garden.

—Joni Mitchell

In one of his many beautiful poems, the Persian mystic, Jelaluddin Balkhi, better known in the West as Rumi, celebrates the special divine intimacy that can only be experienced at night. Night, with all its mystery and wonder, is the privileged time for attaining the "privacy of the beloved" when "that which adoration adores" is beheld:

Don't go to sleep at night.
What you most want will come to you then.
Warmed by a sun inside, you'll see wonders.
Tonight, don't put your head down.
Be tough, and strength will come.
That which adoration adores appears at night.
Those asleep may miss it.
One night Moses stayed awake and asked, and saw a light in
  a tree.
Then he walked at night for ten years, until finally he saw the
  whole tree illuminated.
Muhammad rode his horse through the night sky.
The day is for work, the night for love.
Don't let someone bewitch you.
Some people sleep at night.
But not lovers.
They sit in the dark and talk to God, who told David:
Those who sleep all night every night and claim to be
  connected to us, they lie.
Lovers can't sleep when they feel the privacy of the beloved all
  around them . . .[1]

Rumi, whose writings predate the *Zohar* by some thirty or so years, articulates here with great beauty the power of the nocturnal vigil, the *Qiyam al-Layl*, so beloved of the Sufi masters. Writing somewhat more prosaically, Ibn al-Arabi, "the Great Sheikh," born and raised in al-Andalus in the generations preceding the *Zohar*, and perhaps the most famous of all Sufis, expressed something similar in his magnum opus, *The Meccan Openings*: "If the seeker desires divine loci of witnessing and lordly sciences, he should multiply his nightly vigils and continually multiply within them his concentration."[2] Wakefulness at night, while the majority of humanity slumbers, is a time of special communion with the divine, and according to Rumi, affords the practitioner an experience akin to Moses and Muhammad. Of particular significance in Rumi's poem is the evocation of David, who according to Talmudic tradition was the great minstrel of the night:

> *At midnight I rise to praise You* (Ps. 119:62) . . .
>   *My eyes greet each watch of the night as I meditate on Your words* (Ps. 119:148)
>   Rabbi Oshaya said in the name of Rabbi Aḥa: David said: Midnight never passed me by in my sleep.
>   Rabbi Zeira said: Until midnight he would doze like a horse, from then on he became mighty as a lion.
>   Rav Ashi said: Until midnight he engaged in words of Torah, from then on in songs and praises . . .
>   Did David know the exact moment of midnight? . . . David had a sign . . . Rabbi Shimon the Hasid said: There was a harp suspended above David's bed. As soon as midnight arrived, the north wind came and blew upon it, and it played by itself. Immediately he arose and engaged in Torah until the break of dawn.
>
> —BT *Berakhot* 3b

Like Rumi, the kabbalists of the *Zohar* turn to David as a model for their nocturnal activities, which as we will see, lie at the heart of the zoharic world and its mystical quest. Indeed, perhaps more than any other biblical persona, it is David, not the king or warrior, but the poet and musician, the lover of the night, with whom the kabbalists of the *Zohar* most identify.

The nocturnal delight—the nightly study vigil from midnight till dawn—is, alongside the zoharic praxis of "walking on the way," the most important mystical ritual found in the *Zohar*. The *Zohar* contains dozens of stories outlining this praxis, and frequently we encounter the Companions arising at midnight to ply Torah. Whether in private homes, inns, or even outside on the road, the Companions are punctilious in their observance of this key zoharic ritual. The details of this rich mythical praxis have been artfully explored by *Zohar* scholars and we need not rehearse them here.[3] What is significant for our purposes is a broad understanding of the key participants and arenas in this ritual, as well as the kind of experience attained by the members of the zoharic fraternity. The following passage, to my mind one of the most beautiful articulations of the nocturnal delight found in the entire *Zohar*, provides a convenient entry point:

> At midnight, when birds arouse, the side of the North arouses in a wind. A scepter from the side of the South rises erect and strikes that wind, so it subsides, turning fragrant. Then the Blessed Holy One arouses, following His custom, to delight with the righteous in the Garden of Eden. At that moment happy is the share of the human being who rises to delight in Torah, for the Blessed Holy One and all the righteous in the Garden of Eden listen to his voice, as is written, *You who dwell in the gardens, companions listen for your voice; let me hear!* (Song of Songs 8:13). Further, the Blessed Holy One emanates upon Him a thread of grace, protecting him throughout the world, for higher and lower beings guard him, as is written, *By day YHVH directs His grace, at night His song is with me* (Ps. 42:9).
>
> Rabbi Ḥizkiyah said: Certainly whoever engages in this shares constantly in the world that is coming.
>
> Rabbi Yose asked: What do you mean, constantly?
>
> He replied: So we have learned: Every midnight, when the Blessed Holy One arouses in the Garden of Eden, all the plants of the Garden are watered profusely by the stream called Stream of Antiquity, Stream of Delights, never ceasing. If one rises and engages in Torah, then that stream gushes upon his head, as it were, saturating him among those plants of the Garden of Eden.
>
> Rabbi Yose said: Since all those righteous in the Garden listen to him, he shares in the saturation of that stream; in consequence, he shares constantly in the world that is coming.
>
> —*Zohar* 1:92a (Matt, *The Zohar*)

Midnight is the time of the great arousal—the rousing and rising of the Companions below who assemble together to study Torah, as well as the arousal of the upper worlds, the male aspect of divinity, the Blessed Holy One, who enters the Garden of Eden, a dimension of reality associated with the *Shekhinah*, to delight in the righteous. Throughout the night, the Companions' words of Torah below emit an aphrodisiacal quality, arousing the male and female grades of divinity, who, after a night of playful courtship, finally unite in the intermingling of the day and night immediately preceding the dawn. In this special praxis the Companions are simultaneously present below in their bodies, as well as above in the Garden of Eden in their spiritual or astral garb. The ritual climaxes at dawn with the first rays of light, which the assembled mystics experience as the outpouring of the divine, the erotic fluids flowing from the sexual union of the male and female aspects of divinity, the stream that flows from the world that is coming. The use of the verse from the Song of Songs, "You who dwell in the gardens," as well as the verse from Psalms, "at night His song is with me," is central to the *Zohar*'s construction of the nocturnal vigil, and these verses appear repeatedly throughout the *Zohar*. The Companions, like the earliest Jewish mystics who "entered the orchard" (see *Tosefta Ḥagiga* 2:3), dwell in the garden, and throughout the night, through their song, by virtue of their special mystical-poetic engagement with Torah, heal the primal breach and return to the Garden of Eden.

Perhaps above all else, the nocturnal vigil is significant because it is during these hours that the mystics of the *Zohar* are best able to attain contact with the ultimate object of their desire, the river that flows from Eden, the stream of divinity as it flows forth from concealment into the world and into human consciousness. The Companions of the *Zohar* "stand nightly in the house of YHVH" (Ps. 134:2), and in reward for their steadfast service and presence, receive the gift of saturation from the fountain of the deep stream that flows from Eden—the supernal sanctuary, the sefirah *Ḥokhmah*—through the divine organism and the divine phallus—Zion, the sefirah *Yesod*—and onto to those below:

> *Now bless YHVH all you servants of YHVH [who stand* **nightly** *in the house of YHVH]* (Ps. 134:1) . . . this is the praise of all the sons of faith.
>
> And who are the sons of faith? They are the ones who engage Torah and know how to unify the holy name as is fitting.
>
> And the praise of those sons of faith, the ones who awaken at midnight with Torah . . . *who stand* **nightly** *in the house of YHVH*—these are called *servants of YHVH*, these are worthy to bless the King and their blessing is indeed a blessing, as it is written: *Lift your hands toward the sanctuary and bless YHVH* (Ps. 134:2). You are worthy that the Holy King should be blessed by you, and the blessing uttered by you is a real blessing.
>
> *Lift your hands toward the sanctuary.* What is the sanctuary? The supernal place from which issues the fountain of the deep stream, as it is written, *A river issues from Eden to water the garden* (Gen. 2:10). And Eden is called supernal sanctuary, hence, *Lift up your hands toward the sanctuary.*

And of the man who does so and merits this, what do they
proclaim about him?
May YHVH bless you from Zion (Ps. 134:3).
—*Zohar* 3:12b–13a

Although mystical experience in the *Zohar* can transpire at any time of
the day, it is the hours between midnight and dawn, the temporal
domain of the *Shekhinah*, characterized by the soft and mysterious light
of the moon and stars, where the mystic of the *Zohar* enjoys the greatest intimacy with the divine.

···

While many zoharic treatments of the nocturnal delight are found
embedded within complex narratives (see chapter 9), our passage contains no such plot and is woven around the homilies of Rabbi Shimon,
the grand master, and then Rabbi Abba, the most senior of the disciples.
Following the opening narrative statement, which does no more than
provide the barest of details about the cast and their rising at midnight,
Rabbi Shimon begins the nocturnal vigil with a seemingly straightforward homily. As we shall see, though, his exposition provides a neat
illustration of the zoharic method, conveying in a highly condensed
form many of the key elements of both the nocturnal delight in particular and the zoharic quest in general:

Rabbi Abba was sitting before Rabbi Shimon. Rabbi Shimon
rose at midnight to ply Torah. Rabbi El'azar and Rabbi Abba
rose with him.

Rabbi Shimon opened, saying: *Like a hind craving running
streams, so my soul craves for You, O Elohim* (Ps. 42:2). This
verse has been established by the Companions.

Happy are Israel of all the nations, for the Blessed Holy
One gave them a holy Torah and bequeathed them holy souls
from a holy realm in order to perform His commandments and
delight in Torah; for whoever delights in Torah does not fear
anything, as it is written, *Were not Your Torah my delight, I
would have perished in my affliction* (Ps. 119:92).

What is *my delight*? Torah. For the Torah is called delight,
as it is written, *a source of delight every day* (Prov. 8:30).

And this is as we have learned: The Blessed Holy One
comes to delight with the righteous in the Garden of Eden.

What is meant by *to delight*? In order to rejoice in them.

As we have learned: Happy are the righteous about whom it is written, *Then you will delight in YHVH* (Isa. 58:14), in order to delight from the potion of the stream, as it is said, *He will satisfy your thirst with sparkling flashes* (ibid. 58:11).

The Blessed Holy One, as it were, delights in them, from the potion of the stream in which the righteous delight, and therefore He comes to delight with the righteous.

Whoever engages Torah merits to delight with the righteous from the potion of the stream.

Rabbi Shimon's opening verse, "Like a hind craving running streams, so my soul craves for You, O Elohim," to which he returns only after some preliminary programmatic remarks about the nocturnal delight, might easily serve as a summary statement for the zoharic mystic's deepest desires—to be watered and saturated by the flow of divinity. Not only does the verse evoke an image of intense longing, the broader context of the Psalm, described by Mitchell Dahood as the biblical version of the "dark night of the soul,"[4] opens to a scene of painful yearning, combined with the anticipation of entering the temple of God amid song and praise.

> As a hind cries aloud for running streams, so my soul cries
>   aloud for you, O God.
> My soul thirsts for God, for the living God.
> When shall I begin to drink in deeply the presence of God?
> My tears have been my food day and night, when it was being
>   said to me all day long, "Where is your God?"
> These things I shall remember, and shall pour out my soul
>   before Him, when I cross the barrier and prostrate myself
>   near the temple of God, amid loud shouts of thanksgiving,
>   amid a festal throng.
>   —Psalms 42:1–5 (trans. Mitchell Dahood)

The continuation of the psalm, which contains the key verse "By day YHVH commands His grace, at night His song is with me," is also replete with water imagery and the desire to be saturated from the flowing streams of divinity: "the roar of Your streams, Your waves and breakers sweep over me."

The zoharic author's ability to evoke an entire landscape and emotional tone through citing only a fragment of a verse is undoubtedly one of the distinguishing features of zoharic literary art, and in reading zoharic texts, we need also be aware of the broader context of the verses cited, which, in many cases, resonate and echo with the particular theme the *Zohar* wishes to discuss. The *Zohar* is more than just a theoretical presentation of kabbalistic doctrine, and often we find that a particular verse is cited, not merely because it serves as a proof text for whatever point the *Zohar* wishes to make, but because it opens to an emotional or visual terrain in harmony with the kind of mystical-poetic consciousness the composition seeks to engender. Another case in point from Rabbi Shimon's opening homily is the reference to the Torah as "a source of delight every day" from Proverbs 8. Beyond evoking the well-known rabbinic midrash describing the Blessed Holy One consulting with and delighting in the preexistent Torah before the creation of the world (see *Genesis Rabbah* 1:1), and beyond establishing a connection between the Torah (God's delight) and the nocturnal delight, the context of the verse is also significant.

> It is Wisdom calling . . .
> I was with Him as a confidant, a source of delight every day,
> Rejoicing before Him at all times,
> Rejoicing in His inhabited world,
> Finding delight with mankind . . .
> Happy is the person who listens to me,
> Coming early to my gates each day,
> Waiting outside my doors.
> For he who finds me finds life
> And obtains favor from YHVH
> —Proverbs 8:1, 30–31, 34–35

Particularly pronounced here is the joy and play that characterizes not only the Companions' nocturnal endeavors (they delight in God's delight), but the broader zoharic religious sensibility. Indeed, one of the endearing features of the *Zohar* is its general tone or "vibe" in which the majesty of God is balanced by intimacy, joy, and delight. Noteworthy also in this "hyper-landscape" is the reference to "coming early to my gates each day," in reward for which the Companions achieve contact with the ultimate source of life.

In some cases, when discussing the nocturnal delight, we are treated to a lavish description of all the varied phases of this complex ritual (see, for example, *Zohar* 2:195b), while on other occasions the *Zohar* is content merely to evoke the ritual in bare outline. In this case, Rabbi Shimon cites two verses from Isaiah 58, which although quoted only in part, are sufficient to alert the seasoned *Zohar* reader to the ultimate object of the nocturnal quest. The first verse, "Then you will delight in

YHVH," *az titanag al YHVH*, is read hyper-literally by the *Zohar* and is understood to signify an attainment of divinity, *al YHVH*, that is, over and beyond YHVH, namely, beyond the sefirah *Tiferet*. The *Zohar* here, in extremely condensed form, is signaling to the reader the possibility of coming into contact with the unitary and undifferentiated source of the stream of divinity, whose origins lie beyond *Tiferet* in the innermost depths of the divine being. The continuation of the verse, not cited by the *Zohar*, is also significant: "I will set you astride the heights of the earth and let you enjoy (*haakhaltikha*, lit., feed you) the heritage (*nahalat*) of your father Jacob—for the mouth of YHVH has spoken." Aside from the promise of attainment beyond the earth, that is, beyond the sefirah *Malkhut*, there seems little doubt that the author of this passage also saw in this verse the zoharic quest to ingest the flowing river (*nahal*) of divinity and touch the mouth of the divine.

The second verse cited by Rabbi Shimon is no less suggestive. In fact the entire passage in Isaiah from which the verse is excerpted is particularly important in the *Zohar*:[5]

> Then shall your light burst forth like the dawn, and your healing spring up quickly.
>
> Your Vindicator (*tzidkekha*) shall march before you, the glory of YHVH shall be your rear guard.
>
> Then when you call, YHVH will answer, when you cry, He will say: Here I am . . .
>
> Then shall your light shine in darkness, and your gloom shall be like noonday.
>
> YHVH will guide you always and slake your thirst in parched places and give strength to your bones.
>
> You will be like a watered garden, like a spring whose waters do not fail.
>
> —Isaiah 58:8–11

Once again, these verses contain the zoharic quest in condensed form—to radiate the light of God, to be filled with the divine bounty and imbibe the fluids of divinity. Of special note is the expression "slake your thirst in parched places (*tzahtzahot*)," which as Daniel Matt has suggested, the *Zohar* connects with the Hebrew word *tzah*, meaning bright or sparkling, and which therefore ought to be rendered "satisfy your soul with sparkling flashes."[6] The reference to the dawn, as well as the poignant divine-human intimacy evoked in these verses, an intimacy attained by the mystics of the *Zohar* during the nocturnal ritual, is yet another example of the way the *Zohar* uses "hyper-landscapes" to convey its mystical goals.

Following these preliminary remarks, Rabbi Shimon begins his exposition in earnest. His homily is extremely dense and follows the associative method of the *Zohar*—the unique fluid poetics where verses and images flow and melt into one another—and takes us through the myth of the nocturnal delight into the heart of mystical experience itself. The homily that follows, characteristic of many throughout the *Zohar*, beautifully illustrates the *Zohar*'s capacity to use the verses of the Bible as a launch pad for mythical narrative as well as mystical experience:

> It has been taught:
> *Like a hind craving running streams* (Ps. 42:2)—this is the Assembly of Israel, as it is said, *My strength (eyaluti) hasten to my aid* (Ps. 22:20).
> *Craving running streams*—indeed. To be watered with potions from the fountains of the stream through the Righteous One.[7]
> *Craving (taarog)*—as it is said, *to the beds (arugot) of spices* (Song of Songs 6:2).
> *So my soul craves for You, O Elohim*—to be watered by You in this world and in the world that is coming.
> What are the fountains of the stream? There is one fountain above, as it is written, *A river issues from Eden to water the garden* (Gen. 2:10), and from there it issues and flows and waters the garden. All the streams issue and flow and gather in the two fountains called *Nezah* and *Hod* and these are called *running streams*, at the level of the Righteous One, from where they gush and flow, watering the garden . . .

Rabbi Shimon connects the hind from his opening verse to the Assembly of Israel, the *Shekhinah*, and thereby evokes one of the richest mythical symbols employed throughout the *Zohar*.[8] His proof text, "My strength (*eyaluti*) hasten to my aid," is chosen not merely because of the resonance between hind (*ayal*) and my strength (*eyaluti*), but also because this verse is taken from Psalm 22, a psalm wholly dedicated to *ayelet ha-shahar*, the hind of the dawn. Together, the beginning of the psalm and the verse cited by Rabbi Shimon open to a complex, yet central mythical "story" about the divine being:

> *The hind of the dawn* (Ps. 22:1). What is the hind of the dawn? It is a particular animal, a merciful one, of whom there is none more merciful among the animals of the world; for when time

presses, and she needs food both for herself and for all the animals, she goes far away on a distant journey and comes back bringing food . . . When she returns all the other animals assemble near her, and she stands in the middle and distributes to each one of them . . . When does she distribute to them? When the morning is about to dawn, while it is still night and darkness reigns and day is about to break . . . when the morning shines forth they are all sated with her food . . . She goes in the day and is revealed at night and makes her distribution in the morning, and she is therefore called *the hind of the dawn.*
—*Zohar* 3:249a–b (Tishby and Goldstein, modified; see also *Zohar* 2:219b)

Employing a very earthly image of a hind journeying to obtain food, the *Zohar* describes here the celestial ascent of the *Shekhinah* to the upper regions of the divine being to draw down the divine bounty for those below. The hind craving running streams is the *Shekhinah* seeking to be filled with the flowing fluids from above. As noted, the night is her domain and Rabbi Shimon evokes in real time her perilous journey, the end of which marks, as we will soon see, the culmination of the Companions' nocturnal mystical endeavors. The verse "My strength, hasten to my aid," part of this same mythical story,[9] is here repeated by Rabbi Shimon as a direct call for intimacy and contact with the divine.

Having begun to unpack the symbolic valence of the hind from his opening verse, Rabbi Shimon now turns to the running streams. As we have already seen, flowing fluids—wine, oil, and especially water—are central images for the *Zohar*'s dynamic conception of divinity. Divinity in the *Zohar* is not static, and the divine being seeks constantly to flow forth from itself into itself and on to those below. The God of the *Zohar* is in a perpetual state of becoming and unfolding, and the task of the mystic is at once to enable, attain, and enjoy this movement. This flow, it should be stressed, has a pronounced erotic quality, subtly evoked here through the verse from Song of Songs connecting craving, *taarog*, with the word *arugot* (beds), an unlikely derivation, but one that enables the author to introduce the erotic landscape of the song (6:2)— "My love has gone down to his garden, to the beds of spices, to graze and gather lilies." The love of course is the Blessed Holy One who will soon unite with his garden, *Malkhut*, the female face of the divine. The dynamism of divinity, however, is most dramatically conveyed through the *Zohar*'s favorite verse, "A river issues from Eden to water the garden," quoted hundreds of times in the *Zohar* to describe the flow of divinity from Eden, the sefirah *Hokhmah* or the cluster of sefirot *Keter-*

Hokhmah-Binah into the garden, the sefirah *Malkhut*, as well as on to human beings below. As Melila Hellner-Eshed has noted, this verse functions as a code verse in the *Zohar*, signaling to the reader the ever present possibility of coming into contact with the perpetually flowing river whose "waters never cease."[10] Like the verse itself, whose key verb *yatza*, issues, is in the present tense, contact with divinity, according to the *Zohar*, is not only the patrimony of heroes of old but is available here and now.

Continuing his nocturnal "riff" on the hind, Rabbi Shimon now cites another verse from Psalms, "The voice of YHVH induces hinds and strips forests bare" (Ps. 29:9), a verse familiar to many from the Friday night *Kabbalat Shabbat* liturgy. In a masterful display of zoharic exegesis, he uncovers in this verse a description of the *Shekhinah*'s labor and then birthing of the fluids and nourishment with which she is filled, as well as the secret of enlightenment through live contact with divinity.

> It has been taught:
> *The voice of YHVH induces hinds (yehollel ayalot)* (Ps. 29:9).
> *Ayalot*, hinds—it is written *ayelet*, hind, deficient [i.e., missing the *vav*].[11] This is the hind of the dawn (*ayelet ha-shahar*).[12]
> It has been taught:
> At midnight, when the Blessed Holy One enters the Garden of Eden to delight with the righteous, this voice goes forth and causes pain to all those hinds surrounding the holy throne of glory, as it is written, *encircled by sixty warriors* (Song of Songs 3:7).
> Another interpretation:
> *Induces hinds (yehollel ayalot)*—as it is said, *His hand brought on (hollelah) the elusive serpent* (Job 26:13).
> *And strips forests (yearot) bare* (Ps. 29:9)—as it is said, *into the honeycomb (be-yaarat ha-dvash)* (1 Sam. 14:27), and it is written, *I have eaten my honey and honeycomb* (Song of Songs 5:1), and she suckles them like a mother suckling her children.

Rabbi Shimon's homily, to my mind one of the more complex and most brilliant in the *Zohar*, turns on the multiple understandings of the verb *yehollel*. Translated here as induce, this rich word conveys many meanings, including frighten, cause, create, generate, bring forth, pierce, as well as dance, among many others.[13] Of particular note is the associated verb stem *hal*, to writhe in pain, as in the verse from Isaiah 26:17, "like a woman with child, approaching childbirth, writhing (*taḥeel*) and screaming in her pangs." The genius of the zoharic homilist is precisely in his ability to keep so many of these different meanings and nuances in play as he creates his mythical/mystical midrash. While the picture is not entirely clear in all its phases, we find here an account of the laboring *Shekhinah*, pregnant with the fluids of divinity, culminating with her birth and the ensuing mystical ecstasy. Let us try and unpack this dense mythological narrative ingeniously read out of the verses of Scripture.

Following his opening exegetical move connecting the writhing/ birthing/dancing hinds of our verse with the Assembly of Israel, the hind of the dawn, Rabbi Shimon describes the onset of midnight, the beginning of the nocturnal delight, marked by a dramatic transition in the divine realm.[14] The striking of the hinds encircling or dancing around the *Shekhinah*, the sixty warriors encircling the holy throne of glory, might either be understood as the removal of the forces of judgment associated with the *Shekhinah* prior to her birthing, with *yeḥollel* understood as frightens or pierces,[15] or alternately as a more general account of the onset of labor for the *Shekhinah* and her associated angelic camps, in which case *yeḥollel* might signify writhing or causing to writhe. Whatever the case, it is the next phase in the "story" that is decisive. Playing again on the word *yeḥollel* (so far, the homilist has employed the verb as induce, dance, cause pain, or make writhe), Rabbi Shimon connects our keyword with a verse from Job, "His hand pierced (*ḥollelah*) the elusive serpent." Where the verse from Job describes the subjugation of the forces of evil by God in a theomachy, the *Zohar* here reads the verse differently, understanding *ḥollelah* not as pierce but as create, cause, or bring forth. Rabbi Shimon's reading of the verse "His hand brought on the elusive serpent" thereby returns us to the myth of the hind's nocturnal journey we encountered earlier. In the continuation of that rich mythological scene, we find the following astonishing conclusion:

> When the world needs rain, all the other animals assemble near her, and she goes up to the top of a high mountain, and, bowing her head between her knees, she utters lowing sounds, one after the other, and the Blessed Holy One hears her voice and is filled with Mercy and takes pity on the world . . . When she is pregnant she is closed up. When the time comes for her to give birth, she lows and utters cries, cry after cry . . . The Blessed Holy One brings forth a great snake from among the mountains of darkness and it comes through the hills, its mouth

licking the dust. It draws near to the hind and bites her twice at
the appropriate place. The first time, blood comes out, and it
licks it up. The second time, water comes out and all the animals in the mountains drink, and she is opened and gives birth
. . . At that very time when the Blessed Holy One took pity
upon the young of this animal, what is written, *The voice of
YHVH induces hinds and strips forests bare* (Ps. 29:9). *The
voice of YHVH induces hinds*—those pains and travails . . .
And then immediately, *He strips forests bare*—in order to bring
the snake through . . .

—*Zohar* 3:249a–b (Tishby and Goldstein, modified;
see also *Zohar* 2:52b; BT *Baba Batra* 16b)

The serpent "brought on" (*hollelah*) by God in Rabbi Shimon's associative homily is none other than the mythological face of the other side,
the demonic realm, who must bite the genitalia of the hind/*Shekhinah*
thereby enabling her to give birth and bestow her bounty. The *Zohar* is
a bold work and, on occasion, even seasoned *Zohar* readers are struck
by its daring and surprising imagery. In this fantastic mythological
scene—a scene that recurs nightly according to the *Zohar*—we find
birth and sex (the snake is after all a phallic symbol) juxtaposed in a
most unexpected way. The *Shekhinah*'s birth or delivery of the celestial
bounty is accompanied by an act of piercing or penetration, and it is
only after her erotic encounter with the other side that she can open and
reveal or bring forth her offspring, the sweet flowing fluids within her,
"the running streams" from above.

Having expounded the first part of the verse, "The voice of YHVH
induces hinds," Rabbi Shimon turns to the conclusion of the verse,
"and strips forests bare." His exposition is concise, elusive, and extraordinary, and takes us from a discussion about the nocturnal drama into
the very heart of mystical experience itself. Rabbi Shimon's homily
hinges on his connecting *yearot*, forests, with the Hebrew word for honeycomb, *yaarat ha-devash*. While Rabbi Shimon cites only two words
from the book of Samuel, the biblical scene to which he sends us, seemingly devoid of mystical content, must be kept in mind:

And the fighting moved on past Beth-aven. And the men of
Israel were hard pressed on that day. And Saul made the troops
take an oath, saying, "Cursed be the man who eats food until
evening, until I take vengeance upon my enemies!" And all the
troops tasted no food. And the whole country came into the

forest, and there was honey on the ground. And the troops entered the forest and, look, there was a flow of honey, but none touched his hand to his mouth, for the troops feared the vow. But Jonathan had not heard when his father made the troops swear, and he reached with the tip of the staff that was in his hand and dipped it into the honeycomb and brought his hand back to his mouth, and his eyes lit up.

—1 Samuel 14:24–27[16]

Rabbi Shimon's allusion would place Jonathan, David's beloved friend, in the role of the archetypal mystic, daring to dip his staff, a phallic symbol, into the flow of honey, the sweetness of divinity, as a result of which his face shines with enlightenment. This juxtaposition of ingesting the honey of divinity and illumination is found also in one of the Hebrew works of Moses de Leon, *Or Zarua* (Sown Light) where after recounting a beautiful parable about a man who wasted his whole life studying only the law rather than contemplating the deeper mysteries of being, Moses exclaims, "See now how my eyes shine, for I have tasted a bit of this honey! O house of Jacob, come, let us walk in the light of YHVH."[17] As Gershom Scholem famously observed, the mystical quest might be summarized by the words of the Psalmist, "Taste and see that the Lord is good" (Ps. 34:9),[18] and in citing the verse from the Song of Songs, "I have come into my garden, my sister, my bride. I have gathered my myrrh and my spices. I have eaten my honey and honeycomb. I have drunk my wine and my milk," the *Zohar* provides a sensual and erotic image for the mystical climax. In the space of one verse, Rabbi Shimon has evoked a dynamic mythological and mystical realm, describing the labor and then birth of the *Shekhinah*, "the voice of YHVH induces hinds," as well as the bestowal of her life-giving bounty—"stripping forests bare" (*va-yeḥesof yearot*), understood by the *Zohar* as "exposing the forest," namely, exposing the opening of the womb for birth, or as "revealing the honey," that is, suckling her children (the Companions) who are ever ready to imbibe the milk of divinity. "The voice of YHVH induces hinds, exposing forests of honey": labor, crisis, birth, and then suckling. As is so often the case when reading *Zohar*, we can only wonder at the author's capacity to find in seemingly innocent verses of Scripture the story of the divine being and the secrets of live contact with God. While the nocturnal delight is usually figured in erotic terms of flirtation and sexual union, the picture presented here is very different. The hours from midnight till dawn mark the process of the *Shekhinah*'s ripening and opening, culminating in birth and then suckling, the active bestowal of mystical nourishment.[19] The Companions, the "initiates of the *Matronita*'s palace," are with her throughout the night, at once her midwives, children, and lovers.

Rabbi Shimon's exposition complete, it is now time for Rabbi Abba to play his role in this nocturnal assembly:

> Rabbi Abba said to him:
> *My soul, I desire You (ivitikha) at night, my spirit within me, I seek You at dawn (ashaḥreka)* (Isa. 26:9).[20]
> *Ivitikha, I desire You*—it should have said, *desires You (ivtekha).*
> *Ashaḥreka, I seek You at dawn*—it should have said, *seeks You at dawn.*
> He said to him: Behold they have already established [this verse], as it is said, *In His hand is every living soul and the spirit of all humankind* (Job 12:10).

As is the *Zohar*'s way, the verse chosen for exposition by Rabbi Abba is well attuned to the temporal landscape of the narrative. Seated before Rabbi Shimon during the nocturnal vigil, Rabbi Abba recites a verse that evokes both the night and the dawn. Insisting on reading the verse hyper-literally, Rabbi Abba creates a difficulty with the text, which in turn creates the space for his novel interpretation. Employing one of the *Zohar*'s favorite exegetical strategies—"it should have said"—Rabbi Abba tells us that the verse should have read, "My soul desires You in the night, my spirit within me seeks You at dawn," which is how the verse is usually understood and translated, rather than the clumsy and seemingly inexplicable, yet more literal, "My soul, I desire you at night, my spirit . . . I seek you at dawn." As Rabbi Abba astutely points out, the Hebrew text reads *ivitikha*, "I desire you," in the first person, rather than *ivtekha* "desires you" in the third person, as we would expect, thus raising the question whether the soul is the agent or object of longing in the verse. Expressed differently, Rabbi Abba is asking: is the soul that which desires or that which is desired? The peculiar formulation of the verse sustains both readings. This problem, he says, has already been resolved elsewhere, and in citing the verse from Job (12:10), "In His hand is every living soul and the spirit of all humankind," Rabbi Abba alludes to a rabbinic idea, which the *Zohar* adopts and expands, of the soul's nightly ascent to God.[21] In *Deuteronomy Rabbah*, a late rabbinic midrash (5:15), we read: "While [people] sleep all souls ascend to Him, as it is written, *In His hand is every living soul and the spirit of all humankind*, and in the morning He returns the soul to each and every person."²² Although Rabbi Abba does not make the connection between this idea and his opening verse explicit, a short homily found just before our narrative does exactly this:

> Rabbi Yose said: When a human being sleeps in his bed his soul departs and ascends and testifies about him concerning all that he has done throughout the day. The body says to the soul: *My soul, I desire you at night, my spirit within me, I seek you at dawn.*
>
> —*Zohar* 3:67a–b

The oddity of the verse is thus revealed as containing an allusion to the mysteries of the soul's celestial nocturnal journey, as the body, the "I" of the verse from Isaiah, calls out to the soul and spirit respectively, seeking reunion and reunification.

Not content merely to cite the words of others, however—after all, innovation is the order of the night!—Rabbi Abba now offers a new interpretation of the same verse:

> Come and see:
>   Soul and spirit are always joined as one.
>   It has been taught: The consummate worship with which a person should serve the Blessed Holy One is as we have learned: *You shall love YHVH your God with all your heart and with all your soul and with all your might* (Deut. 6:5), that one should love the Blessed Holy One with love of the soul, literally!
>   This is consummate love, the love of his soul and spirit. Just as these cleave to the body and the body loves them, so a person should cleave to love the Blessed Holy One, cleaving to Him with the love of his soul and spirit. This is what is written, *nafshi ivitikha,* **with** *my soul I desire You*—with my soul, literally!

Rabbi Abba's homily is about "consummate worship" and cleaving to God. Evoking the figure of Rabbi Akiva, the greatest rabbinic mystic and martyr, who loved YHVH with all his soul, "even if he takes your soul" as the Talmud writes (see BT *Berakhot* 61b), Rabbi Abba presents a model of selfless and total devotion to God. Such consummate love is the subject of a short and related discussion in the Introduction of the *Zohar:*

The second commandment . . . this is love, loving one's Lord consummately . . .

Abounding love is consummate love, consummate in two aspects. Unless embracing both, it is not consummate fittingly.

So we have learned: Love—love of the Blessed Holy One—branches in two directions. There is the person who loves Him because he has wealth, longevity, children surrounding him; he dominates his enemies, his paths are paved. Because of this he loves Him. If things were overturned—the Blessed Holy One turning the wheel of strict judgment against him—then he would hate Him, not love Him at all. So this love is not rooted.

The love called consummate abides both aspects, whether judgment or favor. The ripening of the way is to love one's Lord as we have learned, "even if he plucks your soul." Such love is consummate, embracing both aspects.

—*Zohar* 1:12a (Matt, *The Zohar*)

Rabbi Abba's homily, however, does not merely allude to Rabbi Akiva's greatest teaching, namely cleaving to God even unto death, but extends it. Not only does consummate worship require loving God with all one's soul—literally—in the manner of Rabbi Akiva, but one must also love God with one's soul, with one's actual soul, "with my soul, literally."[23] Rabbi Abba seems to be talking here about a mode of cleaving to the divine—*devekut*—based on the Neoplatonic idea of connecting or uniting with God through the soul as the straight path or line to God. As Moshe Idel has observed, early kabbalistic writing on *devekut* was heavily influenced by Neoplatonic thought. Rabbi Ezra of Gerona, for example, a contemporary of Nahmanides, wrote of the human soul as "linked to the supernal soul," a kabbalistic variant of the Neoplatonic Universal Soul to which the individual human soul cleaves by an act of ascent.[24] According to Rabbi Abba, one must love God with the soul—*with my soul I desire You*—because it is the soul alone that can cleave to the divine. According to a well-established medieval hierarchy, the soul occupies an intermediate position between matter and the divine, and just as the body and the soul cleave to one another, the soul instinctively and automatically desires God. This "natural" link between the soul and God is expressed elsewhere in the *Zohar*: "Happy is the portion of the righteous, for all is connected, this to that: *Nefesh* to *Ruaḥ*, *Ruaḥ* to *Neshamah*, and *Neshamah* to the Blessed Holy One" (*Zohar* 3:71b). Although Rabbi Abba does not refer in his exposition to God as the supernal or Universal Soul, a short homily that expounds the same verse from Isaiah, and found immediately prior to our narrative, comes close to such a formulation:

> Rabbi Ḥiyya opened: *My soul, I desire You at night* . . . it should have said, *My soul desires You at night.* What is the meaning of *My soul, I desire You?* . . .
>
> Rather, so has it been taught: The Blessed Holy One is the spirit and soul of all, and Israel say: You are my soul and my spirit.
>
> Therefore, *I desire You*—to cleave to You.
>
> —*Zohar* 3:67a

Combined with Rabbi Abba's innovative exposition, the verse from Isaiah is read by the *Zohar* as containing the secret of mystical union: *Nafshi ivitikha*, "My soul, I desire You"—my soul, namely, God, the soul of all, I desire You. And how do I desire and come to know you? *Nafshi ivitikha*, "with my soul I desire You"—precisely through my soul. Rabbi Abba's homily thus picks up on something unsaid but nevertheless latent in Rabbi Shimon's opening verse, "Like a hind craving running streams, so my soul craves for You, O Elohim," insofar as it is the soul that is the agent of craving and that which seeks and attains contact with God. Rabbi Abba's homily, then, aside from being a concise and innovative piece of kabbalistic exegesis, attains its full symphonic force when read as an amplification of the second part of Rabbi Shimon's opening verse. Where Rabbi Shimon expounded the hind and the running streams, Rabbi Abba takes as his focus the soul and its unique capacity to crave and cleave to the divine.[25]

As Rabbi Abba's homily makes clear, night is the privileged time for union and contact with the divine. The small hours of the night present the mystic with the opportunity to "cleave with his spirit and soul above to the holy King." While such cleaving is accompanied by joy and delight on the part of the practitioner—"a thread of grace (*ḥesed*) is extended upon him"[26]—it is important to point out that in the *Zohar*, mystical union is rarely the goal in and of itself. The mystic, rather, seeks live contact with God, not only for his own benefit, but in order to influence God and the world.

It has been taught:
The righteous person who cleaves with his spirit and soul above to the holy King in love as is fitting, rules over the earth below, and all that he decrees for the world endures.

From where do we know this? From Elijah, as it is written, *As YHVH lives, the God of Israel, whom I serve, there will be no dew or rain these years except at my bidding* (1 Kings 17:1).

Devekut, itself predicated on love, functions here as a precondition for theurgic power and the ability to open up a pathway between the upper and lower worlds.[27] Like Elijah who controlled the rain, the mystics of the *Zohar* are responsible for the descent of the divine flow into the world, which in turn is dependent on their nightly soul to Soul cleaving to God. And like Elijah the Companions are among the spiritual elect— those special souls designated by God for every generation—who "ascend, soar throughout the world and join the bundle of life," not only in death, but every night as part of the nocturnal vigil.

·•·

We do not know how texts like this were written. Are they the fruit of a single mind, bringing forth from his imagination a mythical world known only to him, or are they perhaps the product of real nocturnal assemblies, the reconstructed "transcript" of actual encounters between mystic masters from late thirteenth-century Castile? As tempting as it is to think of these texts as reflective of actual nocturnal gatherings, we possess no historical evidence to the effect that kabbalists from the time of the *Zohar* assembled to perform this ritual. That said, however, the absence of evidence is not the evidence of absence, and we cannot dismiss the possibility that small groups of kabbalists did in fact assemble on occasion from midnight till dawn to study Torah together.[28] As we have already seen, nocturnal poetry parties were an important part of Andalusian culture, and while the focus of such gatherings was very different from the content of the zoharic nocturnal vigil, we are not unjustified in viewing this quintessential zoharic praxis as part of the same Andalusian tradition. Where the Muslim upper classes would gather in stately gardens to imbibe, recite, and compose poetry, the Companions of the *Zohar*, real or imaginary, would assemble to sing the song of Torah throughout the night and enter the Garden of Eden. Whatever the historical practice behind these texts, there can be no doubt they were written with mystical inspiration, in states of ecstasy and union with the divine. Decoding the images and symbols, understanding the associations and exegetical moves, activates in us, the readers, even if only briefly, the same kind of poetic consciousness experienced by the author(s)—the song of the night in the Garden of Eden.

•◆•

CHAPTER EIGHT

The Great Chain of Being and the Light of the World

Midrash ha-Ne'elam, Bereshit 15b–d, *Zohar Ḥadash*

Rabbi Abbahu, Rabbi Ḥiyya, and Rabbi Natan were walking on the way.

Rabbi Natan said: Are you not astounded by those Masters of Mishnah?! For the instruction of their mouth is like the instruction of the holy angels!

And I have recalled what they have said: The sun's light is emanated from the splendor of the speculum above and its light is not its own. This is the meaning of what is written, *Let there be lights, yehi meorot* (Gen. 1:14)—it should have said, *yehi orot*. What is *meorot*? Rabbi Zeira said: *min orot*, from the lights, the *mem* is an addition. That is to say, *min orot, from the lights*, and the word is really *orot*, lights.

Rabbi Ḥiyya said: Do not be surprised by this, for the Torah was emanated from the supernal wisdom and the heavens were emanated from the supernal firmament that is above the heads of the creatures, and thus when you contemplate—all that is above and below was emanated, this from that and one from another, and the Blessed Holy One is above all. From the Throne of Glory they began to emanate, one from another, and the Throne of Glory from Him. And all are as naught compared to Him, as it is written, *All the inhabitants of the earth are of no account* (Dan. 4:32).

Rabbi Abbahu said: Let this not trouble you, for to put it differently [*le-havdil*], our leader begins at first by teaching Torah to the translator and the translator to those near him, and those near him to those near them. Thus we find that when the teaching is completed, all is dependent on the leader. In a like vein you will find above and so in all the worlds.

Rabbi Abbahu said further: Moses was illuminated from the supernal splendor. Joshua was illuminated by Moses, the elders illuminated by Joshua, the prophets illuminated by the elders, the chiefs and the leaders of the people from the prophets—all of them, one from another.

While they were walking, they met Rabbi El'azar.

They said: Behold, one of the masters of the academy is coming.

They said to him: Is it true that you have said that the sun's light is illuminated from the splendor of the speculum above?

He said: It is so.

He opened, saying: *A spring in the garden, a well of living waters, a flowing stream from Lebanon* (Song of Songs 4:15). [Scripture] calls her a spring, afterward a well, afterward a flowing stream. This verse requires contemplation. The spring extends from the well and the well from the flowing stream and the flowing stream from Lebanon—to convey that they were all emanated this from that and one from another.

So it is with the sun. Its light is not its own, but rather one thread of splendor extends that irradiates the sun.

We have learned in our Mishnah: With the light that the Blessed Holy One created at first, Adam would gaze and see from one end of the world to the other.

Come and see: The light of the sun is one sixty thousand and seventy-fifth of the light of the speculum of the concealed light. If even at this light of the sun a person cannot gaze, how much more so at that light?! [But] behold, we have said that a person could see with it from one end of the world to the other!?

Rather, so have we instructed in our Mishnah: With that light (*nehiruta*) a person could know and see with the radiance (*nehiru*) of wisdom all that was and all that will be, from the beginning of the world to the end of the world, and it has been concealed for the righteous in the world to come. What is meant by in the world to come? When the holy soul leaves this world and goes to the world that is coming.

Come and see: It is written, *And he was there with YHVH forty days and forty nights; he ate no bread and drank no water* (Exod. 34:28). What is the reason? For he enjoyed of that splendor. And even though he descended from there and the light did not descend with him, they could not gaze upon Moses's face because of what he had seen previously when he was there, and his face remained radiant like this sun.

Rabbi El'azar turned [to go] on his way and they walked after him to accompany him on his way for three miles.
They said to Rabbi El'azar: Happy are you Masters of Mishnah, for you were behind Moses's shoulders when the Torah was given by him.
Rabbi Ḥiyya and Rabbi Natan walked on while Rabbi Abbahu did not wish to part from him and walked with him on his way.

Rabbi El'azar opened his mouth, saying: *And God said, Let there be lights.*
Come and see: The Blessed Holy One made eighteen firmaments that travel on their journeys and orbit the entire world. Each one is suspended [*mitakev*] the measure bestowed upon it by its Master. And when a particular firmament completes is measure, many good and mighty decrees [*pitgamin*] are innovated in the world.
Now, the fool-hearted think in their minds that this is on account of the orbiting of the firmament. It is not so! For each and every day, from morning to evening, the Blessed Holy One innovates supernal, mighty, and forceful decrees.
Sometimes, when a particular firmament completes its journey, a decree of the Supernal King transpires in the world, and the fool-hearted think that this was on account of that firmament—yet their hearts err in foolishness.
And the Blessed Holy One made for the fourth firmament and placed within it the sun, which orbits the entire world according to the seasons and times for the benefit of the world and humanity.
And we have learned in our Mishnah: The sun moves through three hundred and forty apertures, ascending and descending according to the seasons and times. It moves and begins from the window of the east, from the window called *Noga* and moves in a circular fashion until it reaches the window called *Karbosa*. Then it travels six months to the extremity of the north, until it reaches the window called *Zahara*, and travels six months to complete the year for the benefit of the creatures, for sowing and harvesting, as it is written, *So long as the earth endures, seedtime and harvest, cold and heat, summer and winter, [day and night shall not cease]* (Gen. 8:22).
In completing [its journey] to the side of the south, according to the inhabitants of the earth—*harvest, heat* and *summer*; and in completing [its journey] to the extremity of the north—*seedtime, cold* and *winter*.

All is according to the habitation of the earth, as we have said.

And in this way, literally, just as people use (*mishtamshin*) the light of this firmament, so all the hosts of heaven use the light of the firmament that is above the heads of the creatures.

Rabbi Abbahu said: *Lights, meorot,* מארת—why is it written without the *vav*s?

He said to him: It is as we have said previously, that its light is not complete. For its light is only that which it receives from the light above like a single ray from beyond the wall, and therefore its light is not called complete, nor is it fitting that [any light] be called complete, aside from that light referred to as, *the light dwells with Him* (Dan. 2:22). And [the light] that was concealed for the righteous is one sixty thousand and seventy-fifth of the light that dwells with the Blessed Holy One, and the light of the sun is one sixty thousand and seventy-fifth of the light that was concealed for the righteous in the world that is coming. Therefore the light of the sun is not called complete light, nor is it fitting that it be called so. Therefore the Blessed Holy One said: Do not be troubled in that it is written, *me'erat* [lit., curse] and that it is not complete, for I did not make it except for that which is written, *to shine upon the earth* (Gen. 1:15), to serve (*le-shamsha*) the people of the earth, and let it be enough for you, people of the earth, that this luminary will serve you.

Rabbi El'azar said: And if at this small light people cannot gaze, how much more so at the light concealed for the righteous!?

Rabbi Abbahu said: And how much more so at the light of the luminary that dwells before the Blessed Holy One!?

He [Rabbi Abbahu] came to kiss Rabbi El'azar's hand.

He said: Now I know that in truth *meorot,* lights, is deficient [lacking the *vav*s], and what's more that it is fitting that it be deficient.

He said: Woe to the world when you will depart from it, for until this day I have asked this question yet did not find the essence of the word until now! The way on which you set forth will be for me a sign of blessing (*siman brakhah*) in that I encountered you.

He sat with him thirty days and learned every doubt and question he had.

He [Rabbi El'azar] taught him sixty insights concerning the chapter of creation.

He walked on his way.

He found Rabbi Ḥiyya.

He said to him: May it please you Rabbi Abbahu that I might taste of the sweetness of the honey that you sucked from the instruction of the supernal holy ones?

He said to him: Bits of excrement and the goodness of honey do not go together!

Nevertheless he taught him.

Rabbi Ḥiyya wept, saying: I hereby swear that until I learn before the Masters of the Supernal Mishnah I will not return here.

He sat there for twelve years. When he came, they called him Rabbi Ḥiyya the Great.

Rabbi Yitzḥak said: Light is concealed for the righteous in the future to come—that which is concealed, as it is written, *light is sown for the righteous, joy for the upright in heart* (Ps. 97:11).

Commentary on *Midrash ha-Ne'elam, Bereshit* 15b—d, *Zohar Hadash*

> *With You is the fountain of life; by Your light we see light.*
>
> —Psalms 36:10

> *It is a brilliant light that gives off rays on every side and therein His glory is enveloped.*
>
> —Habakkuk 3:4

In the seventh canto of his poetic masterpiece, *Keter Malkhut* (The Kingly Crown), Solomon Ibn Gabirol (1021–ca.1058), among the first of the great Jewish poets of Andalusia as well as the author of the influential Neoplatonic treatise *Mekor Ḥayyim*, or *Fons Vitae* as it came to be known among Latin scholars, describes God through a dialectic of hidden and revealed lights:

> You are the light of the upper regions
> and the eye of every soul that's pure
> will take you in—
> and the clouds of sin
> in the sinner's soul will obscure you.
> Your invisible light in the world
> will be seen in the world to come
> on the mountain of God:
> You are the light everlasting the eye
> of the mind longs to behold
> and may yet glimpse in extremity—
> but the whole of will not see.[1]

Figuring the divine as a brilliant light is of course not new in Judaism. The Bible and the rabbinic literary corpus are filled with images of God as light. What is new in Ibn Gabirol's poem, however, is the fusion of this light imagery with the Neoplatonic structure of being and theory of emanation as it came to be understood, first by medieval Islamic philosophers and mystics, and then through them by the first of the Jewish Neoplatonic thinkers: "Yours is the real which becomes existence in light's reflection, and in whose shadow we live."[2] It is to Plotinus (204–270 CE) that we owe the philosophically and mystically fecund idea of the world as an emanation of divinity. According to Plotinus, the One, the unknowable and inscrutable source of all being, "overflows" and in bubbling over brings forth from itself the totality of being, from the Divine Mind to the All Soul and on to the physical universe itself. For Plotinus and the countless mystics and philosophers influenced by his thought, the origin of the physical world is explained then not through the analogy of some created thing fashioned by an artisan, but as the necessary extension or flow from the One, which by virtue of its perfection must beget the Many. According to this view, the entirety of reality is linked in the chain of emanation: "The One is all things and no one of them; the source of all things is not all things; and yet it is all things in a transcendent sense—all things, so to speak, having run back to it . . . "3

The details of Plotinus's doctrine need not detain us now.4 What is significant for our purposes are some of the central images and metaphors employed by him to convey this idea. While flowing water and even the passing of knowledge from master to disciple figure prominently, it is the image of radiant light, its brilliance undiminished at the core, yet its luminosity decreasing at it moves further from the source, that appears again and again throughout the *Enneads* as the chief metaphor for the undiminished plenitude that is emanation from the One:

> Given this immobility in the Supreme, it can neither have yielded assent nor uttered decree nor stirred in any way towards the existence of a secondary. What happened then? What are we to conceive as rising in the neighbourhood of that immobility? It must be a circumradiation—produced from the Supreme but from the Supreme unaltering—and may be compared to the brilliant light encircling the sun and ceaselessly generated from that unchanging substance.5
>
> There is, we may put it, something that is centre, about it a circle of light shed from it; round centre and first circle alike, another circle, light from light; outside that again, not another circle of light but one which, lacking light of its own, must borrow. The last we may figure to ourselves as a revolving circle, or rather a sphere, of a nature to receive light from that third realm, its next higher, in proportion to the light which that itself receives. Thus all begins with the great light, shining self-centred; in accordance with the reigning plan (that of emanation) this gives forth its brilliance . . . 6

Jewish mystics in the generations preceding the *Zohar* employed nearly identical language and imagery in their explanations of the emanation of the sefirot from *Ein Sof*. Rabbi Azriel of Gerona, for example, wrote in his *Explanation of the Ten Sefirot*:

I have already informed you that the One is the foundation of the many and that in the many no power is innovated—only in Him. He is more than them and each of them is superior to its antecedent, and the potency of one is in the other. Nevertheless, the first is the dynamic of all the others . . . The metaphor for this is the fire, the flame, the sparks and the aura: They are all of one essence even though they are different one from the other and divisible into separate components.[7]

These similarities are of course not coincidental. In the rich intellectual environment of thirteenth-century Spain, Jewish scholars had access to a wide array of Greek philosophical works that had been translated into Hebrew. The *Theology of Aristotle*—a misnomer as the book is in fact an Arabic paraphrase of certain sections of Plotinus's *Enneads*—was available in Hebrew and was widely read, a small portion of it even appearing in one of Moses de Leon's Hebrew works, where he cites under the name of "*moreh ha-tzaddik*," the righteous teacher, a description of Plotinus's ecstatic ascent to the One.[8]

.•.

As has been noted by numerous scholars, the language of lights is the central language of the theosophical Kabbalah.[9] From *Sefer ha-Bahir* (The Book of Brilliance), the first kabbalistic work, through to *Sefer ha-Zohar* (The Book of Radiance), the greatest of the theosophical works, the Kabbalah of the sefirot abounds with the brilliance and varied hues and intensities of light. In one of his Hebrew works, *Sefer Shekel ha-Kodesh*, Moses de Leon suggests that it is the contemplation of the divine lights that constitutes the very mystery transmitted to "the wise who know religion and law":

For He, may He be blessed, made manifest the mystery of His being and emanated the radiance of the *aspaklaria* (speculum) which He drew forth from His light. And even so, the worlds could not endure Him, until He created light for His light and created worlds, and this light is called garment . . . He gave the mystery of these matters to the wise who know religion and law, to gaze at and contemplate the supernal matters.[10]

The *Zohar* itself contains numerous passages that might best be described as guided contemplative ascents through the various lights comprising divinity (see for example *Zohar Ḥadash*, Song of Songs, 61d–62b; *Zohar* 2:23a–b). These texts, like so many throughout the

Zohar, have an important performative element, and beyond the doctrinal or technical information they seek to convey, are also visual-contemplative practices designed to bring the reader into an awareness of the varied dimensions of being and its unitary source. The passage from *Midrash ha-Ne'elam* quoted at the beginning of this chapter, while not a typical zoharic contemplation of the sefirotic lights, is one such meditation that, through a gradation of lights, leads the reader through the emanatory structure of being.

.•.

As is immediately apparent when reading a text from *Midrash ha-Ne'elam*, we sense that we are not fully in the zoharic world as it emerges in the main part of the *Zohar*. While the format here is identical to the classical zoharic narrative—wandering mystics talking Torah on the way—the cast is different, as is the subject matter and mode of interpretation. Instead of the companions familiar to us from the main body of the *Zohar* gathered around Rabbi Shimon, the pages of *Midrash ha-Ne'elam* are filled with a more varied rabbinic cast. Alongside Rabbi Shimon we encounter other heroes, including Rabbi Akiva and Rabbi Eliezer the Great, as well as a range of other *tannaim* and *amoraim* about whom we will hear no more in the *Zohar* proper. Absent also are the thick bonds that bind the companions to their master, as well as the complex interrelationships between individual narratives. Sefirotic symbolism is present in a more limited form, and the impact of medieval philosophy and cosmology is readily discernable. As Scholem noted in some his earliest philological studies of the *Zohar*, *Midrash ha-Ne'elam* (The Concealed Midrash, or perhaps better rendered as The Midrash of Concealed Matters) represents a distinct literary stratum within the zoharic corpus. In fact, according to Scholem, *Midrash ha-Ne'elam* represents the earliest literary layer of the *Zohar* and reveals a younger Moses de Leon, still under the influence of Maimonidean philosophy and cosmology as well as Neoplatonic thought, searching for a literary center around which to weave his masterpiece.[11] Although we refer to the *Zohar* as *Sefer ha-Zohar* or *The Book of Radiance*, it is important to bear in mind that the *Zohar* is no ordinary book. The *Zohar* is comprised of numerous literary layers and compositions diverse in style and content. While Scholem was of the opinion that all but the later layers of the zoharic corpus were to be attributed to Moses de Leon, current trends in *Zohar* scholarship favor the view of "multiple authorship" and even extend the writing of the *Zohar* over numerous generations. Rather than viewing the *Zohar* entire as the fruit of a single genius, *Zohar* scholars today speak of the "zoharic literary corpus" and think

of the *Zohar* more as a literary movement or renaissance in late thir-
teenth- and early fourteenth-century Spain than as single literary composition.[12] As for *Midrash ha-Ne'elam*, *Zohar* scholars are divided.
Yehuda Liebes argues that *Midrash ha-Ne'elam* is so different in style
from both the *Zohar* proper and Moses de Leon's other Hebrew writings that it is most unlikely to have emerged from the hand of the same
author, while Ronit Meroz has suggested that it is *Midrash ha-Ne'elam*
alone (and not the remainder of the *Zohar*) that ought to be attributed
to de Leon.[13]

Despite these arguments, there has been a near universal tendency
among *Zohar* scholars and readers to be dismissive of the literary value
of *Midrash ha-Ne'elam*.[14] This bias is most unfortunate. While it is true
that we do not find the elaborate narratives characteristic of the main
body of the *Zohar*, or the full blown myth of the *ḥevraya*, the Companions, we do nevertheless find many of the elements and motifs that lie at
the heart of zoharic charm—the wandering mystics, the surprising interpretations of biblical verses, as well as the pathos that plays such a central role in the *Zohar* proper. In fact it is to *Midrash ha-Ne'elam* that
we can ascribe the original "literary breakthrough" that is the *Zohar*.
The strong Neoplatonic and Maimonidean influence, devoid in the
main of the complex zoharic symbolic superstructure, even has peda-
gogical advantages of clarity and simplicity and offers the reader an
alternate mystical-philosophical worldview.

.•.

Rabbi Abbahu, Rabbi Ḥiyya, and Rabbi Natan were walking
on the way.

Rabbi Natan said: Are you not astounded by those Masters
of Mishnah?! For the instruction of their mouth is like the
instruction of the holy angels!

And I have recalled what they have said: The sun's light is
emanated from the splendor of the speculum above and its light
is not its own. This is the meaning of what is written, *Let there
be lights, yehi meorot* (Gen. 1:14)—it should have said, *yehi
orot*. What is *meorot*? Rabbi Zeira said: *min orot*, from the
lights, the *mem* is an addition. That is to say, *min orot, from
the lights*, and the word is really *orot*, lights.

Rabbi Ḥiyya said: Do not be surprised by this, for the
Torah was emanated from the supernal wisdom and the heavens were emanated from the supernal firmament that is above
the heads of the creatures, and thus when you contemplate—all
that is above and below was emanated, this from that and one

from another, and the Blessed Holy One is above all. From the Throne of Glory they began to emanate, one from another, and the Throne of Glory from Him. And all are as naught compared to Him, as it is written, *All the inhabitants of the earth are of no account* (Dan. 4:32).

Rabbi Abbahu said: Let this not trouble you, for, to put it differently, our leader begins at first by teaching Torah to the translator and the translator to those near him, and those near him to those near them. Thus we find that when the teaching is completed, all is dependent on the leader. In a like vein you will find above and so in all the worlds.

Rabbi Abbahu said further: Moses was illuminated from the supernal splendor. Joshua was illuminated by Moses, the elders illuminated by Joshua, the prophets illuminated by the elders, the chiefs and the leaders of the people from the prophets—all of them, one from another.

One of the first things to stand out in this zoharic passage is the use of the term *emanated, itatzel*. Although the *Zohar*'s account of the sefirot is emanatory to the core, we never find this important philosophical term in the main body of the *Zohar* (*Guf ha-Zohar*), which prefers instead to employ the language of illumination, extension, and expansion when describing the emergence of the sefirot from within the depths of *Ein Sof*. As noted previously, the use of classical philosophical terminology is one of the hallmarks of *Midrash ha-Ne'elam*, and our text, like many others in this zoharic stratum, reveals a philosophical-mystical fusion not to be found in the remainder of the *Zohar*. It is important to state at the outset that the emanatory model presented here is different from the accounts of the emanation of the sefirot that occupy so central a position in the *Zohar* proper. Our passage, as far as I can tell, does not refer to the sefirot at all, and in discussing the emanation of being from within divinity, employs a Maimonidean-Neoplatonic synthesis of its own.

Emanationism is not an innovation of the Kabbalah. Not only did Jewish Neoplatonic philosophers adopt this schema, but even Maimonides, the champion of Aristotle, adopted and adapted the mechanism of emanation both in his accounts of creation and revelation.[15] *The Guide of the Perplexed* outlines a cosmology largely in keeping with standard Arabic emanationist cosmology (e.g., Al-Farabi and Avicenna) and presents a multitiered universe of intelligences and invisible rotating spheres emanating from the deity through an "overflow of being" and an "overflow of life."[16]

For the whole intended purpose is to show that the existents
that are below the Creator, may He be exalted, are divided into
three parts: one of them being constituted by the separate intellects; the second, by the bodies of the spheres . . . and the third,
by the bodies subject to generation and corruption, which have
one matter in common. It is further to show that governance
overflows from the deity, may He be exalted, to the intellects
according to their rank; that from the benefits received by the
intellects, good things and lights overflow to the bodies of the
spheres; and that from the spheres—because of the greatness of
the benefits they have received from their principles—forces
and good things overflow to this body subject to generation
and corruption.[17]

While Maimonides is more careful in his legal writings to avoid explicit
philosophical terminology, it is clear that the cosmology presented in
Sefer ha-Mada (The Book of Knowledge), in *Hilkhot Yesodei ha-Torah*
(Basic Principles of the Torah), is equally informed by emanationism,
with the ten intelligences and nine spheres all sustained by the "influence of the Blessed Holy One and His goodness."[18] The details of this
cosmological system need not concern us here,[19] and we shall return
later to some of the more intricate aspects of this system that directly
inform our passage. At present, it is sufficient that we appreciate the
centrality of emanation in medieval Jewish discourse and its view of
reality as the extension and outpouring (either necessary or volitional)[20]
of the divine being.

    Midrash ha-Ne'elam, as has been noted by many scholars, is partic-
ularly concerned with cosmology and the structure of the divine and
extra-divine worlds,[21] and the opening section of our passage artfully
employs a number of devices to convey the idea of interlinking domains
of reality emerging and descending from divinity. Beginning with a neat
interpretation of the verse from Genesis describing the creation of the
luminaries, the *Zohar* reads the word *meorot*, lights, hyper-literally as
me-orot, from the lights, thereby finding in the Torah an allusion to the
splendor that lies beyond the sun. That there is a domain of reality
beyond the sun should not be a surprise, Rabbi Hiyya suggests, as reality is in fact comprised of a series of emanations descending from the
Blessed Holy One. A separate passage appearing just after our text outlines the structure of the cosmos concisely:

For Rabbi El'azar said in the name of Rabbi Tanhum: The
angels that are nearest [to God] are the first to receive the
power that flows from the celestial mirror (*koah shefa' aspak-*

laria shel mala), and from them it descends to those that are not so near, and from there to the heavens and all their host and from them to man. Rabbi Jose said: The Throne of Glory receives first, and from it it flows to the most exalted angels and from them to those that are not so high and exalted as they, and from them to the heavens and from them to man.
—*Midrash ha-Ne'elam, Zohar Ḥadash,*
Genesis 16c (Tishby and Goldstein)

According to Isaiah Tishby, *Midrash ha-Ne'elam* employs a four-tiered hierarchy for domains outside the Godhead—the Throne of Glory, the angels, the heavens, and the earth:[22]

The Blessed Holy One gave the angels dominion over the heavens and the heavens dominion over the earth, but they are all dependent on His Throne, may His name be blessed, to show that *one height watches over the other* (Eccles. 5:7).
—*Midrash ha-Ne'elam, Zohar Ḥadash* Genesis 7d[23]

The extension of the divine being from its own singularity and self-enclosed purity to engender a variegated and manifold universe is depicted in our text with classical Neoplatonic imagery, and much of the charm of this particular zoharic passage lies in the artistic and creative manner in which the author translates this imagery into a Jewish key. As noted earlier, the transmission of knowledge from teacher to student is a common motif employed by Neoplatonic writers to convey the extension of divinity beyond itself without suffering any diminution.[24] Here, the *Zohar* employs two such chains of transmission, the first taken from the world of the rabbis describing the formal mode of Torah study in the academy, and the second a paraphrase of the opening of *Pirke Avot*, which recounts the chain of tradition starting with Moses. Significantly, the word for emanation in Hebrew, *atzilut/etzel*, is derived from a verse in Numbers (11:24–26) that narrates the effusion of the spirit of prophecy from Moses onto the seventy elders: "Then YHVH came down in a cloud and spoke to him. He drew upon (*va-yatzel*) the spirit that was on him and put it upon the seventy elders." The choice of this verb to denote this central Neoplatonic concept is no doubt connected with the midrashic observation that in passing on his prophetic effluence, Moses's radiance suffered no diminution:

The Blessed Holy One said to Moses: *I will draw upon (ve-atzalti) the spirit that is on you and put it upon them* (Num. 11:17). This can be compared to a lit candle from which were kindled many candles and the candle from which they were lit is not diminished.

—*Midrash Tanḥuma, Be-ha'alotekha* 12[25]

Like a teacher whose insights are passed on to her students without her losing any of her own essence, so the Blessed Holy One, the One, the inscrutable source of being, gives of itself, begetting the Many, without losing any of its essence.

The emanatory chain of being, however, is most succinctly captured in the interpretation of a verse from the Song of Songs by Rabbi El'azar (presumably the son of Rabbi Shimon although he might also be Rabbi El'azar ben Arakh), who chances upon the wandering rabbis. In its original context, the verse "A spring in the garden, a well of living waters, a flowing stream from Lebanon" (Song of Songs 4:15), is part of the lover's praise to his beloved and is far indeed from bearing a mystical or philosophical meaning. For the Neoplatonic author of our passage, however, the multiple images of flowing water are readily transformed, and the verse from the song is read as containing the secret of the downward flow of divinity from its source in Lebanon, perhaps understood here as whiteness (*laban*) and thus signifying the purity of the hidden One, through the various grades of the divine and then extra-divine world:

> *A spring in the garden, a well of living waters, a flowing stream from Lebanon* (Song of Songs 4:15). [Scripture] calls her a spring, afterward a well, afterward a flowing stream. This verse requires contemplation. The spring extends from the well and the well from the flowing stream and the flowing stream from Lebanon—to convey that they were all emanated this from that and one from another.

As we have seen throughout this book, the idea of divinity as a flow, bursting the banks of its own nothingness and pouring into reality and onto human consciousness, is a central image in the *Zohar*, and the verse from the song just cited appears on numerous occasions to convey this dynamic aspect of God (see *Zohar* 3:201b, 3:298a). While in our passage this verse from the Song of Songs does not have the same dynamism that we find elsewhere in the *Zohar*, it does nevertheless illustrate with great precision the philosophically and mystically rich idea of reality as the outward extension and flow of a hidden divine being.

Having clarified that reality is a series of emanations extending back to the Blessed Holy One, our passage now returns to its original esoteric teaching conveyed in the name of the "Masters of Mishnah":[26]

> So it is with the sun. Its light is not its own, but rather one thread of splendor extends that irradiates the sun.
>
> We have learned in our Mishnah: With the light that the Blessed Holy One created at first, Adam would gaze and see from one end of the world to the other. Come and see: The light of the sun is one sixty thousand and seventy-fifth of the light of the speculum [*aspaklaria*] of the concealed light. If even at this light of the sun a person cannot gaze, how much more so at that light?!
>
> [But] behold, we have said that a person could see with it from one end of the world to the other!?
>
> Rather, so have we instructed in our Mishnah: With that light (*nehiruta*) a person could know and see with the radiance (*nehiru*) of wisdom all that was and all that will be, from the beginning of the world to the end of the world, and it has been concealed for the righteous in the world to come. What is meant by in the world to come? When the holy soul leaves this world and goes to the world that is coming.

The teaching outlined here and in the continuation of our narrative turns on an important mythological theme found in the writings of the sages—the myth of the concealed light (*or ha-ganuz*):

> Rabbi El'azar said: [With] the light the Blessed Holy One created on the first day, one could gaze and see from one end of the universe to the other. When the Blessed Holy One saw the generation of the Flood and the generation of the Dispersion and saw that their deeds were corrupt, He immediately hid it from them, as is written, *The light of the wicked is withheld* (Job 38:15). For whom did he hide it? For the righteous in the world to come.[27]

This myth also occupies an important place in the prezoharic kabbalistic work *Sefer ha-Bahir*, where the primal light is treasured away, not on account of the wicked, but as an act of grace enabling the worlds to endure:

> Before the world was created, an impulse arose in the divine mind to create a great shining light. A light so bright was

created that no creature could control it. When God saw that
no one could bear it, he took one seventh and gave it to them in
its place. The rest He hid away for the righteous in the time to
come, saying: If they prove worthy of this seventh and guard it,
I will give them the rest in the final world.[28]

Another text from the *Bahir* suggests that the concealed light, the
"good" of the opening verses of Genesis was in fact concealed in the
Torah, the "doctrine of good," raising the possibility that in reading the
Torah one can in fact come into contact with "the good that You have
hidden away":

And Rabbi Yoḥanan said:
    There are two types of light, as it is written, *[let there be
light] and there was light*. Regarding both of them it is written,
[And God saw the light] that it was good (Gen. 1:4).
    The Blessed Holy One took one and stored it away for the
righteous in the World to Come. Regarding this it is written,
*How great is the good that You have hidden away for those
who fear You, that You have accomplished for those who find
shelter in You . . .* (Ps. 31:20).
    We learn that no creature could look at the first light. It is
thus written, *And God saw the light that it was good* (Gen. 1:4)
. . .
    He took of that good and included it in the 32 paths of
wisdom, giving it to this world. This is the meaning of the
verse, *I have given you a doctrine of good, My Torah, do not
abandon it* (Prov. 4:2).[29]

In our passage the concealed light is none other than the luminous
source that illuminates the sun, the *aspaklaria*, the speculum of the concealed light. This light beyond the sun is the original primal light with
which Adam could gaze and see from one end of the universe to the
other. This light whose brilliance is sixty thousand and seventy-five
times[30] the luminosity of the sun cannot of course be apprehended
physically, but is rather a "light of wisdom"[31] through which one can
know "all that was and all that will be." It is tempting to associate it
with something akin to the Platonic Forms or the Plotinan Divine Mind,
the object of mystical contemplation. One thinks of Maimonides' statement in *Hilkhot Yesodei ha-Torah*: "The forms that are incorporeal are
not seen by the eye, rather they are known through the eye of the heart,
just as we know the Lord of everything without vision of the eye."[32] Be

that as it may, this is the light that awaits the righteous in the world to come. In *Perek Ḥelek*, in his discussion of the ultimate good awaiting humanity, Maimonides refers to the "goodness which You have hidden away for them that fear You" (Ps. 31:20) as "the immortality of the soul being in firm possession of the Idea which is God the creator."[33] Our text seems to have something similar in mind. While our passage appears to suggest that such "seeing," although properly part of our original visionary capacity, is attainable only in death, we are nevertheless informed that it was this hidden light that Moses accessed upon his ascent to Mount Sinai, and that was in turn the source of his radiance. Significantly, the "Masters of Mishnah"—a term that reveals much about the zoharic authors' self-consciousness as the authors of a new Torah rivaling the oral Torah of the sages—were behind Moses's shoulders, suggesting that even if they themselves cannot apprehend this light, they can at least bask in its glow here and now.[34]

Now alone with Rabbi Abbahu (Rabbi Natan and Rabbi Ḥiyya have gone on their way), Rabbi El'azar continues his account of the luminaries. His exposition is part medieval cosmology and part religious polemic:

> Rabbi El'azar opened his mouth, saying: *And God said, Let there be lights.*
>
> Come and see: The Blessed Holy One made eighteen firmaments that travel on their journeys and orbit the entire world. Each one is suspended the measure bestowed upon it by its Master. And when a particular firmament completes is measure, many good and mighty decrees are innovated in the world.
>
> Now, the fool-hearted think in their minds that this is on account of the orbiting of the firmament. It is not so! For each and every day, from morning to evening, the Blessed Holy One innovates supernal, mighty, and forceful decrees.
>
> Sometimes, when a particular firmament completes its journey, a decree of the Supernal King transpires in the world, and the fool-hearted think that this was on account of that firmament—yet their hearts err in foolishness!
>
> And the Blessed Holy One made for the fourth firmament and placed within it the sun that orbits the entire world according to the seasons and times for the benefit of the world and humanity.
>
> And we have learned in our Mishnah: The sun moves through three hundred and forty apertures, ascending and descending according to the seasons and times. It moves and

begins from the window of the east, from the window called *Noga* and moves in a circular fashion until it reaches the window called *Karbosa*.[35] Then it travels six months to the extremity of the north, until it reaches the window called *Zahara*, and travels six months to complete the year for the benefit of the creatures, for sowing and harvesting, as it is written, *So long as the earth endures, seedtime and harvest, cold and heat, summer and winter, [day and night shall not cease]* (Gen. 8:22).

In completing [its journey] to the side of the south, according to the inhabitants of the earth—*harvest, heat* and *summer*; and in completing [its journey] to the extremity of the north—*seedtime, cold* and *winter*. All is according to the habitation of the earth, as we have said.

And in this way, literally, just as people use (*mishtamshin*)[36] the light of this firmament, so all the hosts of heaven use the light of the firmament that is above the heads of the creatures.

We need not concern ourselves with all the technical details in this passage. It is, however, important that we appreciate the influence of first, Maimonidean cosmology, and by extension, Arabic cosmology on the author's picture of the universe. Even a cursory reading of the third chapter of *Hilkhot Yesodei ha-Torah*, where Maimonides outlines the structure and order of the cosmos, reveals the extent to which our author has drawn on the Great Eagle's scientific account. Following Maimonides, our text also imagines the world surrounded by eighteen spheres[37] (termed here firmaments) with the sun placed in the fourth sphere. The medieval picture of the universe was of course very different from our own, and imagined a world surrounded by a series of invisible concentric spheres in which were placed all the heavenly bodies. While clearly "primitive" when viewed against modern cosmological understandings, we must not forget that this picture of the universe was able to explain with great precision the movement of the celestial bodies and had the force of scientific truth for hundreds of years. In addition to Maimonides, the influence of Solomon Ibn Gabirol's poem *Keter Malkhut*, the second part of which is comprised of a celebration of the spheres culminating in the sphere of Mind and the Throne of Glory, is readily apparent.[38] More than two hundred years before the *Zohar*, Ibn Gabirol also polemicized against those who maintained that it was the rotation of the spheres, and not God, that was responsible for events in the world. According to Ibn Gabirol, while the moon does indeed excite new events in our world every month, he is categorical in his assertion that "always her own creator's will she heeds" (Canto 11). Our passage too is firm in its assertion that it is the Blessed Holy One who lies at the origin of all astrological influences: "the fool-hearted think that this was on account of that firmament—yet their hearts err in foolishness."

Following Rabbi El'azar's cosmological aside, Rabbi Abbahu now asks the "master of the academy" about the spelling of the word *lights*, *meorot*, in the Torah verse they have been expounding. The word is written *ḥaser*, deficiently, without the *vav*s, and in classical zoharic form, Rabbi Abbahu insists that this must mean something. The exchange that follows takes us to the mystical-philosophical heart of this narrative unit:

> Rabbi Abbahu said: *Lights, meorot, מארת*—why is it written without the *vav*s?
>
> He said to him: It is as we have said previously, that its light is not complete. For its light is only that which it receives from the light above like a single ray from beyond the wall, and therefore its light is not called complete, nor is it fitting that [any light] be called complete, aside from that light referred to as, *the light dwells with Him* (Dan. 2:22).
>
> And [the light] that was concealed for the righteous is one sixty thousand and seventy-fifth of the light that dwells with the Blessed Holy One, and the light of the sun is one sixty thousand and seventy-fifth of the light that was concealed for the righteous in the world that is coming. Therefore the light of the sun is not called complete light, nor is it fitting that it be called so. Therefore the Blessed Holy One said: Do not be troubled in that it is written, *me'erat* [cursed], and that it is not complete, for I did not make it except for that which is written, *to shine upon the earth* (Gen. 1:15), to serve (*le-shamsha*) the people of the earth, and let it be enough for you, people of the earth, that this luminary will serve you.
>
> Rabbi El'azar said: And if at this small light people cannot gaze, how much more so at the light concealed for the righteous!?
>
> Rabbi Abbahu said: And how much more so at the light of the luminary that dwells before the Blessed Holy One!?

The word *meorot*, we learn, is written deficiently, precisely because the light of the sun is deficient. As we learned at the beginning of our passage—the sun's light is not its own but is emanated from the splendor of the speculum above. Rabbi El'azar now completes his teaching and adds a third light to the series. Beyond the sun lies the light concealed for the righteous, and beyond the concealed light lies yet another light, the light of the luminary that dwells before the Blessed Holy One, the light referred to in the verse from Daniel, "the light dwells with Him." This light alone is complete and undiminished, the others in the series being but dim reflections in comparison. This image of the Blessed Holy One as the ultimate light is found also in the Muslim philosopher-mystic Al Ghazali's *Mishkat al-Anwar* (Niche of Lights) where he describes God as the "highest ultimate light" and the "light of lights," based on the famous verse from the Koran (24.35) "God is the light of the heavens and the earth . . . .a light above light." The *Theology of Aristotle* too refers to the First Cause and the One in similar terms.

Rabbi El'azar's teaching, however, does not reach its conclusion with the completion of the series of lights. In fact, the central teaching of this passage is found in the divine injunction "not to be troubled in that it is written, *me'erat*, and that it is not complete." This passage in *Midrash ha-Ne'elam* is of course not the first to notice and comment on the absence of the *vav*s in our key word from the opening of Genesis. The Palestinian Talmud, *Taanit* 4:4 already found in the verse an allusion to diphtheria, reading the word *meorot* as *me'erat*, curse. The divine injunction not to be troubled is thus a profound comment on how one ought to view our reality predicated as it is on the diminution of the divine light. In contrast to certain Gnostic and even Neoplatonic positions, our text affirms our domain of being—reality is not cursed. The absence of the *vav*s, the absence of perfection, and the diminution of the divine light are all part of the necessary order. Indeed the diminution of the divine light is actually an act of grace, enabling the overwhelming brilliant light to diffuse such that we can enjoy it, shining upon the earth. In the main body of the *Zohar*, this verse from Genesis is interpreted along similar lines, with the absence of the *vav*s signifying the diminution of the light that actually enables the overpowering light of divinity to be filtered into our reality:

> The primordial point is inner radiance—there is no way to gauge its translucency, tenuity, or purity until an expanse expanded from it. The expansion of that point became a palace, in which the point was clothed . . . This palace, a garment for that concealed point is a radiance beyond measure, yet not as gossamer or translucent as the primordial point, hidden and treasured. That palace expanded an expanse: primordial

light. That expansion of primordial light is a garment for the palace, which is a gossamer, translucent radiance, deeper within. From here on, this expands into this, this is clothed in this, so that this is a garment for this, and this for this. This, the kernel; this, the shell . . . Shells upon shells were created for concealing the kernel, all for arraying the kernel. So, *Let there be meorot, lights*, is spelled deficiently. All this for arraying the world, as is written: *to shine upon earth* (Gen. 1:15).

—*Zohar* 1:20a (Matt, *The Zohar*)[39]

Unlike his original traveling companions, Rabbi Abbahu's encounter with Rabbi El'azar has led him to the ultimate source of being, as well as to an understanding of the nature of our reality—deficient, only partially illuminated—but necessarily so as a way of seeding the light into the kernels of our material existence.

The mystery of the lights explained—*me-orot* and *me'erat*—our passage resumes its narrative thread, concluding with classical zoharic pathos:

He [Rabbi Abbahu] came to kiss Rabbi El'azar's hand.

He said: Now I know that in truth *meorot*, lights, is deficient, and what's more that it is fitting that it be deficient.

He said: Woe to the world when you will depart from it, for until this day I have asked this question yet did not find the essence of the word until now! The way on which you set forth will be for me a sign of blessing (*siman brakhah*) in that I encountered you.

He sat with him thirty days and learned every doubt and question he had.

He [Rabbi El'azar] taught him sixty insights concerning the chapter of creation.

He walked on his way.

He found Rabbi Ḥiyya.

He said to him: May it please you Rabbi Abbahu that I might taste of the sweetness of the honey that you sucked from the instruction of the supernal holy ones?

He said to him: Bits of excrement and the goodness of honey do not go together![40]

Nevertheless he taught him.

Rabbi Ḥiyya wept, saying: I hereby swear that until I learn before the Masters of the Supernal Mishnah I will not return here.

> He sat there for twelve years. When he came, they called
> him Rabbi Ḥiyya the Great.

His doubts removed, Rabbi Abbahu becomes a disciple of Rabbi
El'azar; he stays with him thirty days and learns yet further cosmological secrets. Rabbi Abbahu's perseverance and diligence are now brought
into sharp relief through the surprising encounter with Rabbi Ḥiyya. It
should be recalled that he alone of the original companions walked on
with Rabbi El'azar while Rabbi Natan and Rabbi Ḥiyya mysteriously
chose to go their own way. Rabbi Abbahu's decision to accompany the
master was certainly the right one, for whereas Rabbi Natan and Rabbi
Ḥiyya only learned about the concealed light, Rabbi Abbahu's
encounter with Rabbi El'azar culminated in the ultimate light, "the light
dwelling with Him," as well as the secret of its diminution. Upon completing his studies with Rabbi El'azar, Rabbi Abbahu chances upon
Rabbi Ḥiyya, who pleads with him to teach him some of "the sweetness
of the honey" that he learned during his stay with "the supernal holy
ones." This equation of wisdom and honey is widespread in Jewish
texts (see for example Ezekiel 3:1–3; Psalms 19:11; BT *Ḥagiga* 13a) and
appears again in *Midrash ha-Ne'elam* (*Zohar Ḥadash* 12b): "Why does
your mouth not drip the sweetness of the honey of wisdom?" Rabbi
Abbahu's response is at once terse, enigmatic, and a sharp rebuke of
Rabbi Ḥiyya, presumably for having forfeited his chance to study with
a grand master. Torah masters, it seems, are rare, and when the opportunity to learn presents itself, one must seize it and extract the nectar
that awaits those who persevere. Rabbi Ḥiyya, for his part, humbly
accepts his rebuke and, like the talmudic Rabbi Shimon and Rabbi
El'azar who spent thirteen years in a cave learning the mysteries of
Torah (BT *Shabbat* 33b–34a), now undergoes a mystical initiation of
his own, learning the "supernal Mishnah" for twelve years, at the end
of which time he emerges as Rabbi Ḥiyya the Great.[41]

⋯•⋯

Reading the *Zohar* can be a difficult task. Deciphering the text's exegetical moves as well as its narrative details can lead us, on occasion, to
miss the forest for the trees. The passage elucidated here, while
grounded in medieval cosmology, is also the bearer of a profound religious sensibility, and it is this sensibility, this unique picture of the
world and its relation to the divine, that must not be lost. It is important to stress yet again that a deep reading of religious texts does not
require that we believe them literally or that we abandon "everything
else we know to be true" in our efforts to find meaning in them. The

truth value of this text, for example, does not stand or fall with the accuracy of its particular cosmology. It does not matter that the sun does not orbit the earth in the fourth sphere, or whether reality "really" is constructed as a series of descending lights. What does matter, however, is the philosophically and mystically compelling view of reality as the extension and outward flow of divinity. The idea that "all that is above and below was emanated, this from that and one from another," that all that we see is connected in a series leading back from the many and variegated world of our experience to a unitary source is as challenging as it is extraordinary. We inhabit a world of great diversity and multiplicity. Yet these variegated phenomena, the mystics and philosophers tell us, are all connected and all the outward expression of the divine. The universe is indeed, as Plato suggests in the *Timaeus* (92c), "a blessed visible God," or perhaps we might say, the self-extension of God, the One made Many. Let us be clear. It is not that the One created the Many or that God created the world. Our world, rather, is the material expression of the divine desire to expand and flow forth from its own nothingness and concealment. Our world is God—hidden and inscrutable—made manifest.

Scholem was certainly correct in noting that much work is required to unveil the hidden pantheistic core of the *Zohar*.[42] The *Zohar* does not offer us a simple or straightforward confession of faith, but a labyrinth of images and symbols, bewildering in their complexity and diversity and dazzling in their brilliance. Nevertheless, throughout its varied layers and literary strata the *Zohar* does present us with a consistent picture of an "uninterrupted continuity [that] permeates and connects all levels of existence from top to bottom" and the consequent insight that there is therefore "a basic similarity of all things to the divine."[43] This divine/world relationship, termed theomonism by one leading contemporary scholar, is perhaps the central teaching of the entire theosophical Kabbalah, the belief "that the oneness of being is manifest through the multiplicity of epiphanies that constitute the different names of the ineffable truth beyond all discrimination."[44] From the words of a contemporary master to the words of the greatest master of them all, we can find no better statement of this religious insight than the following passage from one of Moses de Leon's Hebrew works, *Sefer ha-Rimmon* (The Book of the Pomegranate):

> God is unified oneness—one without two, inestimable. Genuine divine existence engenders the existence of all of creation. The sublime, inner essences secretly constitute a chain linking everything from the highest to the lowest, extending from the upper

pool to the edge of the universe.[45] There is nothing—not even the tiniest thing—that is not fastened to the links of this chain. Everything is catenated in its mystery, caught in its oneness. God is, God's secret is one, all the worlds below and above are all mysteriously one. Divine existence is indivisible . . .

The entire chain is one. Down to the last link, everything is linked with everything else; so divine essence is below as well as above, in heaven and on earth. There is nothing else . . .

And this is what the sages mean when they say: When God gave the Torah to Israel, He opened the seven heavens to them, and they saw that nothing was there in reality but His Glory; He opened the seven worlds to them and they saw that nothing was there but His Glory; He opened the seven abysses before their eyes, and they saw that nothing was there but His Glory. Meditate on these things and you will understand that God's essence is linked and connected with all worlds, and that all forms of existence are linked and connected with each other, but derived from His existence and essence.[46]

•◆•

CHAPTER NINE

Rabbi Ḥiyya, Rabbi Yose, and the Merchants in the Cave

The Mystical Poetics of Zoharic Narrative

Zohar 3:20a–23a

Rabbi Ḥiyya and Rabbi Yose were walking on the way.
While they were walking Rabbi Yose said to Rabbi Ḥiyya: Let us engage words of Torah, words of the Ancient of Days . . .

They walked on.
While they were walking they saw a place of lush grasses with a stream of water flowing by.
They sat down.
While they were sitting a bird flew past, murmuring before them.
Rabbi Ḥiyya said: Let us get up from here, for assuredly mountain quarriers are present here.
They got up and walked on.
While they were turning their heads they saw bandits running after them.
A miracle occurred for them and they found in front of them a rock with a cave inside it.
They went in and sat there the whole of that day and night.

Rabbi Ḥiyya opened, saying: *But you, have no fear My servant Jacob, declares YHVH, be not dismayed, O Israel! I will deliver you from far away, your folk from the land of captivity. And Jacob shall again have calm and quiet with none to trouble him* (Jer. 30:10).

From far away—it should have said *from nearby*!

They have already established this verse: *from far away*—as it is said, *and they shall return from a far land.*[1]

But, *from far away*—as it is written, *from afar did YHVH appear to me* (Jer. 31:3), and *bringing her food from afar* (Prov. 31:14).

What does this mean?

The depth of the river, the place from which the river issues and flows.

And Jacob shall again (shav) have calm—since it is written, *have no fear My servant Jacob*, what does *and Jacob shall again have calm and quiet with none to trouble him* mean?

Rather, it is as we have taught: The Blessed Holy One ascends higher and higher, as it is written, *Why O YHVH do you stand so far off?* (Ps. 10:1), and from that distant place *I will deliver you.*

And Jacob shall return (shav)—to his place to have intercourse with the Assembly of Israel.

Calm—this is *Yesod*.

Quiet—to place his abode in Her.

With none to trouble him (maḥrid)—from Isaac, as it is said, *Isaac was seized with very violent trembling (ḥaradah)* (Gen. 27:33), and therefore it is written, *the Fear of Isaac* (Gen. 31:42).

When this fear is aroused, *Yesod* departs and ascends to another place, as it is written, *Sinners in Zion are frightened* (Isa. 33:14). *In Zion* precisely! Therefore it says, *with none to trouble him.*

Now the Blessed Holy One has saved us from afar and has hidden us in this place in calm and quiet and there is nothing at all to trouble us. For when the Blessed Holy One performs a miracle, He performs its completely . . .

They sat in the cave the entire day.

When night arrived, the moon shone into the cave and two merchants passed by with their donkeys loaded with wine, and food for themselves resting on their loads.

They said to one another: Let us sleep here. Let us give food and drink to the donkeys and we will enter this cave.

His companion said to him: Before we enter, explain this verse that isn't clear.

He said to him: Which one?

He said to him: This is the matter. It is written, *I praise You forever (le-*

*olam) for You have done, I will wait for Your name for it is good in the
presence of Your faithful ones* (Ps. 52:11). What does it mean by *for
You have done* without specifying what?!
It is also written, *good in the presence of Your faithful ones*—for others
then is He not good?!
He could not answer him.
He said: Alas that on account of my trade I have neglected the Blessed
Holy One!
Rabbi Ḥiyya and Rabbi Yose, who were sitting in the cave, rejoiced.
Rabbi Ḥiyya said to Rabbi Yose: Did I not tell you that when the
Blessed Holy One performs a miracle, He performs it completely!
They went out.

When they went out Rabbi Ḥiyya immediately opened, saying: *Peace,
peace to him that is distant (raḥok) and him that is near* (Isa. 57:19).
Peace is said twice here. Once for him that is distant and once for him
that is near, and it is all one. For the one who is distant is brought
near—this is the master of *teshuvah* (repentance/returning). First he was
distant and now he is near.
Further regarding *him that is distant*—when a human being distances
himself from the Torah, he is distant from the Blessed Holy One, while
the one who draws near to the Torah, the Blessed Holy One draws him
near to Himself.
Now, unite with us and enter the cave.
The merchants came and joined them, tethered their donkeys and prepared their food.
They all went out to the mouth of the cave.

One of the merchants said: Let the Masters of Torah explain to us this
verse, *I praise You forever (le-olam) for You have done, I will wait for
Your name for it is good in the presence of Your faithful ones.*
For You have done—what does it mean by *for You have done* without
specifying what?!
It is also written, *good in the presence of Your faithful ones*—for others
then is He not good?!
Rabbi Ḥiyya said: *For You have done*, indeed! And what have You
done? The world (*le-olam*). Because of this world that the Blessed Holy
One has made and arrayed, a human being ought to praise the Blessed
Holy One every day.
*I will wait for Your name for it is good in the presence of Your faithful
ones*—assuredly it is so. For before the righteous, the name of the
Blessed Holy One is good, not so before the wicked, who spurn it every

day and do not engage Torah.

He said to him: This is fine but I have heard a word from behind the curtain yet I am afraid to reveal it.

Rabbi Ḥiyya and Rabbi Yose said to him: Say your word for the Torah is not the inheritance of one place alone.

He said to them: One day I was walking to Lod. I entered the city and positioned myself behind a certain wall. Rabbi Shimon bar Yoḥai was in that house and I heard from his mouth this verse, *I praise You forever (le-olam) for You have done.*

I praise You—King David, peace be upon him, said this about the last world He made, for King David held fast to that world and through it inherited kingship (*malkhut*).

I will wait for Your name for it is good—this is the Blessed Holy One, united with this world that is called *good.*

When is it called good? *In the presence of Your faithful ones (ḥasidekha).*

Who are these faithful ones? For there is *ḥesed* and there is *ḥesed*; but these are the ones called *the enduring loves of David (ḥasdei david ha-neemanim)* (Isa. 55:3), and when these *loves of David* are filled with the goodness flowing down from Holy Ancient One, then *Yesod* is called good . . . and perfumes this last world and all abides in blessing.

Therefore would David wait for this grade, to illuminate this world, to which he held fast.

Thus did I hear these words but I did not know what they meant.

Rabbi Ḥiyya and Rabbi Yose came and kissed him on his head.

Rabbi Ḥiyya said: Who shall cover your eyes with dust Rabbi Shimon bar Yoḥai?! For you are in your place and cause supernal mountains to tremble, and even the birds of heaven rejoice at your words. Woe to the world when you depart and ascend from it! . . .

Rabbi Ḥiyya and Rabbi Yose were amazed and they rejoiced that night. After they had eaten, the merchant's companion opened, saying: Let me say before you a word with which I have been occupied this day, regarding what is written in the verse, *A psalm of David, when he was in the wilderness of Judah* (Ps. 63:1).

David said this poem when he was fleeing from his father-in-law.

What did he say? *Elohim, You are my God; I search for You, my soul thirsts for You, my body yearns for You, as a parched thirsty land that has no water* (Ps. 63:2).

Elohim, You are my God—for he always held fast to *gevurah.*

I search for You (ashaḥreka)—how could David search for the Blessed

Holy One in a distant land, exiled from the land where the *Shekhinah* abides?

Well, even though he was exiled from there, he never ceased seeking the Blessed Holy One. And I have heard that *I search for You (ashaḥreka)* is like someone who says: I would go and appear before you except I cannot. Similarly, *I search for You* except I am outside the domain where the *Shekhinah* abides.

My soul thirsts for You—my soul and my body crave You, to appear before You, but I am unable because I am in *a parched thirsty land that has no water*, for any land outside the domain where the *Shekhinah* abides is called *a parched thirsty land*, because living waters are not found there. What are living waters? This is the *Shekhinah* about whom it is written, *a well of living waters* (Song of Songs 4:15) and therefore it is written, *a parched thirsty land that has no water*.

Rabbi Ḥiyya and Rabbi Yose said: Certainly the way is arrayed before us!

They entered the cave and slept.

At midnight they heard the animals of the wilderness growling.

They awoke.

Rabbi Ḥiyya said: It is now time to assist the Assembly of Israel as She praises the King.

They said: Let everyone say something he has heard and knows of Torah.

They all sat down.

Rabbi Ḥiyya opened, saying: *For the leader on ayelet ha-shaḥar (the hind of the dawn). A psalm of David* (Ps. 22:1).

Who is *ayelet ha-shaḥar (the hind of the dawn)*? This is the Assembly of Israel who is called *a loving hind, a graceful mountain goat* (Prov. 5:19).

Is She then a hind of the dawn only and not the entire day?

Rather, She is a hind from that place called dawn, as it is said, *His firm starting place is like dawn* (Hosea 6:3) . . .

Come and see . . .

At midnight a herald rises and proclaims and the openings open. Then a wind arouses from the north side, strikes David's harp, which plays by itself, and She praises the King and the Blessed Holy One delights in the righteous in the Garden of Eden.

Happy is the portion of the one who arises at that time and engages Torah!

Whoever arises at that time and engages Torah is called a companion of the Blessed Holy One and the Assembly of Israel. And what's more they are called His kin and His friends, as it is written, *For the sake of my kin and my friends, I pray for your well-being* (Ps. 122:8), and they are called companions of the supernal angels and supernal legions, as it is written, *companions listen for your voice* (Song of Songs 8:13).

When day comes, a herald rises and proclaims and the openings of the south side are opened, the stars and constellations awaken, the gates of mercy open and the King is seated and receives their praises. Then the Assembly of Israel takes these words and ascends, and all the companions cling to Her wings, and their words come and rest in the lap of the King . . . Happy is the portion of the righteous who engage Torah, especially when the King craves words of Torah . . .

Rabbi Yose opened, saying: *The Oracle of Dumah. A call comes to me from Seir: Watchman, what of the night? Watchman, what of the night?* (Isa. 21:11)

The Companions have established this verse in numerous places.

But, *The Oracle of Dumah (masa dumah)*—each time that Israel was in exile, their time and end was known, and the time and end of that exile. But the exile of Edom is *masa dumah*, a burden of silence, for it has not been disclosed and is not known like the others.

The Blessed Holy One says: *A call comes to me from Seir*—I have heard a voice from the exile of Seir, from those who are oppressed among them, from those who lie in the dust.

What do they say? *Watchman, what of the night? Watchman, what of the night?* They inquire of Me about the *Matronita*, what have I done with my *Matronita*.

Then the Blessed Holy One assembles His court and says: Look at my beloved children who are oppressed in exile yet forget their own sorrow and inquire of Me about the *Matronita*, saying: *Watchman*—You who are called watchman, where is your watching, where is the watching of Your house? *What of the night?* What have You done with the night? Is this how You watched over Her? . . .

Then the Blessed Holy One answers them: Behold, My watching is present, for behold I am destined to receive Her, to be with Her, as it is written, *The watchman replied* (Isa. 21:12)—the one who watched the house. *Morning came and so did night* (ibid.)—for at first He ascended high above, and raised that morning that is ever ready for Him. Now, *morning came*—for He is ready to join with night. *And so did night*— She is also ready. But because of you they are delayed. If you desire this, why are you delaying? *Return!* Return in repentance. Then, *come back*—come back to Me and we will all be in a single abode, and we will all return to our place, as it is written, *And YHVH your God will return (shav) your captivity* (Deut. 30:3). It does not say *will restore*, but *will return*. *Will return* is written twice here—once for the Assembly of Israel and once for the Blessed Holy One, as it is written, *And YHVH your God will return your captivity and have mercy upon you and will return and gather you from all the peoples* (ibid.).

The merchant opened, saying: *When the morning stars sang together and all the divine beings shouted for joy* (Job 38:7).
Come and see: When the Blessed Holy One comes to delight with the righteous in the Garden of Eden, all the words/things of the lower [alt., upper] world, and all the upper and lower [realms] awaken to receive Him, and all the trees in the Garden of Eden open in praise before Him, as it is written, *then shall all the trees of the forest shout for joy before YHVH who comes* (1 Chron. 16:33). Even the birds of the earth all murmur praise before Him. Then a flame goes forth and strikes the wings of the cock, and it calls and praises to the Holy King, and calls out to human beings to engage in Torah and in the praise of their Master and His service. Happy is the portion of those who arise from their beds to engage Torah!
When morning comes, the openings of the south are opened, and the gates of healing go forth to the world, and the east wind awakens and mercy abounds. All the stars and constellations that are appointed under the rule of that morning open in praise and song to the supernal King, as it is written, *When the morning stars sang together and all the divine beings shouted for joy* (Job 38:7).
What do the divine beings (*bnei elohim*) desire here in calling forth the shout (*tru'ah*) in that morning, for behold, all the judgments pass away when *ḥesed*, love, is aroused in the world?
Rather, *And all the divine beings shouted for joy (va-yariu kol bnei elohim)*—behold the might of the harsh judgments has been broken, and their power has been broken, as it is said, *the earth is breaking, breaking (roah hitroaah)* (Isa. 24:19).
All this because that morning awakens in the earth, and Abraham awakens and comes to plant a tamarisk in Beer Sheva. This matter I have heard as follows—in Beer Sheva indeed!
And it is written, *and he invoked there the name YHVH, El Olam* (Gen. 21:33).

The merchant's companion opened, saying: *The morning was light (ha-boker or) and the men were sent off, they and their donkeys* (Gen. 44:3).

What does it mean *the morning was light*?

So we have learned: What is morning (*boker*)? When morning (*tzafra*) comes and judgments pass away, and *ḥesed* desires to arouse, all who come from that side hasten to (*mevakrei*) their place to summon blessings for the world.

This is *the morning was light*, for love settles upon the world and *ḥesed* abides in its place. Then *the morning was light*, and it is written, *Elohim saw that the light was good* (Gen. 1:4).

Come and see:

Everything is in known levels. *Night* is known. *Morning light* (*boker or*) is known—it is a higher level that is found in Her always. When is this? When the sun shines. The *sun* is known and it is a higher level that perfumes all and illuminates all, as it is said, *For YHVH Elohim is sun and shield* (Ps. 84:12). This *morning light* shines from the *sun* and illuminates the *night*, and thus all are dependent on one another. When this *morning light* awakens, all the people of the world come together in unity and joy and abide in the world.

And now, behold the day has dawned; it is a propitious time to walk on the way.

Rabbi Ḥiyya and Rabbi Yose blessed them, kissed them on their heads and sent them on their way.

Rabbi Ḥiyya said to Rabbi Yose: Blessed is the Merciful One who arrayed our way before us! Certainly the Blessed Holy One sent them to us! Happy are they who engage Torah and do not neglect her for even an instant!

Rabbi Ḥiyya and Rabbi Yose went out and continued on their way.

Rabbi Yose said: Truly the love of my heart is bound to those merchants.

Rabbi Ḥiyya said: I am not surprised by this, for in the days of Rabbi Shimon, even the birds of the sky murmur wisdom, for his words are known above and below.

Commentary on *Zohar* 3:20a–23a

In what remains a seminal article in *Zohar* scholarship, Yehuda Liebes, the most original and insightful *Zohar* commentator of our time, lamented the fact that the *Zohar* still awaits recognition as one of the great works of world literature.[2] More recently, and despite the great strides in *Zohar* scholarship, Eitan Fishbane also observed that the *Zohar* "still awaits full appreciation as a book oriented by a complex narrative and poetic craft."[3] While the under-appreciation of the *Zohar* is surely lamentable, it is also understandable. As we have seen, the *Zohar* is an extremely complex work, and appreciation of the *Zohar* as literature is severely hampered by the composition's esotericism. Yet, as all *Zohar* researchers and readers know, the *Zohar* is a literary masterpiece and its discrete compositional units virtuoso displays of narrative and exegetical fusion. Zoharic narratives are much more than repositories of kabbalistic teachings. They are, rather, poetic wonders, which through their very form—fluid, dynamic, and responsive—embody the mystical quest to generate a new understanding of the relationship between Torah and life.

There can be no doubt that much of the charm of the *Zohar* lies in the artful manner in which mystical exegesis is seamlessly integrated with narrative. As we have seen throughout this book, the *Zohar* does not simply present kabbalistic doctrine, but interlaces its teachings with the delightful stories of the Companions' many adventures. While in some cases the narrative is bare and provides no more than a context for the Companions' expositions, on other occasions the integration is more dramatic and profound. In these more developed compositions (of which there are dozens throughout the *Zohar*, some extending for more than twenty folio pages) it is not merely that kabbalistic homilies are housed within quaint accounts of the Companions' travels, but that these two rhetorical modes—narrative and exegetical—interact with one another in dynamic and surprising ways. As Melila Hellner-Eshed has noted, the "objective" reality of the journey and the "reality" of the exposition of verses are not disconnected from one another,[4] and in the *Zohar* we find ourselves in an extraordinary space where these two literary modes intersect. Zoharic composition is thus characterized by a subtle dynamism where narrative generates exegesis and exegesis triggers narrative. We shall return later to the mystical significance of this literary format.

The passage at the beginning of this chapter, in my view one of the most beautiful narratives in the entire *Zohar*, artfully conveys this poetic aspect of zoharic composition. Not only does the unit display the narrative-exegetical weave so central to the *Zohar*, but it also reveals something of the symphonic element in zoharic midrash. While zoharic narratives are comprised of individual homilies that may be appreciated in isolation, it is as integrated compositions, as the homilies play on and respond to one another, that zoharic literary craft comes to the fore. As in a classical symphony or jazz improvisation where discrete movements or solos each have their theme to convey yet which assume their full meaning and power when appreciated in the context of the entire piece, so zoharic homilies combine to produce a whole much greater than the sum of their parts. The author(s) of the *Zohar* was undoubtedly one of the greatest literary talents in the Jewish tradition and his compositions are masterful symphonies composed with a dynamic fusion of scriptural exegesis and narrative.[5]

·••·

The unit above is found in the *Zohar*'s commentary to the opening chapters of the book of Leviticus and is woven around the adventures and homilies of first, Rabbi Ḥiyya and Rabbi Yose, the *Zohar*'s favorite traveling pair, and then two anonymous traveling merchants. The placement of the unit in printed editions of the *Zohar* in *parashat Va-Yikra* is determined, presumably, by the opening homily about confession, one of the key themes of the Torah portion, as well as one of the ensuing homilies in the unit that explores the meaning of Leviticus 4:13, "And if all the community of Israel should err, and the matter be hidden from the eyes of the assembly." The *Zohar* explains that "the eyes of the assembly" are in fact the leaders of the people, "the eyes of the nation," and quoting a verse from Isaiah (3:12), "Your leaders are misleaders, they have confused the course of your paths (*orḥotekha*)," explains that the Roman exile and the destruction of the temple occurred as a direct result of the nation's leaders. The verse from Leviticus, it should be noted, does not play a major role in the narrative, although, as we shall see, the motifs of eyes, leaders being in the dark, and the arraying of the way (*orḥa*) (as opposed to the confusion of the paths) establish a series of echoes with the verse.

The unit begins with the now familiar zoharic opening:

> Rabbi Ḥiyya and Rabbi Yose were walking on the way.
>   While they were walking Rabbi Yose said to Rabbi Ḥiyya:
> Let us engage words of Torah, words of the Ancient of Days
> . . .

This invocation to engage "words of the Ancient of Days" is more than just an opening to learn and innovate Torah. The epithet "Ancient of

Days," taken from the book of Daniel (7:9), refers to the most primal
and ancient countenance of divinity, the most recondite, singular, and
undifferentiated aspect of the divine. The zoharic quest is not only to
innovate words of Torah, but more specifically, to uncover in the
Torah's verses the story of divinity from its most primal manifestation.
To paraphrase Walter Benjamin, "origin is the goal,"[6] and the zoharic
homily is particularly attuned to this dimension of reality.

As noted, our unit begins on a sombre and dark note, and the first
homilies expounded by our protagonists take as their focus themes of
guilt, shame, confession, and exile. From this melancholic context the
wandering Companions then chance upon a paradisiacal garden.

> They walked on.
> While they were walking they saw a place of lush grasses
> with a stream of water flowing by.
> They sat down.
> While they were sitting a bird flew past, murmuring before
> them.
> Rabbi Ḥiyya said: Let us get up from here, for assuredly
> mountain quarriers (*nagrei turraya*) are present here.
> They got up and walked on.
> While they were turning their heads they saw bandits run-
> ning after them.
> A miracle occurred for them and they found in front of
> them a rock with a cave inside it.
> They went in and sat there the whole of that day and night.

The Companions find themselves in a classical zoharic landscape, first
"a place of lush grasses with a stream of water flowing by," and then
following their flight from their mysterious assailants,[7] in the inner
recesses of a cave. Both the stream and the cave, key loci for zoharic
narratives, are highly symbolic, and as we shall see, brimming with
associations. The "way" is unpredictable, offering both enchanted sites
of beauty and protection, as well as exposure to many perils. "Walking
on the way" also demands a special state of consciousness, and the
Companions are able to both notice and then decipher seemingly
innocuous signs and symbols. In this heightened mystical-poetic state
everything is meaningful, with all of reality grasped as a semantic field
where everything is a sign pointing beyond itself.[8]

Rabbi Ḥiyya's homily responds directly to the narrative context:

> Rabbi Ḥiyya opened, saying: *But you, have no fear My servant
> Jacob, declares YHVH, be not dismayed, O Israel! I will deliver*

you from far away, your folk from the land of captivity. And Jacob shall again have calm and quiet with none to trouble him (Jer. 30:10).

From far away—it should have said from nearby!

They have already established this verse:[9] *from far away*— as it is said, *and they shall return from a far land.*[10]

But, *from far away*—as it is written, *from afar did YHVH appear to me* (Jer. 31:3),[11] and *bringing her food from afar* (Prov. 31:14).

What does this mean?

The depth of the river, the place from which the river issues and flows.

And Jacob shall again (shav) have calm—since it is written, *have no fear My servant Jacob*, what does *and Jacob shall again have calm and quiet with none to trouble him* mean?

Rather, it is as we have taught: The Blessed Holy One ascends higher and higher, as it is written, *Why O YHVH do you stand so far off?* (Ps. 10:1), and from that distant place *I will deliver you.*

And Jacob shall return (shav)[12]—to his place to have intercourse with the Assembly of Israel.

Calm—this is *Yesod.*

Quiet—to place his abode in Her.

With none to trouble him (maḥrid)—from Isaac,[13] as it is said, *Isaac was seized with very violent trembling (ḥaradah)* (Gen. 27:33), and therefore it is written, *the Fear of Isaac* (Gen. 31:42).

When this fear is aroused, *Yesod* departs and ascends to another place, as it is written, *Sinners in Zion are frightened* (Isa. 33:14). *In Zion* precisely![14] Therefore it says, *with none to trouble him.*

Now the Blessed Holy One has saved us from afar and has hidden us in this place in calm and quiet and there is nothing at all to trouble us. For when the Blessed Holy One performs a miracle, He performs its completely . . .

Rabbi Ḥiyya begins by quoting a verse from Jeremiah: "But you, have no fear My servant Jacob, declares YHVH, be not dismayed, O Israel! I will deliver you from far away, your folk from the land of captivity. And Jacob shall again have calm and quiet with none to trouble him" (Jer. 30:10). The choice of verse is determined both by the Companions' sense of terror and then their sense of deliverance. In an exceptional display of kabbalistic hermeneutics, Rabbi Ḥiyya then proceeds to expound the verse according to the "mystery of faith," that is to say, to uncover the great drama of the unfolding of divinity concealed in the verses of the Bible appropriate to the moment. Rabbi Ḥiyya focuses on a curious phrase in the verse, "I will deliver you from far away," and explains that the word *far* is actually a symbol for the second sefirah *Hokhmah*, the concealed divine thought, the primal seed of being, as well as the depth of the river of emanation, "the place from which the river issues and flows." The stream of the narrative layer has now entered the exposition as the flow of the river of divine plenty. The remainder of the verse, "And Jacob shall again have calm and quiet with none to trouble him," is also interpreted symbolically to refer to unification of the masculine and feminine grades within divinity, the serenity of the divine harmony, paralleling the Companions' sense of deliverance. Even when read in isolation, Rabbi Ḥiyya's homily is worthy of admiration. Yet, it is the connection with the narrative context and echoes with the protagonist's state of mind that is cause for deep wonder. Returning to the narrative context, Rabbi Ḥiyya spells out the connection between his exposition and the rabbis' situation: "Now the Blessed Holy One has saved us from *afar* and has hidden us in this place in *calm* and *quiet* and there is nothing at all to *trouble us*." Even the most seasoned *Zohar* readers frequently miss the comic element in zoharic composition. Yet it is precisely the interlacing of the comic and the profound that is the source of the *Zohar*'s charm. Here a very visual depiction of two rabbis fleeing their assailants and huddled together in a cave leads to a homily about the most recondite aspect of divinity. As readers we can only marvel at the author's daring in juxtaposing such divergent literary moments.

Following a brief remark by Rabbi Yose that it is their engagement with the Torah that accounts for their deliverance, the narrative unfolds in yet another direction:

They sat in the cave the entire day.

When night arrived, the moon shone into the cave and two merchants passed by with their donkeys loaded with wine, and food for themselves resting on their loads.

They said to one another: Let us sleep here. Let us give food and drink to the donkeys and we will enter this cave.

His companion said to him: Before we enter, explain this verse that isn't clear.

He said to him: Which one?

He said to him: This is the matter. It is written, *I praise You*

*forever (le-olam) for You have done, I will wait for Your name
for it is good in the presence of Your faithful ones* (Ps. 52:11).
What does it mean by *for You have done* without specifying
what?!

It is also written, *good in the presence of Your faithful
ones*—for others then is He not good?!

He could not answer him.

He said: Alas that on account of my trade I have neglected
the Blessed Holy One![15]

Rabbi Ḥiyya and Rabbi Yose, who were sitting in the cave,
rejoiced.

Rabbi Ḥiyya said to Rabbi Yose: Did I not tell you that
when the Blessed Holy One performs a miracle, He performs it
completely!

They went out.

If the encounter with the mountain diggers triggers feelings of terror
and fear, the encounter with anonymous traveling merchants, who as
we quickly discover are themselves mystical adepts, generates rejoicing
and delight. The way is full of surprises, sometimes for ill and sometimes for good, and the Companions must be alert to all the possibilities
of the journey. The scene before us is at once enchanted, comical, and
ironic. The image of the moon shining into the cave, both symbolic of
the feminine, as well as the image of the wine, a symbol for Torah and
the divine overflow, create a sense of expectation. The seasoned *Zohar*
reader is immediately aware that these are no ordinary donkey drivers,
but like so many of the wondrous characters encountered on the way,
are the bearers of mystical insights. There is of course great irony and
comedy in the merchant's lament that he has neglected the Blessed Holy
One on account of his trade, given that he and his companion, like
Rabbi Ḥiyya and Rabbi Yose, have been talking words of Torah as they
walk. The two merchants, unable to answer their own exegetical problem, function here as a kind of mirror image of the companions of
Rabbi Shimon.

When they went out Rabbi Ḥiyya immediately opened, saying:
*Peace, peace to him that is distant (raḥok) [and him that is
near]* (Isa. 57:19).

Peace is said twice here. Once for him that is distant and
once for him that is near, and it is all one. For the one who is
distant is brought near—this is the master of *teshuvah* (repen-
tance/returning). First he was distant and now he is near.

Further, regarding *him that is distant*—when a human being distances himself from the Torah, he is distant from the Blessed Holy One, while the one who draws near to the Torah, the Blessed Holy One draws him near to Himself.[16]

Now, unite with us and enter the cave.

The merchants came and joined them, tethered their donkeys and prepared their food.

They all went out to the mouth of the cave.

In many zoharic stories, upon encountering mysterious figures, the Companions adopt a posture of superiority, assuming that the travelers they meet can not possibly have anything to teach them. Here the dynamic is more subtle and nuanced. Having overheard the merchants engaging in words of Torah, Rabbi Ḥiyya and Rabbi Yose know that they are not simply ignoramuses. Nevertheless, picking up on the keyword from his earlier homily, *raḥok*, far, which previously was interpreted as referring to the source of the river of divine plenty, Rabbi Ḥiyya quotes a verse from Isaiah employing the same word, but used here as a greeting to the merchants, while simultaneously establishing a hierarchy between the companions of Rabbi Shimon and the anonymous travelers: "Peace, peace to him that is distant (*raḥok*) and him that is near" (Isa. 57:19). The homily that follows engages with the merchant's lament at neglecting the Blessed Holy One, after which Rabbi Ḥiyya, who until this point has been the primary agent in the narrative, invites the merchants to join them inside the cave. If earlier it was the stream that "migrated" from the narrative register into the homily, here we find the inverse, with a keyword moving from a homily back into the narrative.

The cave, no longer merely a site of refuge, is now transformed into the locus of a great banquet with wine, food, and words of Torah. As has often been noticed, zoharic Eros is anti-ascetic and overflowing with pleasure.[17] The transformation of the bare cave into a lavish symposium accompanied by words that ascend and soar and "rest in the lap of the King" brings to mind similar such transformations in another Spanish literary marvel, *Don Quixote* by Miguel de Cervantes. Like the Ingenious Hidalgo who sees in a humble inn a grand castle, a paradise with "stars and suns to accompany the heaven you have brought with you" (DQ 1.42), the zoharic author generates forth from the human collectivity gathered in the cave a mystical and celestial realm.[18] Significantly, the exchanges that now follow take place at the "mouth of the cave." Although they have joined as one, the Companions and the anonymous merchants are still checking one another out, as it were, and total intimacy has not yet been attained. Only later will the narrative move into the innermost recesses of the cavern.

> One of the merchants said: Let the Masters of Torah explain to us this verse, *I praise You forever (le-olam) for You have done, I will wait for Your name for it is good in the presence of Your faithful ones.*
>
> *For You have done*—what does it mean by *for You have done* without specifying what?!
>
> It is also written, *good in the presence of Your faithful ones*—for others then is He not good?!
>
> Rabbi Hiyya said: *For You have done,* indeed! And what have You done? The world (*le-olam*). Because of this world that the Blessed Holy One has made and arrayed, a human being ought to praise the Blessed Holy One every day.
>
> *I will wait for Your name for it is good in the presence of Your faithful ones*—assuredly it is so. For before the righteous, the name of the Blessed Holy One is good, not so before the wicked, who spurn it every day and do not engage Torah.

Having united as one, the merchant then returns to his original exegetical difficulty. Perhaps responding to Rabbi Hiyya's subtle posturing the merchant opens by asking the "Masters of Torah" to explain the difficult verse from Psalms.[19] Rabbi Hiyya offers a solution to the merchant's difficulty, and although his response is based on a neat exegetical device (he reads the word *le-olam*, which can mean forever but also for the world), it is by no means dazzling. The merchant too is not satisfied with the Master of Torah's response.

> He said to him: This is fine but I have heard a word from behind the curtain [*pargod*] yet I am afraid to reveal it.

The merchant informs Rabbi Hiyya that while his response is adequate, he has a deeper intimation, "from behind the curtain" (a rabbinic allusion to divine sources of knowledge)[20] about the meaning of the verse. Having been unable to provide a satisfactory answer to the merchant's query, Rabbi Hiyya and Rabbi Yose now drop their posturing and invite the merchant to share his thoughts. This carnivalesque switch whereby the masters are transformed into students, characteristic of many zoharic narratives, especially those containing Rabbi Hiyya and Rabbi Yose,[21] resonates with the verse from Leviticus "and the matter be hidden from the eyes of the assembly," the eyes it will be recalled having been interpreted as referring to the leaders of the people.

Rabbi Ḥiyya and Rabbi Yose said to him: Say your word for the Torah is not the inheritance of one place alone.[22]

He said to them: One day I was walking to Lod. I entered the city and positioned myself behind a certain wall. Rabbi Shimon bar Yoḥai was in that house and I heard from his mouth this verse, *I praise You forever (le-olam) for You have done.*

I praise You—King David, peace be upon him, said this about the last world[23] He made, for King David held fast to that world and through it inherited kingship (*malkhut*).

I will wait for Your name for it is good—this is the Blessed Holy One,[24] united with this world that is called *good*.[25]

When is it called good? *In the presence of Your faithful ones (ḥasidekha).*

Who are these faithful ones? For there is *ḥesed*, love, and there is *ḥesed*, love;[26] but these are the ones called *the enduring loves of David (ḥasdei david ha-neemanim)* (Isa. 55:3), and when these *loves of David*[27] are filled with the goodness flowing down from Holy Ancient One, then *Yesod* is called good . . . and perfumes this last world and all abides in blessing.

Therefore would David wait for this grade, to illuminate this world to which he held fast.

Thus did I hear these words but I did not know what they meant.

The merchant proceeds to relate his interpretation, the source of which we learn is none other than Rabbi Shimon, the grand master, an interpretation he once heard when he positioned himself "behind a wall." The playful interpretation connecting the rabbinic expression "behind the curtain" with the narrative detail of how the merchant came to obtain this insight by positioning himself "behind the wall" to overhear Rabbi Shimon's teaching at once establishes Rabbi Shimon as a (semi)divine source of knowledge, while simultaneously confusing the reader's sense of the merchant's source of knowledge. The merchant's claim that he has heard a word from "behind the curtain" seems to suggest a revelatory moment, that is, that he has just now received some inspiration, while the narrative detail about Rabbi Shimon suggests something entirely different. It will be recalled that until now the merchant has been unable to answer his own exegetical difficulty, a situation that would be difficult to account for if he had indeed previously heard these words from Rabbi Shimon. Can we perhaps sense in this ambiguity and *ars poetica* expression of the zoharic author's own source of inspiration, at once just now, from behind the curtain, while simultaneously garbed in the authoritative voice of second-century rabbis?[28]

Be that as it may, the merchant's homily is a brilliant display of theosophical exegesis. Quoting Rabbi Shimon the merchant uncovers in the verse the sefirotic structure of divinity, from the innermost depths of the divine through to *Malkhut*, the *Shekhinah*, the last of the sefirot, and like Rabbi Ḥiyya's opening homily, finds in the verse a description of the "goodness flowing down from the Holy Ancient One" (the word *in the presence of*, *neged*, is interpreted here from the Aramaic, *negidu*, flowing). It should be noted that in expounding the verse as describing the flow of divinity from the Holy Ancient One, the most recondite aspect of the godhead, into the sefirot of *Nezaḥ* and *Hod* symbolized by the expression "David's (= the *Shekhinah*'s) enduring loves," into *Yesod* and finally into the last world, namely *Malkhut*, the *Shekhinah*, the merchant has also accomplished the task set by Rabbi Yose at the beginning of our unit, namely, to engage words of the Ancient of Days.

Rabbi Ḥiyya and Rabbi Yose respond in classical zoharic fashion:

> Rabbi Ḥiyya and Rabbi Yose came and kissed him on his head.
>
> Rabbi Ḥiyya said: Who shall cover your eyes with dust Rabbi Shimon bar Yoḥai?! For you are in your place and cause supernal mountains (*turraya*) to tremble, and even the birds of heaven rejoice at your words. Woe to the world when you depart and ascend from it! . . .

Rabbi Ḥiyya's invocation of Rabbi Shimon, while a key feature in many zoharic narratives and not unexpected in this context given that it is Rabbi Shimon's teaching they have just heard, resonates both with the verse from Leviticus ("who shall cover your eyes?") and the earlier narrative scene with the omen bird ("birds of heaven rejoice at your word"). Rabbi Ḥiyya's observation that Rabbi Shimon causes mighty mountains (*turraya*) to tremble also echoes with the earlier narrative detail about the mountain diggers (*nagrei turraya*) from whom the Companions have fled. This lament about a world without Rabbi Shimon will return at the end of our unit explicitly connected to the verse from Leviticus.

> Rabbi Ḥiyya and Rabbi Yose were amazed and they rejoiced that night.
>
> After they had eaten, the merchant's companion opened, saying: Let me say before you a word with which I have been occupied this day, regarding what is written in the verse, *A*

psalm of David, when he was in the wilderness of Judah (Ps. 63:1).

David said this poem when he was fleeing from his father-in-law.

What did he say? *Elohim, You are my God; I search for You, my soul thirsts for You, my body yearns for You, as a parched thirsty land that has no water* (Ps. 63:2)[29] . . .

I search for You (ashaḥreka)—how could David search for the Blessed Holy One in a distant land, exiled from the land where the *Shekhinah* abides?

Well, even though he was exiled from there, he never ceased seeking the Blessed Holy One. And I have heard that *I search for You (ashaḥreka)* is like someone who says: I would go and appear before you except I cannot. Similarly, *I search for You (ashaḥreka)* except I am outside the domain where the *Shekhinah* abides.

My soul thirsts for You—my soul and my body crave You, to appear before You, but I am unable because I am in *a parched thirsty land that has no water*, for any land outside the domain where the *Shekhinah* abides is called *a parched thirsty land*, because living waters are not found there. What are living waters? This is the *Shekhinah* about whom it is written, *a well of living waters* (Song of Songs 4:15) and therefore it is written, *a parched thirsty land that has no water*.

Following the description of Rabbi Ḥiyya and Rabbi Yose's amazement and delight, and after being told that the Companions along with the merchants sit down to eat together, the merchant's companion, until now silent, begins his own homily. Significantly, he does not preface his exposition with the honorary yet ironic epithet "Masters of Torah," perhaps an indication that the dialectics of hierarchy have now come to an end. Indeed, from this point on, the narrative is constructed through the equal participation of all the protagonists. Once again, the verses chosen for exposition—"A psalm of David, when he was in the wilderness of Judah. Elohim, You are my God. I search for You, my soul thirsts for You, my body yearns for You, as a parched thirsty land that has no water" (Ps. 63:1–2)—are connected to the narrative context. As we learn toward the end of the unit, the Companions and the merchants have indeed been wandering through the wilderness, and as we have already seen, rivers, streams, and flowing fluids have been a crucial part of both the narrative and their exegetical endeavors. The second part of the verse, "I search for You," *ashaḥreka*, sets the scene for the homilies that follow, which as we will soon see, are all elaborations and explorations of the verb root *shaḥar*. The word *ashaḥreka* is laden with possibilities and resonances, at once alluding to the blackness (*shaḥor*) of night, the yet distant dawn (*shaḥar*), as well as the quest to behold the Blessed Holy One and experience His presence (*le-shaḥer*), a quest actualized in desire if not in action by the merchants who earlier lamented having neglected the Blessed Holy One on account of their trade. To return to the symphony metaphor, the merchant's homily is thus the principal theme around which Rabbi Ḥiyya, Rabbi Yose, and the anonymous merchants will make their music.

> They entered the cave and slept.
> At midnight they heard the animals of the wilderness growling.
> They awoke.
> Rabbi Ḥiyya said: It is now time to assist the Assembly of Israel as She praises the King.
> They said: Let everyone say something he has heard and knows of Torah.
> They all sat down.

The stage is now set for the nocturnal delight, the central mythical drama of the *Zohar*. Having slept through the dangerous hours of the night, from dusk to midnight, when the forces of evil are at their height, the Companions and the merchants awaken together to the sounds of animals in the wilderness. Rabbi Ḥiyya, displaying none of his earlier arrogance, invites everyone to share words of Torah and thereby participate in assisting the female grade of divinity, the Assembly of Israel, to praise and ultimately unite with Her beloved, the King, the Blessed Holy One. This is the structural center of the narrative; the Companions and the merchants have united as one (marked by the narrator through the expression "they all sat down"),[30] and significantly transpires in the inner recesses of the cave. The passage from the mouth of the cave to the depths of the cave, it should be stressed, is more than just an incidental flourish or narrative detail. The Companions and the merchants are poised to participate in the *zivvug ha-kadosh*, the holy union/intercourse of the male and female grades of divinity, and their physical location, *inside* and *within* the cave, functions as a neat narrative analogue to the divine union that will soon follow.

> Rabbi Ḥiyya opened, saying: *For the leader on ayelet ha-shaḥar (the hind of the dawn). A psalm of David* (Ps. 22:1).

Who is *ayelet ha-shaḥar (the hind of the dawn)?* This is the Assembly of Israel who is called, *a loving hind, a graceful mountain goat* (Prov. 5:19).[31]

Is She then a hind of the dawn only and not the entire day?

Rather, She is a hind from that place called dawn, as it is said, *His firm starting place is like dawn* (Hosea 6:3) . . .

Come and see . . .

At midnight, a herald rises and proclaims and the openings open. Then a wind arouses from the north side, strikes David's harp, which plays by itself, and She praises the King and the Blessed Holy One delights in the righteous in the Garden of Eden.

Happy is the portion of the one who arises at that time and engages Torah!

Whoever arises at that time and engages Torah is called a companion of the Blessed Holy One and the Assembly of Israel. And what's more they are called His kin and His friends, as it is written, *For the sake of my kin and my friends, I pray for your well-being* (Ps. 122:8), and they are called companions of the supernal angels and supernal legions, as it is written, *companions listen for your voice* (Song of Songs 8:13).

When day comes, a herald rises and proclaims and the openings of the south side are opened, the stars and constellations awaken, the gates of mercy open and the King is seated and receives their praises. Then the Assembly of Israel takes these words and ascends, and all the companions cling to Her wings, and their words come and rest in the lap of the King . . .

Happy is the portion of the righteous who engage Torah, especially when the King craves words of Torah.[32]

Rabbi Ḥiyya's homily ingeniously picks up on the keyword of the merchant's previous exposition, *ashaḥreka*, I search for You. Rabbi Ḥiyya, however, explores a different resonance of the word, connecting the phrase from Psalms to *ayelet ha-shaḥar*, the hind of the dawn, namely the Assembly of Israel, the female grade of divinity, whom the Companions and merchants must now adorn and assist in the nocturnal delight. Having evoked the presence of the *Shekhinah*, Rabbi Ḥiyya proceeds to outline the well-known *mythos* of the nocturnal vigil. Beginning with the onset of night, when the forces of judgment hold sway, a period best spent asleep, as the Companions and merchants have just done, Rabbi Ḥiyya then describes the celestial drama—the arousal of the upper worlds and the role of humanity in bringing harmony and joy to the divine realm—and concludes by focusing on the moment of the dawn. It should be noted that the exegesis is not merely a theoretical presentation of the dynamics of this key zoharic praxis. Rather, the description of the nocturnal delight serves to describe what is transpiring here and now within the narrative. We will return to the function of this exegetical device later.

> Rabbi Yose opened, saying: *The oracle of Dumah. A call comes to me from Seir: Watchman, what of the night? Watchman, what of the night?* (Isa. 21:11)
>
> The Companions have established this verse is numerous places.[33]
>
> But, *The oracle of Dumah (masa dumah)*—each time that Israel was in exile, their time and end was known, and the time and end of that exile.
>
> But the exile of Edom is *masa dumah*, a burden[34] of silence, for it has not been disclosed and is not known like the others.
>
> The Blessed Holy One says: *A call comes to me from Seir*— I have heard a voice from the exile of Seir, from those who are oppressed among them, from those who lie in the dust.
>
> What do they say? *Watchman, what of the night? Watchman, what of the night?* They inquire of Me about the *Matronita*, what have I done with my *Matronita*.[35]
>
> Then the Blessed Holy One assembles His court and says: Look at my beloved children who are oppressed in exile yet forget their own sorrow and inquire of Me about the *Matronita*, saying: *Watchman*—You who are called watchman, where is your watching, where is the watching of Your house? *What of the night?* What have You done with the night? Is this how You watched over Her?

If Rabbi Ḥiyya's homily largely focused on the joy and delight of the nocturnal celestial drama, culminating in the grace of dawn, Rabbi Yose's exposition switches key, exploring some of the darker associations of the night, namely exile and separation in the divine realm. To borrow Hellner-Eshed's delightful comparison between zoharic homiletics and jazz improvisation, Rabbi Yose's exposition begins with the blues. Night, with all its wonder, mystery, and fear, is one of the chief designations for the female aspect of the divine, the tenth sefirah *Malkhut*, the *Shekhinah*, and in quoting the verse from Isaiah (21:11),

"The Oracle of Dumah. A call comes to me from Seir: Watchman, what of the night? Watchman, what of the night?," Rabbi Yose evokes the tragic and fragile existence of the *Shekhinah* in the world—in exile (in Seir, meaning Rome, meaning Christendom) with the people of Israel and separated from her lover, the Blessed Holy One, the male grade of divinity. Reading the word *Dumah* hyper-literally as silence (in its biblical context it designates the name of a people), the homily opens to a vision of the silent and endless night. In a masterful display of classical midrashic and kabbalistic hermeneutics, Rabbi Yose uses the verses from Isaiah to construct a picture of Israel's deep identification with the *Shekhinah* and has them inquire, or better yet, demand of God that He come to her aid: "*Watchman*—You who are called watchman, where is your watching, where is the watching of Your house? *What of the night?* What have You done with the night? Is this how You watched over Her?"

Then the Blessed Holy One answers them: Behold, My watching is present, for behold I am destined to receive Her, to be with Her, as it is written, *The watchman replied* (Isa. 21:12)— the one who watched the house, *Morning came and so did night* (ibid.)—for at first He ascended high above, and raised that morning[36] that is ever ready for Him. Now, *morning came*—for He is ready to join with night. *And so did night*— She is also ready. But because of you they are delayed. If you desire this, why are you delaying? *Return!* Return in repentance. Then, *come back*—come back to Me and we will all be in a single abode, and we will all return to our place, as it is written, *And YHVH your God will return (shav) your captivity* (Deut. 30:3). It does not say *will restore*, but *will return. Will return* is written twice here—once for the Assembly of Israel and once for the Blessed Holy One, as it is written, *And YHVH your God will return your captivity and have mercy upon you and will return and gather you from all the peoples* (ibid.).[37]

As if to mark the midpoint of the night, and the passage from the despair of being caught in an endless night to the expectation and yearning for the arrival of the dawn, Rabbi Yose expounds the very next verse from Isaiah, "The watchman replied: Morning came and so did night." Continuing the dialogue between the Blessed Holy One and the people of Israel, the exposition reads out of the biblical verses a description of the unification of the male and female grades of divinity, morning and night. Still in the space of the verse from Isaiah, Rabbi Yose's homily concludes with a vision of an anticipated harmony and unity, "we will all be in a single abode, and we will all return to our place." Without even a single narrative statement and relying on exegesis alone, Rabbi Ḥiyya and Rabbi Yose have led us from midnight and the arousal of the upper worlds into the darkness of the night and onto the expectation of the impending dawn.

Now, the two merchants play their part in the zoharic symphony. With the first stirrings of dawn, one of the merchants, continuing exactly where Rabbi Yose left off, begins his exposition:

> The merchant opened, saying: *When the morning stars sang together and all the divine beings shouted for joy* (Job 38:7).
>
> Come and see: When the Blessed Holy One comes to delight with the righteous in the Garden of Eden, all the words/things of the lower [alt., upper] world, and all the upper and lower [realms] arouse to receive Him, and all the trees in the Garden of Eden open in praise before Him, as it is written, *then shall all the trees of the forest shout for joy before YHVH who comes* (1 Chron. 16:33). Even the birds of the earth all murmur praise before Him. Then a flame goes forth and strikes the wings of the cock, and it calls and praises to the Holy King, and calls out to human beings to engage in Torah and in the praise of their Master and His service. Happy is the portion of those who arise from their beds to engage Torah!
>
> When morning comes, the openings of the south are opened, and the gates of healing go forth to the world, and the east wind awakens and mercy abounds. All the stars and constellations that are appointed under the rule of that morning open in praise and song to the supernal King, as it is written, *When the morning stars sang together and all the divine beings shouted for joy* (Job 38:7).
>
> What do the divine beings (*bnei elohim*) desire here in calling forth the shout (*tru'ah*) in that morning, for behold, all the judgments pass away when *ḥesed*, love, is aroused in the world?
>
> Rather, *And all the divine beings shouted for joy (va-yariu kol bnei elohim)*—behold the might of the harsh judgments has been broken, and their power has been broken, as it is said, *the earth is breaking, breaking (roah hitroaah)* (Isa. 24:19).
>
> All this because that morning awakens in the earth, and Abraham awakens and comes to plant a tamarisk in Beer

Sheva. This matter I have heard as follows—in Beer Sheva indeed![38]

And it is written, *and he invoked there the name YHVH, El Olam* (Gen. 21:33).

The first light of morning is stirring and the merchant's homily that expounds the verse from Job, "When the morning stars sang together and all the divine beings shouted for joy," is wonderfully attuned to the temporal landscape of the narrative. The merchant then evokes the celestial joy of dawn, when love and healing go forth to the world. The same verse is then expounded to indicate the subjugation of the forces of judgment. Darkness, fear, and judgment are now totally defeated (*yariu*, shout, is read as *roah hitroah*, breaking, breaking); love and mercy have been aroused (Abraham = *ḥesed*, love) and the male and female grades of divinity are united (the combination of two divine epithets *YHVH* and *El Olam* are understood as symbolizing the masculine and feminine respectively).

The merchant's companion opened, saying: *The morning was light (ha-boker or) and the men were sent off, they and their donkeys* (Gen. 44:3).

What does it mean *the morning was light*?[39]

So we have learned: What is morning (*boker*)? When morning (*tzafra*) comes and judgments pass away, and *ḥesed*, love, desires to arouse, all who come from that side hasten (*mevakrei*) to their place to summon blessings for the world.

This is *the morning was light*, for love settles upon the world and *ḥesed* abides in its place. Then *the morning was light*, and it is written, *Elohim saw that the light was good* (Gen. 1:4).[40]

Come and see:

Everything is in known levels. *Night* is known. *Morning light (boker or)* is known—it is a higher level that is found in Her always. When is this? When the sun shines. The *sun* is known and it is a higher level that perfumes all and illuminates all, as it is said, *For YHVH Elohim is sun and shield* (Ps. 84:12). This *morning light* shines from the *sun* and illuminates the *night*, and thus all are dependent on one another. When this *morning light* awakens, all the people of the world come together in unity and joy and abide in the world.

And now, behold the day has dawned; it is a propitious time to walk on the way.

The verse chosen by the merchant in the final exposition of this part of the narrative is ingenious—at once appropriate to the time of day as well as the more concrete narrative context, namely, the impending departure of the merchants and their donkeys. Beginning with a neat midrashic play, connecting hastening (*mevakrei*) with morning (*boker*), the merchant's homily summarizes and concludes the nocturnal vigil. Sun, night, and morning light, three grades of divinity, *Tiferet*, *Malkhut*, and *Yesod*, in unity and joy: "This morning light shines from the sun and illuminates the night and thus all are dependent on one another." The mythical celestial drama now complete, we return to the narrative, which seems to almost spill out of the exegesis. If earlier we saw the stream of the narrative tier enter the exegetical domain, now it is the morning light that flows from the homily into the story.

> Rabbi Ḥiyya and Rabbi Yose blessed them, kissed them on their heads, and sent them on their way.
>
> Rabbi Ḥiyya said to Rabbi Yose: Blessed is the Merciful One who arrayed our way before us! Certainly the Blessed Holy One sent them to us! Happy are they who engage Torah and do not neglect her for even an instant!
>
> Rabbi Ḥiyya and Rabbi Yose went out and continued on their way.
>
> Rabbi Yose said: Truly the love of my heart is bound to those merchants.
>
> Rabbi Ḥiyya said: I am not surprised by this, for in the days of Rabbi Shimon, even the birds of the sky murmur wisdom, for his words are known above and below.

Taking their cue from the verse in Genesis (44:3), "The morning brightened and the men were sent off, they and their donkeys," the merchants are sent on their way. The Companions reflect on all that has befallen them, express their joy and invoke once again the greatness of their master, Rabbi Shimon. (In fact, the Companions attribute the merchants' mystical knowledge to the "days of Rabbi Shimon," evoking once again the murmuring birds of the sky thereby recalling an earlier motif.) This penultimate paragraph neatly ties together a number of threads that have been running through our narrative. Rabbi Ḥiyya exclaims: "Happy are those who engage Torah and do not neglect her even for an instant!" returning us to the merchant's original lament about neglecting the Blessed Holy One on account of his trade.

Having parted and invoked the greatness of Rabbi Shimon, our narrative has essentially come to a close. One final homily, however,

returns us to the verse from Leviticus we encountered at the beginning
of our story. The homily is at once a celebration of the "generation of
Rabbi Shimon,"[41] a unique time in the annals of human spiritual history, yet like the beginning of our unit, which began on the sombre note
of confession, exile, and confused leaders, laments a future world without Rabbi Shimon, when "matters will be hidden from the eyes of the
assembly." Like a jazz solo or piece of classical music, the narrative concludes by artfully returning to its dark opening movement:

> Rabbi Ḥiyya opened, saying: *YHVH said to Moses, "You are
> soon to lie with your fathers"* (Deut. 31:16).
>
> Come and see. As long as Moses was present in the world,
> he would chastise Israel so that they would not be found guilty
> before the Blessed Holy One. And since Moses was present
> among them, there will never be a generation like that one until
> the generation when King Messiah comes—when they will see
> the glory of God as they did, for they attained what no other
> generation has ever attained.
>
> We have taught: A handmaiden at the sea saw what Ezekiel
> the prophet never saw.[42]
>
> If they attained so much—all the more so the women of
> Israel, their children, the men, the Sanhedrin, the princes! And
> all the more so the supernal, faithful prophet Moses, who is
> higher than them all!
>
> And now, if these donkey drivers of the wilderness possess
> so much wisdom—all the more so the wise of this generation,
> and all the more so those who stand before Rabbi Shimon and
> learn from him every day, and all the more and all the more so
> Rabbi Shimon who is supreme above all!
>
> After Moses died, what is written? *The people will go
> astray* (Deut. 31:16). Woe to the world when Rabbi Shimon
> will depart, for the springs of wisdom will be sealed to the
> world, and a person will seek a word of wisdom and will not
> find anyone who can speak. And the whole world will err in
> Torah for there will not be found among them anyone to be
> aroused in wisdom.
>
> About that time it is written, *If all the community of Israel
> should err* (Lev. 4:13)—and if they err in Torah and do not
> know her way about some matter, *since the matter be hidden
> from the eyes of the assembly*, for they cannot find anyone who
> knows how to reveal the profundity of Torah and her ways.
> Woe to those generations who are present then in the world!

•••

This narrative is without doubt the most complex and developed composition examined in this book. Not only is the unit considerably longer than the other narratives examined so far, its thematic range and variation are also considerably greater. In many ways, this narrative is also a perfect zoharic narrative, if we can speak of such a thing. In the space of three folio pages (in the context of the *Zohar*, this is a mid-length composition), we are treated to a stunning display of zoharic literary artistry. This composition has it all, one might say—the wandering sages, mysterious bandits, traveling merchants, a nocturnal delight, as well as surprising, daring, and touching exegesis of biblical verses. The narrative is also a wonderful illustration of the poetic sensibility of the *Zohar*, its delight in wordplay and visual imagination. Although much of the *Zohar* is far from what we understand by the term *poetry*, zoharic narratives do most definitely have a strong poetic sense to them. To borrow Elliot Wolfson's incisive formulation about the Kabbalah, the stories that fill the pages of the *Zohar* display "a poetic orientation to being in the world,"[43] and much of the joy of reading the *Zohar*, and I would add, part of the mystical task, is to grasp this element of poetic play that so underwrites the *Zohar*'s world.

In our case this poetic orientation is most clearly revealed through the high level of integration between the narrative and exegetical registers of the composition. As we have seen, the narrative is far more than a literary flourish framing theosophical content. Narrative and exegesis are thoroughly intertwined, combining together in a masterful and imaginative way to create the symphony that is zoharic literary art. Narrative context generates exegesis—conventional midrashic and theosophic—which in turn flows back into more narrative only to generate yet more exegesis. Eitan Fishbane neatly captures this aspect of zoharic composition, noting that "a great part of the wonder of zoharic rhythm is this opening and closing of lenses—the advance and withdrawal of two separate modes of rhetoric."[44] A stream from the narrative appears in a homily as the river of divine plenty, while the morning light from a homily (symbolizing the divine grade *Yesod*) suddenly appears in the narrative as the brightening light of day. Classical rabbinic texts do indeed, on occasion, house exegesis in a narrative frame. The Talmud and midrashic literature contain many stories telling of the adventures and lives of the sages, and these stories frequently contain interpretations of Torah. Yet such a highly developed literary form with narrative and exegesis interacting in such a dynamic fashion would appear to be a zoharic innovation. Indeed, this literary dynamism, it might be suggested, is itself an expression of the religious and interpretative way of the *Zohar*. While the *Zohar* is certainly, in part, a theosophical midrash on the Torah, there seems little doubt that one of the composition's deepest desires, above and beyond the imparting of kabbalistic teachings, is the generation of mystical consciousness in its readers.[45] This performative aspect of the *Zohar* is apparent in the work's direct calls to its readers to awaken to a new consciousness, as well as, I would argue, through its modeling of mystical-exegetical consciousness through its literary form. Exegesis and narrative are so thoroughly interlaced not merely because the zoharic author found a convenient way in which to convey his kabbalistic doctrine, but rather, because this interplay reveals something fundamental about the kind of consciousness—the type of exegesis and the manner of being in this world—that the *Zohar* wishes to impart. Exegesis is connected to narrative because the "Torah of the way" must be fresh, new, and responsive. Zoharic narrative and zoharic mysticism are not static theology;[46] rather, the Torah of the way is alive, spontaneous, vital, and in a sense reminiscent of improvisatory writing. The Torah of the way is the Torah of the moment and the literary form itself an expression of the *Zohar*'s quest to arouse "a new and surprising encounter between the Torah and life, so as to discover how divinity resides in them both."[47]

Beyond the integration of narrative and exegesis, the special poetics of the composition are also manifest in the relationship between time and narrative, and time and exegesis. One of the distinguishing features of this text, as well as many others throughout the *Zohar*, is the way in which the time of the narrative overlays with divine time. As readers we are simultaneously drawn in to the real time of the human protagonists of the story (dusk, night, midnight, dawn, morning) that plays out against the background of divine time, marked by shifts and fluctuations in the state of the divine emanations. Temporal time is thus seamlessly juxtaposed with eternal time, and both the protagonists and the reader find themselves in the unique space where these two modalities intersect.[48] Indeed, the inscription of time into the narrative through quoting verses from the Bible as well as through evoking the varied phases of the zoharic myth of the nocturnal delight is one of the most original and noteworthy characteristics of this unit. There are of course numerous ways to convey the passage of time in narrative. The simplest method is through temporal markers—the moon shone, day broke, the companions sat the entire day and night—and the *Zohar* frequently employs such devices. More interesting, however, is the use of exegesis about the varied phases of the night and dawn to mark temporal shifts in the narrative. This intersection of narrative time and exegetical time serves an important performative function, dramatically drawing the reader into the multiple temporal landscapes of the composition, and like the intersection of narrative event and exegetical content is one of the *Zohar*'s key strategies for cultivating a special kind of mystical-temporal consciousness.

We have only scratched the surface of this wonderful narrative, and this narrative is but one of the dozens of discrete compositions that combine to form the *Zohar*. The *Zohar* is a literary marvel, perhaps the brightest jewel in the medieval Jewish literary crown. Not until Rabbi Nahman of Bratslav in the eighteenth century will Jewish narrative soar as high again. Fusing journey narrative with mystical exegesis, the *Zohar* achieves a literary dynamism unrivaled in the Jewish canon and rightly deserves a place alongside the masterpieces of world literature.

•◆•

CHAPTER TEN

The Palace of Love

Zohar 3:267a–b

You shall love YHVH your God with all your heart (Deut. 6:5).
You shall love—for a person must bind himself to Him in supernal love.
For all the service that a person must offer the Blessed Holy One he
must offer in love, for there is no worship like the love of the Blessed
Holy One.
Rabbi Abba said: These words are the essence of Torah, for the ten
commands of Torah are comprised here, and so have the Companions
established . . .

One day Rabbi Yose fell ill.
Rabbi Abba, Rabbi Yehudah, and Rabbi Yitzḥak went to see him and
they saw him lying on his face asleep.
They sat down.
When he awoke they saw that his face was smiling.
Rabbi Abba said to him: Have you seen some new thing?
He said to him: Certainly so. For just now my soul arose and saw the
glory of those who have sacrificed themselves for the sanctity of their
Master, how they were entering thirteen rivers of pure balsam, and the
Blessed Holy One was delighting in them.
And I have seen what they have not given me permission to tell.
I asked them and said: This glory, to whom does it belong?

They said to me: To those who loved their Master in that world.
My soul and my heart were illuminated with what I saw, and therefore
my face is smiling.

Rabbi Abba said to him: Happy is your portion!
But the Torah has already attested to them, as it is written, *No eye has
seen, O God, but You, He acts for those who trust Him* (Isa. 64:3).
Rabbi Yehudah said to him: Behold, the Companions have inquired
about this. It is written, *He acts*. It should have said: *You act*.
He said to him: This has been said. But the mystery of the matter is as it
is written, *to gaze upon the beauty of YHVH, to contemplate in His
temple* (Ps. 27:4).
And they have established, *the beauty of YHVH*—that which comes
from the Holy Ancient One, in which the Blessed Holy One delights, for
that *beauty* flows from the Ancient One.
To contemplate in His temple (heikhalo)—in the most supernal palace
(*heikhala*) of all.
So here, *No eye has seen, O God, but You, He acts for those who trust
Him*.
Who? The Ancient One, most concealed of all, for on Him does this
depend.
He said to him: Certainly it is so. Happy is the portion of those to
whom their Master's love cleaves! There is no measure of their portion
in that world!
Rabbi Yitzhak said: How many chambers upon chambers await the
righteous in that world?! And the most supernal chamber of all is for
those who are bound to the love of their Master, for their chamber is
linked to the most ascendant palace of all. Why so? Because through
this [i.e., love] the Blessed Holy One is crowned.

Come and see:
This palace is called love and everything abides because of love, as it is
written, *Great seas cannot quench love* (Song of Songs 8:7).
And all abides because of love, for behold, so it is with the Holy Name,
as they have established:
Yod—the upper point never separates from the *yod*, for it rests upon
him in love, never separating from him ever.
Hey—for behold they have established, the *yod* never separates from
her and they abide as one in love, never separating from one another
. . . as it is written, *A river flows from Eden* (Gen. 2:10), flowing continuously, forever cleaving in love.
Vav-Hey—when they cleave to one to another, they cleave in love, like

the groom in the bride, whose way is always in love.

Thus: *Yod* in *Hey*, *Hey* with *Vav*, *Vav* with *Hey*, bound to one another in love.

And all is called love, and therefore one who loves the King is bound in this love.

And therefore: *You shall love YHVH your God.*

Commentary on *Zohar* 3:267a–b

Does not everyone know that I based the world solely on love?
I have said: The world is built by love (Ps. 89:3).
It is love that sustains the world.

—*Zohar* 1:10b

As we have seen throughout this book the world of the *Zohar* is brimming with Eros. More than any other work in the Jewish canon before or since, the *Zohar* celebrates and delights in Eros in all its varied manifestations. One can scarcely read a page of *Zohar* without encountering one or another daring Eros-laden account of the divine life, human life, and the life of the Companionship. In fact, so central is Eros to the *Zohar* that one leading *Zohar* scholar has actually gone so far as to make the formal equation between the word *Zohar*, derived from the verse in Daniel (12:3), "The enlightened will shine like the radiance (*zohar*) of the sky," from which *The Book of Radiance* derives its name, with this classical Greek idea, most famously presented in Plato's *Symposium*.[1] Eros in the *Zohar* is the primal force, the motivating principle of the entirety of being, with human sexual relations, the bonds among the Companions, the Companions' relationship with the Torah, with God, and even the complex interactions within the divine realm itself, all manifestations of this overarching generative principle. Even human creativity pertains to this law of Eros/*Zohar*, as through their new and innovative expositions of Torah the Companions too seek to shine like the radiance of the cosmos.

> *The enlightened will shine like the radiance (zohar) of the sky*
> *and those who make the masses righteous will shine like the*
> *stars forever and ever (Dan. 12:3).*
> *The enlightened*—those who contemplate the mystery of wisdom.
> *Will shine*—who sparkle with the mystery of wisdom.
> *Will shine*—they radiate and sparkle with the splendor of supernal wisdom.
> *Like the radiance*—the streaming of the sparks of the river that flows from Eden.
> And this is the concealed mystery called *sky*—there are suspended the stars and planets, the sun and moon, and all the radiant lights.
>
> —*Zohar* 2:2a

The river that flows from Eden is without doubt the most central zoharic expression for the desire of divinity to pour forth and illuminate reality with its diverse qualities. Through this multivalent image (sometimes associated explicitly with *Yesod*, the divine phallus and conduit of the divine flow) the *Zohar* conveys the erotic yearning of divinity to fertilize the varied dimensions of being.[2] Divinity, or if one prefers, the cosmos as a whole, has a pulsating erotic heart and this heart beats through every element and fiber of being.[3]

The short passage at the beginning of this chapter, found in the *Zohar*'s commentary to the Torah portion *Ve-Ethanan*, which contains the famous injunction "You shall love YHVH your God with all your heart and with all your soul and with all your might" (Deut.6:5), provides a stunning illustration of zoharic Eros, as well as a fitting conclusion to our exploration of the kabbalistic masterpiece. As is clear from even a cursory reading, the passage is a meditation on love—love of God, God's love, love among the Companions as well as the love that dominates the divine life itself. In the beautiful formulation of our text, "everything abides because of love." As is the *Zohar*'s way, the passage combines exegesis with a short yet touching narrative, both of which take as their focus the love that must underwrite religious-spiritual life. One must bind oneself to God in supernal love and thereby attain the palace of love, enjoying the flow of divine beauty from *Atika*, the Holy Ancient One, the most primal aspect of divinity and ultimate source of divine love.

This love of God, it should be stressed, is also an act of *imitatio dei*. The divine being itself is love, ruled by the primal law of love, and in loving God one participates in the love which "is all." The injunction to love YHVH is here understood by the *Zohar* as much more than a simple directive to love God. The famous verse from Deuteronomy, whose recitation forms an essential component of the daily Jewish liturgy, actually encodes a great secret, and loving YHVH involves a participation in the same love that radiates through and binds the letters of the divine name. As we find repeatedly throughout the *Zohar*, the letters of the Tetragrammaton, YHVH, יהוה,[4] the explicit name of God, are actually symbols for the sefirot, and the very form of the Name an icon for the totality of the divine being. Like the sefirot whose complex relations are dominated by love, the letters of the divine name are also bound by this law of love:

He [Rabbi Shimon] said to him: El'azar, my son, from now on take care that you write the Holy Name as is fitting, for whoever does not know how to write the Holy Name as is fitting, and to tie the knot of faith, binding one with the other in order to unify the Holy Name, about him it is written, *Because he has despised the word of YHVH and has broken His commandments, that soul shall be utterly cut off* (Num. 15:31)—even if he omits only one rung or one knot from one of the letters.

Come and see:

Yod at the beginning is the sum of all, concealed on all sides, the paths are not open, the sum of male and female, the upper point of the *yod* indicating *ayin*, nothingness.

After this, *yod* brings out the river that flows forth and emerges from it, to become pregnant by it—*hey*.

Of this it is written, *A river flows from Eden* (Gen. 2:10). It says, *flows*, not *flowed* . . .

Yod produces in front of itself the river and two children,[5] whom the mother suckles, for she conceived them and bore them.

After we have *hey* like this: *hey* together with the children that are below the father and the mother.

After she had borne she produced a son and placed him in front of her, and so it is necessary to write *vav*.

This [son] inherits the patrimony of the father and the mother . . . and from him the daughter is nourished, and so it is necessary to write after this *vav-hey* together.

Just as the first *hey* is written *yod-hey* together without disjunction, so also *vav-hey* together without disjunction.

—*Zohar* 3:65b (Tishby and Goldstein, modified,
see also *Zohar* 2:126b–127a)

From the uppermost point of the *yod*, as the white of the page and the black ink first meet at an infinitesimal space, where nothingness/*Keter* and being/*Ḥokhmah* intersect, to *hey*, the primal mother/*Binah* (in Hebrew *hey* is a marker of the feminine), on to *vav*, whose numerical value is six thereby signifying the six sons (often treated as one), the torso of the sefirot, *Tiferet*, and finally on to the lower *hey*, *Malkhut*, the divine name YHVH marks the fullness of divine being from infinity to the very edge of the divine world. Importantly, the letters themselves are bound to one another in love with love functioning like the strong nuclear force, holding the letters, the sefirot and the different domains of being together. In short, love is the central force of the cosmos and when we love YHVH as YHVH loves, as the letters love one another, we are bound in the love that abides within YHVH. The zoharic formulation here comes close to the celebrated expression in 1 John 4:16—"God is love, and he who abides in love abides in God, and God abides in him." *Deus caritas est. Dayka!* precisely, the *Zohar* would say, as the letters themselves participate in the same love that pervades all.

While Jewish readers might be surprised to find this love-God equation, another well-known passage in the *Zohar* does exactly this. Returning once again to the opening declaration by the beloved in the Song of Songs, "Let him kiss me with kisses of the mouth," the *Zohar* finds another four-lettered name hiding, as it were, behind the Tetragrammaton.

> *Let him kiss me with kisses of the mouth* (Song of Songs 1:2).
>
> What did Solomon mean by introducing words of love between the upper and lower world, and by beginning the praise of love . . . with *let him kiss me?*
>
> They have already given an explanation for this. It is that the inseparable love of spirit for spirit can only be by a kiss, and a kiss is with the mouth, for that is the source and outlet of the spirit. And when they kiss one another, the spirits cling to one another, and they are one and then love is one.
>
> In the Book of the Ancient Rav Hamnuna Sava, he says on this verse:
>
> The kiss of love extends into four spirits[6] and the four spirits cling together and they are within the mystery of faith, and they ascend by four letters, and these are the letters upon which the Holy Name depends, and upon which the upper and lower realms depend, and upon which the praise in the Song of Songs depends.
>
> And which are they?
>
> *Alef, hey, bet, hey* אהבה, *(Love).* They are the supernal chariot, and they are the companionship, unison and wholeness of all . . .
>
> There are four spirits in the kiss and each one of them is comprised within its companion . . . and when they spread abroad a single fruit is made from these four spirits, one spirit comprised of four spirits, and this ascends and splits firmaments until it ascends and dwells by a palace called "the palace of love," a palace upon which all love depends . . .
>
> —*Zohar* 2:146a–b (Tishby and Goldstein;
> see also *Zohar Hadash* 60c, 61d–62a)

In its own unique way, the *Zohar* here expresses what mystics of all persuasions know. *Begin ahavah kayma kula*—on account of love all abides.

.⸭.

There can be no thought of really concluding a book on the *Zohar*. No statement, no chapter, no passage can convey the depth and breadth of the zoharic world. Indeed, the *Zohar* itself has no beginning and no end, and the zoharic journey, like the Companions' many travels, is ongoing. The *Zohar* shines with a brilliance unrivaled in the Jewish tradition and those who would take the time to explore its wondrous, enigmatic, and playful world will no doubt encounter moments of illumination, awakening, and discovery. "Happy is their portion!" the *Zohar* might say. But there is no final destination. While reading the *Zohar* can bring about a transformation in the consciousness of its readers, and can enable a more expansive comprehension of divinity and ourselves, mystical insight, the *Zohar* tells us, is elusive and transient. We remain as we were, yet somehow different, having tasted of an enchanting world that knows no peer. Perhaps we should not expect any more.

The *Zohar* is an invitation, a call to open oneself to the life of the world:

> Come and see:
> There is opening within opening, and level within level.
> Through these the Glory of the Blessed Holy One becomes known . . .
> *Open for me the gates of righteousness, this is the gate to YHVH* (Ps. 118:19)
> —*Zohar* 1:103b

May we be opened to the *Zohar* and through the *Zohar* to the Ancient One who illumines all!

Appendix

The Sefirot and Their Symbols

Ein Sof: "infinity," the concealed of concealed

Keter: "crown," nothingness, will/desire, *Atika Kaddisha*/Holy Ancient One, Ancient of Days

Ḥokhmah: "wisdom," point, beginning, thought, *yesh*/being, Eden, the letter *yod*, father

Binah: "understanding," womb, palace, *teshuvah*/return, river, the world that is coming, the letter *hey*, mother

Ḥesed: "love," Abraham, right arm

Din: "judgment," Isaac, left arm

Tiferet: "beauty," the Blessed Holy One, Jacob, voice, sun, day, son, heaven, YHVH, the letter *vav*

Nezaḥ: "eternity," right leg, prophecy

Hod: "majesty," left leg, prophecy

Yesod: "foundation," phallus—covenant, Joseph, righteous one

Malkhut: "kingdom," *Shekhinah*, the Assembly of Israel, David, rose, hind, daughter, speech, earth, moon, night, time, righteousness, the letter *hey*

Notes

Chapter 1. The Way of the *Zohar*

1. On this important passage, see Elliot R. Wolfson, *Through a Speculum That Shines: Vision and Imagination in Medieval Jewish Mysticism* (Princeton: Princeton University Press, 1994), 327–328, and Daniel Boyarin, *Intertextuality and the Reading of Midrash* (Bloomington: Indiana University Press, 1990), 110, 118–122.
2. Wolfson, *Through a Speculum That Shines*, 328–329.
3. On the authorship of the *Zohar*, see Gershom Scholem, *Major Trends in Jewish Mysticism* (New York: Schocken Books, 1946), 156–204; Isaiah Tishby, *The Wisdom of the Zohar,* trans. David Goldstein (London: The Littman Library of Jewish Civilization, 1989), vol. 1:1–128; Yehuda Liebes, "How the Zohar was Written" in *Studies in the Zohar,* trans. Arnold Schwartz, Stephanie Nakache, and Penina Peli (Albany: State University of New York Press, 1993), 85–138; Ronit Meroz, "Zoharic Narratives and Their Adaptations," *Hispania Judaica Bulletin* 3 (2001): 3–63.
4. Yehuda Liebes, "The Zohar as Renaissance," *Daat* 46 (2001): 5–11 [Hebrew].
5. For a classical overview of the origins of the Kabbalah, see Gershom Scholem, *Origins of the Kabbalah*, ed. R. J. Zwi Werblowsky, trans. Allan Arkush (Philadelphia: The Jewish Publication Society, 1987). See also Joseph Dan, "Introduction" in *The Early Kabbalah* (New York: Paulist Press, 1986), 31–42, for a concise discussion of the kabbalistic circles in Provence, Gerona, and Castile prior to the *Zohar*.
6. See Bernard McGinn, "The God beyond God: Theology and Mysticism in the Thought of Meister Eckhart," *Journal of Religion* 61 (1981): 1–19.

7. For a helpful introduction to the sefirot, see David S. Ariel, "The Calculus of the Divine World: The Teaching of the Sefirot" in *The Mystic Quest: An Introduction to Jewish Mysticism* (Northvale: Jason Aronson, 1988), 65–88. See also Moshe Hallamish, "The Doctrine of the Sefirot" in *An Introduction to the Kabbalah*, trans. Ruth Bar Ilan and Ora Wiskind-Elper (Albany: State University of New York Press, 1999), 121–166.

8. Moshe Idel, *Kabbalah: New Perspectives* (New Haven: Yale University Press, 1988), 222–223.

9. See Melila Hellner-Eshed, *A River Issues From Eden: On the Language of Mystical Experience in the Zohar* (Tel Aviv: Am Oved, 2005), 138–148 [Hebrew].

10. "Yehoshuah the son of Levi said: One who walks on the way without accompaniment should engage in Torah" (BT *Eruvin* 54a).

    "Rabbi Ilai the son of Berehaya said: Two students of the wise who are walking on the way with no words of Torah between them deserve to be burned" (BT *Taanit* 10b; see also *Pirke Avot* 3:2, 3:7).

11. Hellner-Eshed, *A River Issues From Eden*, 146–148.

12. Moses Maimonides, *Mishneh Torah, Hilkhot Yesodei ha-Torah* 1:3.

13. Moses Maimonides, *The Guide of the Perplexed*, trans. Shlomo Pines (Chicago: University of Chicago Press, 1963), vol 1:16. On this verse see BT *Berakhot* 54a, 63a; PT *Berakhot* 9:3, 14d. See also *Zohar* 1:116b, 3:62b.

14. See Idel, *Kabbalah:New Perspectives*, 158–159 on this passage.

15. See also *Avot* 5:6: "Ten things were created on Sabbath eve at twilight . . . And some say: Also the demons." See Daniel C. Matt, trans., *The Zohar: Pritzker Edition* (Stanford: Stanford University Press, 2004), 1:47b–48a and notes.

16. On the *Zohar* see especially, Daniel C. Matt, *Zohar: The Book of Enlightenment* (New York: Paulist Press, 1983) and Aryeh Wineman, *Mystic Tales from the Zohar* (Princeton: Princeton University Press, 1998). See also Arthur Green, *A Guide to the Zohar* (Stanford: Stanford University Press, 2004). On the Kabbalah more generally, see David S. Ariel, *The Mystic Quest: An Introduction to Jewish Mysticism* (Northvale: Jason Aronson, 1988); Moshe Hallamish, *An Introduction to the Kabbalah*, trans. Ruth Bar Ilan and Ora Wiskind-Elper (Albany: State University of New York Press, 1999); Byron L. Sherwin, *Kabbalah: An Introduction to Jewish Mysticism* (Lanham: Rowman and Littlefield Publishers, 2006). Arthur Green's popular yet profound works *Seek My Face, Speak My Name: A Contemporary Jewish Theology* (Northvale: Jason Aronson, 1992) and *Ehyeh: A Kabbalah for Tomorrow* (Wood-

stock: Jewish Lights Publishing, 2003) also deserve special mention. Melila Hellner-Eshed's *A River Flows From Eden: On the Language of Mystical Experience in the Zohar*, trans. Nathan Wolski (Stanford: Stanford University Press, 2009), now available in English, will no doubt be welcomed by students of Jewish mysticism.

17. For a more detailed discussion of these themes, see Nathan Wolski, "Mystical Poetics: Narrative, Time and Exegesis in the Zohar," *Prooftexts* 28 (2008): 101–128.

18. Friedrich Nietzsche, "On the Genealogy of Morals" in *Basic Writings of Nietzsche*, ed. and trans. Walter Kaufmann (New York: Modern Library, 1968), 451.

19. Abraham Joshua Heschel, *God in Search of Man: A Philosophy of Judaism* (New York: Farrar, Straus and Giroux, 1976), 45.

20. For an insightful discussion of this phenomenon, see Boaz Huss, "The New Age of Kabbalah: Contemporary Kabbalah, the New Age and Postmodern Spirituality," *Journal of Modern Jewish Studies* 6 (2007): 107–125.

21. Miguel de Cervantes, *Don Quixote*, trans. John Rutherford (London: Penguin Books, 2000), part 2, chapter LXII, 915. See Nathan Wolski, "Don Quixote and Sancho Panza were walking on the way: El Caballero Andante and the Book of Radiance," *Shofar: An Interdisciplinary Journal of Jewish Studies* 27 (2009): 24–47.

22. Daniel C. Matt, trans., *The Zohar: Pritzker Edition*, vols. 1–4 (Stanford: Stanford University Press, 2004, 2004, 2006, 2007).

23. *Shivhei ha-Besht*, ed. Benjamin Mintz (Tel Aviv: Talpiot, 1961), 61 [Hebrew].

Chapter 2. In the Mountains of Kurdistan

1. On this wonderful zoharic composition, see Nathan Wolski and Merav Carmeli, "Those Who Know Have Wings: Celestial Journeys with the Masters of the Academy," *Kabbalah: Journal for the Study of Jewish Mystical Texts* 16 (2007): 83–114.

2. "Rabbi Oshaya opened: *I was with Him as a confidant (amon), a source of delight every day* (Prov. 8:30). *Amon* means tutor; *Amon* means covered; *Amon* means hidden; and some say *Amon* means great . . .

   Another interpretation: *Amon* is an artisan *(uman)*.

   The Torah declares: I was the working tool of the Blessed Holy One.

   In human practice, when a mortal king builds a palace, he

builds it not with his own skill, but with the skill of an architect. The architect moreover does not build it out of his head, but employs plans and diagrams to know how to arrange the chambers and the wicket doors. Thus God consulted the Torah and created the world, while the Torah declared:

> In the beginning God created (Gen. 1:1). Beginning—referring to the Torah, as in the verse, The Lord made me at the beginning of His way (Prov. 8:22)" (Genesis Rabbah 1:1, Soncino modified).

3. The mountains of Kurdistan·appear again in Zohar 1:62a, 63a.

4. See BT Berakhot 43b: "To one person [a demon] shows himself and causes harm; to two he shows himself but does not cause harm; to three, he does not show himself"; Avot 3:6: "Rabbi Halafta of Kefar Hananyah said: When ten sit and occupy themselves with Torah the Shekhinah rests among them . . . even to three . . . " See also Zohar 1:229b, 230a–b for a similar narrative structure to this passage.

5. From the thirteen hermeneutical principles of Rabbi Ishmael found in the introduction to the Sifra.

6. The idea that the Torah is the name of God is famously presented by Nahmanides in his introduction to his commentary on the Torah: "We possess an authentic tradition that the entire Torah consists of the names of God and that the words we read can be divided in a very different way, so as to form [esoteric] names . . . The statement in the Aggadah to the effect that the Torah was originally written with black fire on white fire obviously confirms our opinion that the writing was continuous, without division into words, which made it possible to read it either as a sequence of [esoteric] names or in the traditional way as history and commandments. Thus the Torah as given to Moses was divided into words in such a way as to be read as divine commandments. But at the same time he received the oral tradition, according to which it was to be read as a sequence of names." Nahmanides, Commentary on the Torah. The translation is from Gershom Scholem, "The Meaning of the Torah in Jewish Mysticism" in On the Kabbalah and Its Symbolism, trans. Ralph Manheim (New York: Schocken Books, 1965), 38.

7. Translation from Matt, Book of Enlightenment. Figuring the student's relationship with the Torah as erotic is not a kabbalistic innovation. The sages of the Talmud also understood the Torah in similar terms. See, for example, Tosefta Yevamot 8:7; BT Eruvin 54b. For a masterful discussion, see Daniel Boyarin, "Lusting after Learning" in Carnal Israel: Reading Sex in Talmudic Culture

(Berkeley: University of California Press, 1993), 134–166. On *Sabba de-Mishpatim*, see Scholem, "The Meaning of the Torah"; Elliot R. Wolfson, "Beautiful Maiden Without Eyes: *Peshat* and *Sod* in Zoharic Hermeneutics" in *The Midrashic Imagination: Jewish Exegesis, Thought and History*, ed. Michael Fishbane (Albany: State University of New York Press, 1993), 155–203; Oded Yisraeli, *The Interpretation of Secrets and the Secret of Interpretation: Midrashic and Hermeneutic Strategies in Sabba de-Mishpatim of the Zohar* (Los Angeles: Cherub Press, 2005) [Hebrew]; Hellner-Eshed, *A River Issues From Eden*, 187–197 [Hebrew]; Yehuda Liebes, "Zohar and Eros," *Alpayim* 9 (1994): 67–119 [Hebrew]; Pinchas Giller, *Reading the Zohar: The Sacred Text of the Kabbalah* (New York: Oxford University Press, 2001), 35–68.

8. See *Zohar* 2:98b; see also Hellner-Eshed, *A River Issues From Eden*, 264–267 [Hebrew].

9. Azriel, *Perush Aggadoth*, 37, cited in Scholem, "The Meaning of the Torah," 45.

10. Joseph Gikatilla, *Gates of Light*, trans. Avi Weinstein (London: Altamira Press, 1994), 221.

11. Ibid., 6.

12. Scholem, "The Meaning of the Torah," 42.

13. The shofar blasts that are performed on Rosh Hashanah and Yom Kippur.

14. The commandment to blow the shofar requires that the one blowing *know* the mystery of shofar and its impact on the divine realm. The *Zohar* commentary to the Torah portion *Teztaveh* expounds the mysteries of the shofar and Rosh Hashanah more fully. See also *Zohar* 3:258b for another interpretation of the verse from Genesis about the resting of the ark on the seventeenth day of the seventh month.

15. Glowing marshals renders *tufsirin*, a zoharic neologism derived from Jeremiah 51:27 *tifsar*, where it means official, marshal, or scribe. It may also be connected with *tifsa*, meaning ember or coal in the *Zohar*. See Matt, *The Zohar* 2:30b and notes.

16. Although postdating the *Zohar*, the well-known Cave of Montesinos scene in Don Quixote is perhaps the most famous example.

17. The Near Eastern antecedents of the biblical Menorah are complex and fascinating. See Carol L. Meyers, *The Tabernacle Menorah: A Synthetic Study of a Symbol from the Biblical Cult* (Missoula: Scholars Press, 1976) for an overview. Of particular interest is the suggestion connecting the Menorah, the sacred (almond) tree, and the goddess Asherah, the chief consort of El and sometimes Baal.

(The Greek/Latin name for the almond tree, *amygdale*, derives from the Hebrew *em gedolah*, great mother.) See J. E. Taylor, "The Asherah, the Menorah and the Sacred Tree," *JSOT* 66 (1995): 29–54. Where the Torah furnishes no information about the symbolic meaning of the lamp stand, in Zechariah 4 the Menorah appears as the focal point of the divine presence and as a symbol for God Himself: "These seven (lamps) are the eyes of the Lord, which range through the whole earth." In interpreting the Menorah as reflecting the structure of the lower seven sefirot from *Binah*, the great mother, to *Malkhut*, the last of the sefirot, the *Zohar* thus remythologizes the lamp stand and, as happens frequently throughout the *Zohar*, mythological themes ignored, suppressed, or simply forgotten in the biblical and rabbinic corpus reemerge.

18. The *Zohar*'s treatment of *Tikkun Leil Shavuot*, the special all-night learning vigil that precedes and facilitates the sacred union between *Tiferet* and *Malkhut*, the Groom and the Bride, is perhaps the most well-known example of this motif: "All those Companions initiated into the bridal palace need—on that night when the Bride is destined the next day to be under the canopy with Her Husband—to be with Her all night, delighting with Her in Her adornments in which She is arrayed . . . She enters, escorted by Her maidens . . . The next day She enters the canopy only with them, and they are called members of the canopy." *Zohar* 1:8a (Matt, *The Zohar*).

19. "Come and see: What is the difference between Moses and Aaron? Which of them is superior? Moses is superior. Moses is the attendant of the king; Aaron is the attendant of the *Matronita*.

   A parable: Like a king who had a great queen. What did he do? He gave her a *shushbin* (attendant) to adorn her and to look after the affairs of her house. Therefore, when the attendant comes to the king, he only comes with the queen, as it is written, *With this (zot = Malkut) shall Aaron enter the shrine* (Lev. 16:3)" (*Zohar* 3:53b). See also 2:49b, 3:177a.

20. Judah Goldin, trans., *The Fathers According to Rabbi Nathan* (New Haven: Yale University Press, 1955), 33.

21. On incense in the *Zohar* see *Zohar* 3:11a; 2:218b–219b. The *Zohar* connects the Hebrew word for incense, *ketoret*, with the Aramaic *itkater*, to bind, link, unite: "Come and see: Incense binds bonds, spreading joy from above to below" (1:230a, Matt, *The Zohar*). The Torah combines the offering of incense with the lighting of the Menorah and both are understood by the *Zohar* as affecting unity in the divine realm. Immediately preceding our narrative we find the following succinct statement:

"Come and see: When the priest focuses to light the lamps below and offers the aromatic incense, at that time, the supernal lights illuminate, and all is bound (*itkater*) as one, and joy and delight abide in all the worlds, as is written, *Oil and incense rejoice the heart* (Prov. 27:9), and therefore it is written, *be-ha'alotekha, when you elevate the lamps* (Num. 8:2)" (*Zohar* 3:149a). See also *Zohar* 1:230a.

22. See Rashi and Ibn Ezra ad loc. See BT *Yoma* 15a.

23. See Joel Hecker, *Mystical Bodies, Mystical Meals: Eating and Embodiment in Medieval Kabbalah* (Detroit: Wayne State University Press, 2005), 78–79, on this verse in Moses de Leon's *Sefer ha-Rimmon*. See also *Zohar* 2:153b.

24. On this verse from Proverbs, see *Zohar* 1:192b; 2:197a–b, 259b.

25. See Maimonides, *Mishneh Torah, Hilkhot Tmidin* 3:12—*hatavatam* = *hadlakatam*, dressing = lighting.

26. The equation between good (*tov*) and lit has been commented on by numerous scholars. This interpretation seems to originate with Rabbi Isaac the Blind, one of the first kabbalists:

    "*And God saw the light that it was good (tov)*. This is derived from *when he tends the lamps* (Exod. 30:7). The matter is ignited as if one lights a candle one from the other. Therefore He grants a power to the essences to expand and draw forth." From Rabbi Isaac the Blind, "The Process of Emanation" in *The Early Kabbalah*, ed. Joseph Dan, trans. Ronald C Kiener (New York: Paulist Press, 1986), 81. Rabbi Isaac reads the verse as though it says, "He saw the light that was lit." Apparently this is derived from a no longer extant Aramaic translation of Exodus 30:7, where *heitivo* is rendered as *be-adlakutei*. See also Ezra of Gerona, *Perush Shir ha-Shirim*, 485. See Scholem, *Origins of the Kabbalah*, 292, note 186; see also Elliot Wolfson's gloss in Moses de Leon, *Sefer ha-Rimmon* (Atlanta: Scholars Press, 1988), 196. See *Zohar* 1:230a and Matt note 428. *Zohar* 1:16b conveys a similar idea: "*God saw that the light was good . . . Good*, illumining above and below and all other directions . . . "

27. Cf. BT *Baba Batra* 145b: "*A good-hearted person / contentment (tov-lev) is a continuous feast*—this refers to the one who has a good wife."

Chapter 3. In the Image of God

1. "*Ayeh makom kevodo* / where is the place of His glory?"—from the *Mussaf Kedushah*.

2. See *Tosefta Yevamot* 8:7; see also Moshe Greenberg, "Some Postu-
   lates of Biblical Criminal Law" in *Studies in the Bible and Jewish
   Thought* (Philadelphia: The Jewish Publication Society, 1995),
   25–42. For a comprehensive discussion of this central concept, see
   Yair Loberbaum, *Image of God: Halacha and Agada* (Tel Aviv:
   Schocken Books, 2004) [Hebrew].
3. *The Guide of the Perplexed* 1:2, trans. Shlomo Pines, 24–26.
4. See Moshe Idel, *Kabbalah: New Perspectives*, 112–122; Moshe
   Hallamish, *An Introduction to the Kabbalah*, 141–142.
5. Yehudah Halevi, *The Kuzari: An Argument for the Faith of Israel*,
   trans. Hartwig Hirschfeld, revised ed. (Jerusalem: Sefer ve-Sefel
   Publishing, 2003).
6. See Joseph Dan, ed., *The Early Kabbalah*, 89–96.
7. On the dialogical structure of mystical experience in the *Zohar*, see
   Hellner-Eshed, *A River Issues From Eden*, 133–137 [Hebrew].
8. Rabbi Moses Cordovero, *Or Yakar*, vol. 14, *Shlah*, 28.
9. See *Genesis Rabbah* 8:2: "Rabbi Ḥama the son of Rabbi Ḥanina
   opened: *Do you not know this, from time immemorial, since man
   was set on the earth* (Job 20:4).

   Rabbi Ḥama the son of Rabbi Ḥanina said: This may be compared to a country which received its supplies from donkey drivers
   who used to ask one another: What was the market price today?
   Thus those who supplied on the sixth day would ask those who
   supplied on the fifth day; the fifth of the fourth, the fourth of the
   third, the third of the second, the second of the first; but of whom
   was the first day supplier to ask? Surely of the citizens who were
   engaged in the public affairs of the country.

   Thus the works of each day asked one another: Which creatures did the Blessed Holy One create among you today? The sixth
   asked of the fifth, the fifth of the fourth, the fourth of the third, the
   third of the second, and the second of the first. Of what was the
   first to ask? Surely of the Torah which preceded the creation of the
   world by two thousand years, as it is written, *I was with Him as a
   confidant, a source of delight every day* (Prov. 8:30); now the day
   of the Lord is a thousand years, as it is said, *For in Your sight a
   thousand years are like yesterday that has passed* (Ps. 90:4).

   That is the meaning of *Do you not know this, from time immemorial, since man was set on the earth*. The Torah knows what was
   before the creation of the world, but you have no business to
   inquire apart from *since man was set on the earth*.

   Rabbi El'azar said in the name of Ben Sirah: About what is too
   great for you do not inquire; what is too hard for you do not inves-

tigate; what is too wonderful for you know not; of what is hidden from you do not ask; contemplate what was permitted to you: you have no business with hidden things" (Soncino trans.).

10. See Ephraim E. Urbach, *The Sages: Their Concepts and Beliefs*, trans. Israel Abrahams (Cambridge: Harvard University Press, 1975), 420–436.

11. Translation based on Urbach, *The Sages*, trans. Israel Abrahams, 278–279.

12. See also BT *Berakhot* 10a: "What have you to do with the secrets of the Merciful One? You should have done what you were commanded and let the Blessed Holy One do that which he pleases." See also *Mishnah Ḥagiga* 2:1: "Whoever speculates about four things, it would have been better for him if he had not come into the world: what is beyond [the heavenly realm], what is beyond [the earthly realm], what was before [creation] and what will come afterward. Whoever is not sensitive to the honor of his Creator, it would have been better for him if he had not come into this world."

13. Rabbi Moses Cordovero, *Or Yakar*, vol. 14, *Shlaḥ*, 29.

14. See Ramban, *Introduction to Torah Commentary*; see chapter 2 in this volume, note 6.

15. See Hellner-Eshed, *A River Issues From Eden*, 187–221 [Hebrew]. See also Yehuda Liebes, "The Messiah of the Zohar" in *Studies in the Zohar*, 26–31. See also Moshe Halbertal, *By Way of Truth: Nahmanides and the Creation of Tradition* (Jerusalem: Shalom Hartman Institute, 2006), 297–333.

16. "Come and see: Later generations are destined to arise when the Torah will be forgotten among their children, and the wise of heart will assemble in their places and there will be none to close and open. Woe to that generation! From here on, there will not be a generation like this one until King Messiah comes, and knowledge will be aroused in the world, as it is written, *for all of them, from the least of them to the greatest shall know me* (Jer. 31:34)" (*Zohar* 3:58a, *Idra Rabba*).

"Rabbi Shimon wept and said [to the Companions]: I know for certain that the supernal holy-spirit sparkles among you. Happy is this generation, for behold there will not be another generation like this one until King Messiah comes, for behold the Torah is returning to its antiquity [alt., ancient completeness]!" (*Zohar* 2:147a).

See Liebes, "The Messiah of the Zohar," 31–34, and Hellner-Eshed, *A River Issues From Eden*, 124–131, on the special characteristics of Rabbi Shimon's generation.

17. See *Guide of the Perplexed* 1:56, 58.

18. *Zohar* 1:2a. Idolatry in the *Zohar* is the forgetting of the mystery and the worship of the known only, the *Eleh*, these. This is the secret of the verse uttered by Aaron in the episode of the Golden Calf: "These are your gods, O, Israel" (Exod. 32:8).

19. See Tishby, *The Wisdom of the Zohar* 2:556–557.

20. See also *Zohar* 1:103a and *Sefer ha-Bahir* 131 for similar interpretations based on the *Mussaf Kedushah*.

21. Ḥayyim Yosef David Azulai (the Hida) in his commentary *Nitsotsei Orot* writes of *alma de-peruda* that "this refers to sleep when man's soul ascends and he is present and not present, i.e., his body is present but not his soul."

22. On the earthly Garden of Eden, see Tishby, *The Wisdom of the Zohar* 2:751.

23. Plotinus, *The Enneads*, iv. 8.8; trans. Stephen MacKenna (London: Penguin Books, 1991), 342. Cf. Tishby, *The Wisdom of the Zohar* 2:751–752.

24. The human soul is the offspring of the union of the Blessed Holy One and *Malkhut*. This is the secret of "You are children of YHVH, your God"—children of YHVH, the Blessed Holy One and your God, *Elohekha*, *Malkhut*.

25. *Matronita* = Great Lady, *Malkhut*, the female aspect of divinity.

26. See Moses de Leon, *Sefer ha-Rimmon*, 299. See also Tishby, *The Wisdom of the Zohar* 2:752–754.

27. For a clear and groundbreaking discussion of Nahmanides' views, see Halbertal, *By Way of Truth: Nahmanides and the Creation of Tradition*, 117–148 [Hebrew].

28. "Come and see: Until Adam sinned, he ascended and abode in supernal, radiant wisdom, never parting from the Tree of Life" (*Zohar* 1:52b, Matt, *The Zohar*).

    "Come and see: When Adam sinned by eating from the tree, he transmogrified that tree into a universal source of death; he caused a defect, separating the Woman from Her Husband" (*Zohar* 1:53a, Matt, *The Zohar*).

    "Come and see the secret of the word: Adam was caught in his own sin, inflicting death upon himself and the whole world, causing that tree with which he sinned to be divorced, driven away with him, driven away with his children forever, as it is written, *He drove out (et) Adam* (Gen. 3:24)" (*Zohar* 1:237a, Matt, *The Zohar*).

29. On the *Zohar*'s theory of the tripartite soul, see Tishby, *The Wisdom of the Zohar* 2:684–692; see also Hallamish, *An Introduction to the Kabbalah*, 247–266.

30. Translation based on Gershom Scholem, *Zohar: The Book of Splendor* (New York: Schocken Books, 1949), 69–71.
31. Moses de Leon, *Sefer ha-Nefesh ha-Ḥakhamah* 2, sig. 3, fol. 4a. Cited in Tishby, *The Wisdom of the Zohar* 2:680. See also Scholem, *Major Trends in Jewish Mysticism*, 241.
32. Rabbi Moses Cordovero, *Or Yakar*, vol. 14, *Shlaḥ*, 30.

Chapter 4. The Magical Book in the Cave of Souls

1. *Pirke Avot* 3:1.
2. Theodotus, cited in Clemens Alexandrinus, *Excerpta ex Theodoto*, 78.2. Translation from Hans Jonas, *The Gnostic Religion* (Boston: Beacon Press, 2001 [1958]), 45. See also Elaine Pagels, *The Gnostic Gospels* (New York: Vintage Books, 1989), xix.
3. See Jonas, *The Gnostic Religion*, 48–99; Pagels, *The Gnostic Gospels*, 119–141.
4. See Scholem, *The Origins of the Kabbalah*, 49–198. On the connections between Gnosticism and the theosophical Kabbalah, see Idel, *Kabbalah: New Perspectives*, especially 112–127.
5. Rabbi Yehudah from Akko might be an allusion to Rabbi Yitzḥak of Akko, a well-known kabbalist from the late thirteenth and early fourteenth centuries. As is well known, R. Yitzḥak of Akko played an important role in the "discovery" of the *Zohar*'s authorship. See Matt, *Zohar: The Book of Enlightenment*, 3–4; see also Tishby, *The Wisdom of the Zohar* 1:13–17.
6. On the mysterious books encountered by the Companions on their journeys, see Hellner-Eshed, *A River Issues From Eden*, 426–427 [Hebrew]; see also Boaz Huss, "The Appearance of *Sefer ha-Zohar*," *Tarbiz* 70 (2001): 507–542, especially 516–523 [Hebrew].
7. See *Exodus Rabbah* 15:21 where the verse is interpreted in the context of the future to come and the new light awaiting humanity. Presumably the author of our passage was aware of this interpretation as he constructed his own eschatological interpretation of the verse.
8. The Hebrew word for hell.
9. Cf. *Masekhet Gehinnom*, BhM 1:147–149: "'The leech has two daughters: Give, Give (Hav, Hav)' (Proverbs 30:15), a verse R. Eliezer took to mean that two companies of angels stand at the gate of *Gehinnom* and say, Give, give [the wicked to me]." See also BT *Avoda Zara* 17a.
10. Cf. *Sefer ha-Bahir* 184.

11. See Urbach, *The Sages: Their Concepts and Beliefs*, 236–237, 242, 245, 247 for a detailed overview.
12. Translation based on Urbach, *The Sages*, trans. Israel Abrahams, 245–247.
13. For a concise discussion of these themes in the thought of Plotinus, see Pierre Hadot, *Plotinus or The Simplicity of Vision*, trans. Michael Chase (Chicago: University of Chicago Press, 1993), 23–34.
14. Translation is from Scholem, *Zohar: The Book of Splendor*, 64–67, slightly modified.
15. Cf. "The Hymn of the Pearl" in Jonas, *The Gnostic Religion*, 113–116.
16. Franz Kafka, another great Jewish Gnostic spirit, expressed this uneasy dualism as follows: "He is a free and secure citizen of this earth, for he is attached to a chain that is long enough to make all areas of the earth accessible to him, and yet only so long that nothing can pull him over the edges of the earth. At the same time, however, he is also a free and secure citizen of heaven, for he is also attached to a similarly calculated heavenly chain. Thus, if he wants to get down to earth, he is choked by the heavenly collar and chain; if he wants to get into heaven, he is choked by the earthly one. And in spite of this he has all the possibilities, and feels that it is so; indeed, he even refuses to attribute the whole thing to a mistake in the original chaining." From Franz Kafka, *The Blue Octavo Notebooks*, ed. Max Brod, trans. Ernst Kaiser and Eithne Wilkins (Cambridge: Exact Change, 1991), 32.
17. Plotinus, *The Enneads*, iv. 8.1; trans. Stephen MacKenna, 335.
18. Ibid. vi. 4, 14, 16–31. Translation is from Hadot, *Plotinus or The Simplicity of Vision*, 28.
19. Blaise Pascal, *Pensees*. No. 553 (London: Penguin Books, 1966); see Hadot, *Plotinus or The Simplicity of Vision*, 46–47.
20. BT *Niddah* 30b: "[During the period of gestation] light burns above its head, and it gazes and is able to see from one end of the world to the other. There is no time during which man abides in greater happiness than during those days. At that time he is taught the entire Torah, all of it. But as he comes into the air of the world, an angel appears, strikes him on the mouth, and makes him forget the entire Torah. The foetus does not leave the womb until it is made to swear an oath. What is the oath it is made to swear? 'Be righteous, be not wicked; even if the entire world, all of it tells you, 'You are righteous,' consider yourself wicked. Always bear in mind that the Holy One is pure and His ministers pure, and that the soul I placed in

you is pure; if you preserve it in purity, well and good; but if not I will take it from you'" (Soncino trans.).

21. Plotinus, *The Enneads*, iv. 8.5, 340.

22. Moses de Leon, *Sefer ha-Mishkal*. Translation from Daniel C. Matt, *The Essential Kabbalah: The Heart of Jewish Mysticism* (San Francisco: Harper, 1995), 148. See also Saadia, *Emunot ve-Deot* 4:4.

23. Elsewhere, the *Zohar* explains the drama of the soul's descent in terms of the perfection of the divine. Souls descend because it is through their perfection below that perfection above is attained, and the divine being is only able to flow forth by virtue of the actions of human souls here on earth. See *Zohar* 1:23a.

24. Hans Jonas, *The Gnostic Religion*, 56.

25. See Moses de Leon, *Sefer Shekel ha-Kodesh*, critically edited and with an introduction by Charles Mopsik (Los Angeles: Cherub Press, 1996), 2.

26. See *Zohar* 2:176b, the famous parable of the man in the mountains who "knew nothing of the delights of the world." See Hecker, *Mystical Bodies, Mystical Meals: Eating and Embodiment in Medieval Kabbalah* for a recent treatment of a related theme.

27. See Tishby, *The Wisdom of the Zohar* 2:701.

28. *Zohar* 3:13a–b; 2:150a. On the descent of the soul, see Tishby, *The Wisdom of the Zohar* 2:749–754.

29. *Genesis Rabbah* 20:12. "*And the Lord God made coats of skin (or with an ayin) for the man and his woman, and He clothed them* (Gen. 3:21). In Rabbi Meir's Torah they found written, *ketonot or* (with an *aleph*), coats of light."

30. The Jewish prayer book, the *siddur*, contains its own meditation on soulfulness, traditionally recited upon waking: "*Elohai* (My God), the soul You placed within me is pure. You created her, You fashioned her, You breathed her into me, and You preserve her within me and eventually You will take her from me and restore her to me in the future to come. As long as the soul is within me, I thank You YHVH, My God and the God of my ancestors, Master of all works, Lord of all souls. Blessed are You YHVH, who restores souls to dead bodies."

31. Hadot, *Plotinus or The Simplicity of Vision*, 27.

32. Moses Maimonides, *Perek Helek*. Translation is from Isadore Twersky, ed., *A Maimonides Reader* (Springfield: Behrman House, 1972), 411–412.

33. See also *Zohar* 1:57b: "Come and see: No one departs from the world without first seeing Adam, who asks him why he is leaving the world and how he is exiting. He replies: Woe to you! On

account of you I am leaving the world. He responds: My son, I violated one command and was punished for it. Look at all your sins! Look how many of your Lord's commands you have violated!" (Matt, *The Zohar*).

34. Cf. *Zohar Ḥadash Ruth* 80a, where Ye'azrael appears in a story similar to our passage, although in *Zohar Ḥadash*, Rabbi Perahiah (the flying Rabbi!) learns about the Garden of Eden through a personal tour into the celestial domain rather than through a book.

35. *Dumah*, literally, means silence, and is used in the Bible as a synonym for the netherworld (Ps. 115:17). In rabbinic writings *Dumah* comes to signify the prince of hell or the prince of spirits, see BT *Shabbat* 152b.

36. See *Pirke de'Rabbi Eliezer* 15: "Rabbi Eliezer said: I heard with my ear the Lord of Host speaking. What did He speak? He said: *See, I have set before you this day life and good, and death and evil* (Deut. 30:15). The Blessed Holy One said: Behold, these two ways have I given to Israel, one is good, the other is evil. The one which is good is of life, and the one which is evil is of death. The good way has two byways, one of righteousness and the other of love, and Elijah, be he remembered for good, is placed exactly between these two ways. When a person comes to enter [one of these byways], Elijah, be he remembered for good, cries aloud concerning him, saying: *Open the gates, let a righteous nation enter, the nation that keeps faith* (Isa. 26:2)." Gerald Friedlander, trans., *The Chapters of Rabbi Eliezer the Great* (New York: Sepher-Hermon Press, 1916), 102–103. See also *Zohar* 2:213a.

37. See also *Zohar* 2:211b.

38. See *Zohar* 1:66a: "Come and see: When souls ascend to the site of the bundle of life, there they bask in radiance of the resplendent speculum, shining from the highest site of all. If the soul did not garb herself in the radiance of another garment, then she could not draw near to view that light. The mystery of the matter: Just as the soul is given a garment in which to be garbed, to exist in this world, so she is given a garment of supernal radiance in which to exist in that world, to gaze into the speculum that shines from within the land of the living" (Matt, *The Zohar*). See Gershom Scholem, "*Tselem*: The Concept of the Astral Body" in *On the Mystical Shape of the Godhead*, trans. Joachim Neugroschel (New York: Schocken Books, 1991), 251–274; idem., "The Paradisic Garb of Souls and the Origin of the Concept of *Haluka de-Rabbanan*," *Tarbiz* 24 (1955): 290–306 [Hebrew].

39. See especially *Zohar* 2:209b–210b.

40. Moses de Leon, *Seder Gan Eden*. Translation is from Moshe Idel, *Ascensions on High in Jewish Mysticism: Pillars, Lines, Ladders* (Budapest: Central European University Press, 2005), 106.
41. See *Zohar* 2:127a.
42. See Hellner-Eshed, *A River Issues From Eden*, 331–344 [Hebrew].
43. A reference to Gabriel, "The man clothed in linen with the writing case at his waist," see Ezekiel 9:11 and Daniel 12:7. In rabbinic and medieval kabbalistic literature, Gabriel is a key character in the celestial domain. See *Yalkut*, Isaiah 429; *Seder Gan Eden*. See also *Zohar* 2:231a: "Gabriel was appointed to be a messenger in this world, and every messenger who is appointed for this world has to be clothed in the garments of this world."
44. This sentence and the one immediately following are somewhat obscure and the text in disarray. The account in *Zohar Ḥadash* and the account in the *Tosafot* conflict. The translation here is tentative.
45. See *Zohar* 3:204a where this verse is expounded.
46. "When Adam was in the Garden of Eden, the Blessed Holy One brought down a book for him by the hand of Raziel, the holy angel appointed over supernal, sacred mysteries. In it were engraved supernal engravings, sacred wisdom . . . Just then the holy angel Hadraniel encountered him and exclaimed: Adam, Adam, treasure away the precious glory of your Lord, for permission has not been granted to supernal beings to know it, only to you!

    So he kept it hidden until he left the Garden of Eden, daily wielding treasures of his Lord, discovering supernal mysteries of which supernal ministers are unaware.

    As soon as he sinned, violating his Lord's command, that book flew away from him. Adam slapped himself on the head and wept . . . " (*Zohar* 1:55b, Matt, *The Zohar*; see also *Zohar* 1:118b).
47. See Aryeh Wineman, *Mystic Tales from the Zohar* (Princeton: Princeton University Press, 1998), 42.
48. Moses Maimonides, *The Guide of the Perplexed*, introduction, trans. Shlomo Pines, 7.
49. See Andre Maurois's preface in Jorge Luis Borges, *Labyrinths: Selected Stories and Other Writings*, ed. Donald A. Yates and James E. Irby (London: Penguin Books, 1970), 18.

Chapter 5. "Feast Friends and Drink, Drink Deeply O Lovers"

1. See note 8 in this chapter.
2. See Peter Cole, *The Dream of the Poem: Hebrew Poetry from*

Muslim and Christian Spain, 950–1492 (Princeton: Princeton University Press, 2007).

3. Raymond P. Scheindlin, *Wine, Women and Death: Medieval Hebrew Poems on the Good Life* (Philadelphia: Jewish Publication Society, 1986), 47.

4. Ibid., 55. See also Arie Schippers, *Spanish Hebrew Poetry and The Arabic Literary Tradition: Arabic Themes in Hebrew Andalusian Poetry* (Leiden: Brill, 1994), 105–143; Dan Pagis, "'And drink thy wine with joy': Hedonistic Speculation in Three Wine Songs by Samuel Hannagid" in *Studies in Literature Presented to Simon Halkin*, ed. E. Fleischer (Jerusalem: Magnes Press, 1973), 133–140 [Hebrew].

5. Translation from Ariel Bloch and Chana Bloch, *The Song of Songs: A New Translation* (Berkeley: University of California Press, 1995). See also Song of Songs 2:4, 4:10, 7:9–10, 8:2.

6. See *Zohar* 3:296b, *Idra Zuta*. Meron is the traditional site of Rabbi Shimon's grave.

7. Wine is sometimes associated with the demonic in the *Zohar*, the shadowy other side:

    "Rabbi Shimon said: There is a vine and there is a vine! Supreme, holy vine; *alien vine* (Jer. 2:21), daughter of an alien god . . . When Israel sinned, abandoning this vine, what is written? *From the vine of Sodom is their vine* (Deut. 32:32). So, there is a vine, and there is a vine" (Matt, 1:238b). See *Zohar* 3:12b. See also Rabbi Moses de Leon, *Sefer ha-Rimmon*, 319–320, and *Shekel ha-Kodesh*, 36–37. See Hecker, *Mystical Bodies, Mystical Meals*, 215 note 88.

8. The word *dovev* is enigmatic and unclear. In rabbinic literature the word is understood to mean "causing to speak" or "causing to move"; See Rashi and Ibn Ezra ad loc. See BT *Sanhedrin* 90b and *Song of Songs Rabbah* 7.10.1, where the verse is used to convey the idea that even in the next world, the righteous learn Torah.

9. See Hecker on mystical satiety in *Mystical Bodies*, 57–82.

10. See Hellner-Eshed, *A River Issues From Eden*, 237–267 [Hebrew].

11. Cf. BT *Eruvin* 54a.

12. Symbolizing the sefirah *Gevurah*. See Rashi, BT *Shabbat* 137b.

13. On this narrative, see Matt, *The Book of Enlightenment*, 127–131, and Hellner-Eshed, *A River Issues From Eden*, 383–385 [Hebrew].

14. Symbolizing *Tiferet*, the Blessed Holy One, the divine male in which the qualities of the upper sefirot are merged.

15. The famous "Yanuka" narrative (3:186a–192a), which relates the encounter between two of the Companions and yet another wun-

derkind, portrays something similar. Seated around the table with the Companions, the child begins to expound some of the mysteries of wine:

"We have learned that there are seven firmaments . . . and they all originate from the wine of the Holy Ancient One on high. Jacob brought that wine from afar and squeezed it out from the grapes of the vine. Then Jacob brought the wine, which was suited to him, and rejoiced and drank, as it is written, *and he brought him wine and he drank* (Gen. 27:25) . . . This wine went from one level to the other, and they all tasted it, until Joseph the righteous also tasted it, for he is the faithful beloved, and this is the meaning of *like choicest wine, flowing smoothly to my beloved* (Song of Songs 7:10)." Rabbi El'azar and Rabbi Abba are astonished by the child and exclaim: "This wine belongs to you. You have conquered, holy angel, by means of the holy spirit"—meaning that the child is now filled with the wine, the flow of divinity (trans. based on Tishby and Goldstein).

16. He does not even know the grace after meals.

17. A term designating the secrets of creation. According to rabbinic tradition these esoteric secrets were to be highly guarded.

18. See Ronit Meroz, "Zoharic Narratives and Their Adaptations," *Hispania Judaica Bulletin* 3 (2001): 3–63; Boaz Huss, "The Appearance of *Sefer ha-Zohar*," *Tarbiz* 70 (2001): 507–542 [Hebrew]; and Yehuda Liebes, "How the Zohar was Written" in *Studies in the Zohar*, 85–138, for detailed discussions of the various kabbalistic circles in late thirteenth-century Spain.

19. See Oded Yisraeli, *The Interpretation of Secrets and the Secret of Interpretation*, 111–112 [Hebrew].

20. Interestingly, the verse from the Song of Songs, "Your mouth like choicest wine," also appears in the series of homilies in this narrative unit.

21. "*Prop me up with raisins (ashishot)*—this means with two fires (*eshot*), the heavenly fire and the earthly fire. Another interpretation: *Prop me up with raisins (ashishot)*—with two fires, the written law and the oral law. Another interpretation: *Prop me up with raisins (ashishot)*—with many fires, with the fire of Abraham and of Moriah, and of the bush, with the fire of Elijah and of Hananiah, Mishael and Azariah" (*Song of Songs Rabbah* 2.5.1, Soncino trans.).

22. The triad, *Ḥesed*, *Gevurah*, and *Tiferet*.

23. The ninth sefirah, *Yesod*, the conduit of the divine flow into the *Assembly of Israel*.

24. Elliot R. Wolfson, "The Left Contained in the Right: A Study in Zoharic Hermeneutics," *AJS Review* 11 (1986): 52.

25. Yeisa's exposition picks up on the homily immediately preceding our narrative, which takes as its focus the difference in the nature of the divine service of the priests and the Levites; see later in this chapter.

26. On the expression "those who love me with *yesh*," see *Zohar* 1:4b, 158a, 206a, 242b, and 1:88a, Sitrei Torah. See also *Avot* 5:19, *Mishnah Uqtsin* 3:12, BT *Sanhedrin* 100a.

27. See for example the famous account of Rabbi Ḥiyya's initiation, *Zohar* 2:14a–15b, *Midrash ha-Ne'elam*.

28. Cf. *Pirke Avot* 6:3: "He who learns from his fellows a single chapter, or a single law, or a single verse, or a single utterance, or even a single letter—must treat him with honor."

29. Cf. BT *Sanhedrin* 34a and BT *Shabbat* 88b, where the verse from Jeremiah 23:29, "Behold My word is like fire, declares the Lord, and like a hammer that shatters rock," is used to convey the midrashic principle of multiple interpretation.

30. The context of this verse is significant, as Rabbi Yeisa is compared to the prophet Jeremiah, whom God appointed as a youth:

    "The word of YHVH came to me:

    Before I created you in the womb, I knew you; before you were born I consecrated you; I appointed you a prophet concerning the nations.

    I replied: Ah, my Lord YHVH! I do not know how to speak, for I am still a boy.

    And YHVH said to me: Do not say, 'I am still a boy,' but go wherever I send you and speak whatever I command you . . .

    YHVH put out His hand and touched my mouth, and YHVH said to me: Here, I have put My words into your mouth" (Jer. 1:4–9).

31. Significantly, this epithet appears in the introduction to the *Idra Rabba* (3:127b). It will be recalled that Rabbi Yeisa the Younger comes to fill the place of Rabbi Yeisa the Elder, who died during this mystical gathering.

Chapter 6. Pearls in a Beggar's Wallet

1. On Ecclesiastes, see Robert Gordis, *Koheleth: The Man and His World* (New York: Schocken Books, 1968).

2. *Mishnah Yadaim* 3:5. Oddly enough, the phrase "makes the hands

unclean" signifies that a work is holy and has canonical status. *Avot de Rabbi Natan* 1 provides a different but equally delightful account of the acceptance of the work: "Originally, it is said, Proverbs, Song of Songs and Ecclesiastes were suppressed; for since they were held to be mere parables and not part of the Holy Writings [the religious authorities] arose and suppressed them; [and so they remained] until the men of Hezekiah came and interpreted them." Judah Goldin, trans., *The Fathers According to Rabbi Nathan*, 5.

3. *Leviticus Rabbah* 28:1 contains another reflection on these words that "savored of heresy": "Rabbi Yitzḥak the son of Levi said: The Sages were about to suppress the Book of Ecclesiastes, having found in it words that savored of heresy. They said: Should Solomon have given utterance to advice such as, *Rejoice O young man in your childhood and let your heart cheer you in the days of your youth* (Eccles. 11:9)? Even though Moses had said, *Go not about after your own heart and your own eyes* (Num. 15:39), Solomon said, *Walk in the ways of your heart and in the sight of your eyes* (Eccles. 11:9), as though all restraint were removed and there were neither justice nor judge. But since Solomon went on to say, *But know that for all these things God will bring you into judgment* (ibid.), [the Sages decided] that Solomon had spoken well after all" (Soncino trans.).

4. *Ecclesiastes Rabbah* 3:12.

5. See also *Zohar* 2:39a: "Therefore he [Solomon] composed three books: Song of Songs, Ecclesiastes, and Proverbs and the purpose of them all is to perfect wisdom. Song of Songs corresponds to love (*ḥesed*), Ecclesiastes corresponds to judgment (*din*), and Proverbs corresponds to mercy (*raḥamim*)—in order to perfect wisdom." See also *Zohar* 3:64a.

6. See Hellner-Eshed, *A River Issues From Eden*, 115–123 [Hebrew].

7. This expression is taken from *Ecclesiastes Rabbah* 11:8.

8. See Wolfson, "The Left Contained in the Right."

9. Kohelet here quotes "orthodox" wisdom that he of course rejects.

10. Yeshayahu Leibowitz, *The Faith of Maimonides*, trans. John Glucker (Tel Aviv: MOD Books, 1989), 77.

11. Moses Maimonides, *The Guide of the Perplexed* 3:51, trans. Shlomo Pines, 624–625.

12. On Maimonidean providence and its reception, see Alfred L. Ivry, "Providence, Divine Omniscience and Possibility: The Case of Maimonides" in *Maimonides: A Collection of Critical Essays*, ed. Joseph A. Buijs (Notre Dame: University of Notre Dame Press,

1990), 175–191; Charles M. Raffel, "Providence as Consequent Upon the Intellect: Maimonides' Theory of Providence," *AJS Review* 12 (1987): 25–71. See also Aviezer Ravitzky, "Samuel Ibn Tibbon and the Esoteric Character of the *Guide of the Perplexed*," *AJS Review* 6 (1981): 87–123.

13. Leibowitz, *The Faith of Maimonides*, 78–79.

14. See Dov Schwartz, "The Debate Over Maimonides' Theory of Providence in Thirteenth-Century Jewish Philosophy," *Jewish Studies Quarterly* 2 (1995): 185–196. See 188.

15. Gershom Scholem, *Ha-kabbalah be-Gerona*, ed. J. Ben Shlomo (Jerusalem: Akadamon, 1972), 306–307 [Hebrew]. Translation is from Berger, see next note.

16. David Berger, "Miracles and Natural Order in Nahmanides" in *Rabbi Moses Nahmanides: Explorations in His Religious and Literary Virtuosity*, ed. Isadore Twersky (Cambridge: Harvard University Press, 1983), 107–128.

17. See Halbertal, *By Way of Truth: Nahmanides and the Creation of Tradition* (Jerusalem: Shalom Hartman Institute, 2006), 149–180 [Hebrew].

18. Tishby, *The Wisdom of the Zohar* 1:423.

19. Rabbi Moses Cordovero, *Or Yakar*, vol. 14, *Shlaḥ*, 25–26.

20. William G. Braude and Israel J. Knapstein, trans., *Tanna Debe Eliyyahu: The Lore of the School of Elijah* (Philadelphia: The Jewish Publication Society of America, 1981), 477–478.

21. Cf. *Zohar* 1:72a. See Matt, *The Zohar: Pritzker Edition*, 1:425, note 634.

22. Moses Maimonides, *The Guide of the Perplexed* 3:17, trans. Shlomo Pines, 464.

23. Ibid. 3:17, 471.

24. Yitzḥak Baer, *A History of the Jews in Christian Spain*, vol. 1, trans. Louis Schoffman (Philadelphia: The Jewish Publication Society of America, 1966), 261–305.

25. Moses de Leon, *Sefer ha-Rimmon*, 391. See Matt, *Zohar: The Book of Enlightenment*, 6 for full text. See also Scholem, *Major Trends in Jewish Mysticism*, 397–398, note 154. See also Daniel J. Silver, *Maimonidean Criticism and Maimonidean Controversy 1180–1240* (Leiden: Brill, 1965), 182–198.

26. The wording of this verse is ambiguous and complex. The translation here follows the *JPS Tanakh*. *Ecclesiastes Rabbah* contains the following interpretation, undoubtedly known by the author of our passage: "*I said in my heart: It is because of the sons of men, that God may sift them, and that they may see that they themselves are*

but as beasts (Eccles. 3:18). It is because (*divrat*) means the manner (*middaberot*) in which the wicked conduct themselves in this world, in that they revile and blaspheme in this world; nevertheless the Holy One blessed be He, grants them abundant peace. For what purpose? *That God may sift them* (*le-varam*): i.e., to make manifest to them (*levarer lahem*) what is the Attribute of Judgment for the wicked. *And that they may see that they themselves are but as beasts*: that they should recognise and demonstrate to the world that the wicked are likened to a beast. In the same way that a beast is condemned to death and does not enter the life of the world to come, so are the wicked condemned to death like a beast and do not enter the world to come" (trans. Soncino).

27. Moses Maimonides, *The Guide of the Perplexed* 3:18, trans. Shlomo Pines, 475.

28. In addition to the medieval resonances just outlined, the equation between the fools of the world and beasts also alludes to older rabbinic polemics against the *am ha-aretz*, the simpleton. Tractate *Pesaḥim* 49b from the Babylonian Talmud contains a long discussion about these simpletons who are repeatedly compared to animals. Among a litany of insults, we read, for example, that a person must not marry his daughter to an *am ha-aretz*, a principle buttressed by the following proof text: "cursed be he who lies with any beast" (Deut. 27:21). The *Zohar* frequently employs this rabbinic interpretation and views the *amei ha-aretz* as beasts: "*They shall rule the fish of the sea, the birds of the sky, the beasts* . . . (Gen. 1:26)—*the beasts*, these are the *amei-haaretz*" (*Zohar* 1:252b, *hashmatot*).

29. See *Zohar* 1:57a: "*You are not a God who delights in wickedness; evil cannot abide with you* (Ps. 5:5) . . . one is only called evil if he wastes his way, defiling himself, defiling the earth, empowering the impure spirit called evil . . . He never enters the palace, nor gazes upon the face of the *Shekhinah*, for on account of this *Shekhinah* withdraws from the world" (Matt, *The Zohar*; see also 1:221b).

30. My reading follows Cordovero, *Or Yakar*, vol. 14, *Shlaḥ*, 26–27.

31. The biblical text preserves two readings, the *keri*, the text as read, *yivḥar* /choose/יבחר and the *ketiv*, the text as written, *yehubar* /joined/ יחבר, distinguished only by a small consonantal shift. The *Zohar*'s interpretation brilliantly keeps both in play.

32. Judah Goldin, trans., *The Fathers According to Rabbi Nathan*, 39.

33. According to rabbinic tradition, the members of the wilderness generation have no portion in the world to come. See BT *Sanhedrin* 108a.

34. Rabbi Ḥagai figures in two other stories in the zoharic corpus, *Sitrei Torah*, *Lekh Lekha* 89a, and in *Zohar Ḥadash*, *Lekh Lekha*, *Midrash ha-Ne'elam*, 25c. In both accounts, which are in fact variants of one another, Rabbi Ḥagai appears as master, whose mystical-spiritual prowess outshines the companions he is with.

35. Boaz Huss, "A Sage Is Preferable Than a Prophet: Rabbi Shimon bar Yoḥai and Moses in the Zohar," *Kabbalah: Journal for the Study of Jewish Mystical Texts* 4 (1999): 103–139 [Hebrew]; see in particular 132–133. See also Hellner-Eshed, *A River Issues From Eden*, 214–216 [Hebrew]. See also Yehuda Liebes, "The Zohar's Relation to the Land of Israel" in *Zion and Zionism Amongst the Jews of Spain and the Orient*, ed. Z. Harvey et. al (Jerusalem: Misgav Yerushalayim, 2002), 31–44, especially 36 [Hebrew]. See also *Zohar* 1:96b—the conclusion to the famous Tarsha narrative—where the villagers of Tarsha are exiled to Babylon, presumably because they need to learn to conceal their esoteric wisdom.

Chapter 7. Midnight in the Garden of Delight

1. Rumi, "The Vigil" in *Selected Poems*, trans. Coleman Barks with John Moyne, A. J. Arberry, and Reynold Nicholson (London: Penguin, 2004), 85–86.

2. Cited in William C. Chittick, *The Sufi Path of Knowledge: Ibn al-Arabi's Metaphysics of Imagination* (Albany: State University of New York Press, 1989), 223.

3. See Elliot R. Wolfson, "Forms of Visionary Ascent as Ecstatic Experience in the Zoharic Literature" in *Gershom Scholem's Major Trends in Jewish Mysticism, 50 Years After*, ed. Peter Schäfer and Joseph Dan (Tubingen: J.C.B. Mohr, 1993), 209–235; Hellner-Eshed, *A River Issues From Eden*, 149–176 [Hebrew]. See also Gershom Scholem, "Tradition and New Creation in the Ritual of the Kabbalists" in *On the Kabbalah and Its Symbolism*, 118–157; Moshe Idel, *Nocturnal Kabbalists* (Jerusalem: Carmel, 2006), esp. 36–44 [Hebrew].

4. Mitchell Dahood, *Psalms 1, 1–50*, Anchor Bible Series (New York: Doubleday, 1965), 255.

5. See *Zohar* 2:97a, 142b, 210b. See Hellner-Eshed, *A River Issues From Eden*, 303–304 [Hebrew].

6. Matt, *Zohar: The Book of Enlightenment*, 94, 235.

7. *Tzadik*, Righteous One, symbolizes the ninth sefirah, *Yesod*, the divine phallus, the conduit for the divine flow into *Malkhut*.

8. On the image of the gazelle/hind in prezoharic Hebrew poetry, see Raymond P. Scheindlin, *The Gazelle: Medieval Hebrew Poems on God, Israel and the Soul* (Oxford: Oxford University Press, 1991).

9. "It is written, *And You O YHVH be not far off, my strength hasten to my aid* (Ps. 22:20). King David said this when he was arranging praises for the King, so as to unite the sun with the moon . . .

   Be not far off—when She [*Malkhut*] ascends to be adorned by Her husband, and everything is situated in the upper world, He [*Tiferet*] seeks to rise from there to *Ein-Sof*, so that all might be bound together, higher and higher, and therefore, *Be not far off*—do not depart from us or forsake us . . .

   My strength (eyaluti)—when a hart (*ayal*) or gazelle runs away it soon comes back to the place where it was. So with the Blessed Holy One—even though He moves away higher and higher toward *Ein-Sof*, He soon returns to His place. Why is this? Because Israel take hold of Him and do not allow Him to slip away and leave them. Therefore, *my strength, hasten to my aid.* Consequently, we need to take hold of the Blessed Holy One and restrain Him, like someone drawing another down from above . . . " (*Zohar* 2:138b, Tishby and Goldstein, modified).

10. See Hellner-Eshed, *A River Issues From Eden*, 268–296 [Hebrew].

11. Apparently so in the text before the author of this *Zohar* passage. In standard versions of the Bible today, the word is written correctly with the *vav*.

12. The text here is confused and the translation tentative.

13. See Avraham Even-Shushan, *Ha-milon he-Ḥadash*, vol. 2, entries for *ḥollel* (Jerusalem: Kiryath Sepher, 1979), 729, 756. See Rashi and Ibn Ezra ad loc. on Psalms 29:9. See Ramban ad loc. Job 26:13.

14. See *Zohar* 2:36b where the verse, "the voice of YHVH makes hinds writhe" is also used to mark the onset of the nocturnal delight: "At midnight, they saw a hind pass before them, shouting and crying loudly. Rabbi Ḥiyya and Rabbi Yose arose and trembled. They heard a voice proclaiming: Those who are awake, arise! Those who are asleep, awake! Worlds, prepare for your Master, for your Master is going forth to the Garden of Eden, which is His palace, to delight in the righteous, as is written, *And in His Temple, all say 'Glory!'* (Ps. 29:9).

   Rabbi Ḥiyya said: Now it is precisely midnight and this voice is the voice that goes forth and causes pain to the hind above and below, as is written, *the voice of YHVH makes hinds writhe* (Ps. 29:9). Happy is our portion that we merited to hear this!"

See Mordechai Pechter, "Between Night and Day" in *The Zohar and Its Generation*, ed. Joseph Dan (Jerusalem: The Hebrew University, 1989), 311–346 [Hebrew] on this fascinating narrative.

15. The *Shekhinah* is surrounded by angelic camps and both she and they are at times dominated by forces of severity. See *Zohar* 3:60; see also *Zohar* 1:37a. Although not likely to be the *peshat* of the *Zohar* here, it is tempting to think of the Companions as the sixty warriors surrounding the *Shekhinah*. They are her midwives and will be with her throughout the birth.

16. Translation from Robert Alter, *The David Story: A Translation with Commentary of 1 and 2 Samuel* (New York: W.W. Norton, 1999).

17. Moses de Leon, *Or Zarua*, ed. Alexander Altman, *Qovez al Yad*, n.s. 9 (1980): 249. Cited in Matt, *Zohar: The Book of Enlightenment*, 7, 193.

18. Scholem, *Major Trends in Jewish Mysticism*, 4.

19. On the motif of suckling in the Kabbalah, see Daniel Abrams, *The Female Body of God in Kabbalistic Literature: Embodied Forms of Love and Sexuality in the Divine Feminine* (Jerusalem: Magnes Press, 2004), 123–140 [Hebrew].

20. See *Genesis Rabbah* 3:1.

21. On sleep in the *Zohar*, see Tishby, *The Wisdom of the Zohar* 2:809–813. See also *Zohar* 1:83a on the same verse from Isaiah, which is expounded in the context of the soul's nocturnal ascent.

22. See also *Pesikta Rabbati* 31:2 on this verse from Job. The first prayer recited in the morning upon rising also alludes to this idea: "I thank You O living and eternal King for you have returned my soul within me with compassion—abundant is Your faithfulness."

23. See Radak ad loc. who also reads the verse as "with my soul I desire You."

24. Idel, *Kabbalah: New Perspectives*, 42–43. See also Alexander Altman, "The Ladder of Ascension" in *Studies in Mysticism and Religion Presented to Gershom Scholem on His Seventieth Birthday*, ed. E. E Urbach, R. J. Z Werblowsky, C. Wirszubski (Jerusalem: Magnes Press, 1967), 1–32. On *devekut*, cleaving in the *Zohar*, see also Hellner-Eshed, *A River Issues From Eden*, 345–351, and Tishby, *The Wisdom of the Zohar* 3:994–998.

25. While the *Zohar*'s understanding of the soul's "natural" inclination to cleave to God is colored by the composition's Neoplatonic influences, the idea that the soul possesses a distinct identity from the "I" of the speaker of the verse from Psalms and that the soul shares a particular affinity with God is quite likely the literal meaning of the verse in its biblical context. See James L. Kugel, *The Great*

Poems of the Bible (New York: The Free Press, 1999), 44–53.

26. See BT *Avoda Zara* 3b: "Resh Lakish said: Whoever engages Torah by night, the Blessed Holy One extends upon him a thread of grace by day, as it is said, *By day YHVH commands His grace, at night His song is with me* (Ps. 42:9)."

27. See Idel, *Kabbalah: New Perspectives*, 53, on this part of our text.

28. See Wolfson, "Forms of Visionary Ascent," 234.

Chapter 8. The Great Chain of Being and the Light of the World

1. Solomon Ibn Gabirol, *Keter Malkhut*, Canto 7. Peter Cole, trans., *Selected Poems of Solomon Ibn Gabirol* (Princeton: Princeton University Press, 2001), 146. See also Bernard Lewis, trans., *The Kingly Crown*, introduction and commentary by Andrew L. Gluck (Notre Dame: University of Notre Dame Press, 2003); David R. Slavitt, trans., *A Crown for the King* (Oxford: Oxford University Press, 1998).

2. Solomon Ibn Gabirol, *Keter Malkhut*, Canto 1. Cole, *Selected Poems*, 140.

3. Plotinus, *The Enneads*, v. 2.1., trans. Stephen MacKenna, 361.

4. For a succinct overview, see Arthur O. Lovejoy, *The Great Chain of Being: A Study of the History of an Idea* (Cambridge: Harvard University Press, 1933), 62–63.

5. Plotinus, *The Enneads*, v. 1.6, trans. MacKenna, 354; see also v. 3.12.

6. Ibid. iv. 3.17, trans. MacKenna, 270.

7. Rabbi Azriel of Gerona, *Explanation of the Ten Sefirot*, in Joseph Dan, ed., *The Early Kabbalah*, 92.

8. See Scholem, *Major Trends in Jewish Mysticism*, 203, 398.

9. Wolfson, *Through a Speculum That Shines*, 270–288.

10. Rabbi Moses de Leon, *Sefer Shekel ha-Kodesh*, 16 [Hebrew].

11. See Scholem, *Major Trends in Jewish Mysticism*, 181–190; idem, *Kabbalah* (Jerusalem: Keter, 1974), 217. See also Pinchas Giller, *Reading the Zohar: The Sacred Text of the Kabbalah*, 8.

12. See Daniel Abrams, "The Zohar as a Book: On the Assumptions and Expectations of the Kabbalists and Modern Scholarship," *Kabbalah: Journal for the Study of Jewish Mystical Texts* 12 (2004): 201–232 [Hebrew]; idem, "The Invention of the Zohar as a Book: On the Assumptions and Expectations of the Kabbalists and Modern Scholars," *Kabbalah: Journal for the Study of Jewish Mystical Texts* 19 (2009): 7–142.

13. Liebes, "How the Zohar Was Written" in *Studies in the Zohar*, 87; Ronit Meroz, "The Original Structure of the Zohar," *Proceedings of the Twelfth World Congress of Jewish Studies*, forthcoming [Hebrew].

14. See Liebes, "How the Zohar Was Written," 87: "There also seems to be a difference in literary taste here—the *Midrash ha-Ne'elam* lacks the refined taste which gives the *Zohar* its tremendous force."

15. On Jewish Neoplatonism, see Alfred L. Ivry, "Neoplatonic Currents in Maimonides' Thought" in *Perspectives on Maimonides: Philosophical and Historical Studies*, ed. Joel L. Kramer (Oxford: Oxford University Press, 1991), 115–140; Arthur Hyman, "From What Is One and Simple Only What Is One and Simple Can Come to Be" in *Neoplatonism and Jewish Thought*, ed. Lenn E. Goodman (Albany: State University of New York Press, 1992), 111–135.

16. Moses Maimonides, *The Guide of the Perplexed* 2:12.

17. Ibid. 2:11, trans. Shlomo Pines, 274–275. See also 2:6.

18. Moses Maimonides, *Mishneh Torah, Hilkhot Yesodei ha-Torah* 2:5.

19. For a detailed and clear overview of medieval cosmological systems, see Herbert A. Davidson, *Alfarabi, Avicenna and Averroes on Intellect: Their Cosmologies, Theories of the Active Intellect and Theories of Human Intellect* (Oxford: Oxford University Press, 1992). In particular, see 44–45.

20. The question of the necessary or divinely willed nature of creation/emanation was a central one for medieval Jewish thought and lies at the heart of the some of the more famous passages in the *Guide of the Perplexed*. See Kenneth Seeskin, *Maimonides on the Origin of the World* (Cambridge: Cambridge University Press, 2005) for a recent discussion.

21. See Tishby, *The Wisdom of the Zohar* 1:77, where he notes the strong influence of *Sefer ha-Mada* and *The Guide of the Perplexed* on *Midrash ha-Ne'elam*.

22. Tishby, *The Wisdom of the Zohar* 2:557

23. See Maimonides, *Hilkhot Yesodei ha-Torah* 2:5, where the same verse from Ecclesiastes in used to describe the separate intelligences. The Throne of Glory is of particular significance in this hierarchy signifying the first emanation of divinity. In *Midrash ha-Ne'elam*, the throne is also the source of the soul. See *Midrash ha-Ne'elam*, *Zohar Ḥadash* 24a–b. Cf. *The Guide of the Perplexed* 2.26; *Pirke d'Rabbi Eliezer* 3; BT *Ḥagiga* 12b–13a. See also *Keter Malkhut*, Canto 26: "Who could approach the place of your dwelling, in your raising up over the sphere of mind the Throne of Glory in the fields of concealment and splendour, at the source of the secret and

matter, where the mind reaches and yields?" (trans. Peter Cole).

24. Hallamish, *Introduction to the Kabbalah*, 190–191.

25. See also *Zohar* 2:86b, where the same verse is used to describe Rabbi Shimon: "Rabbi Ḥizkiyah said: This is the meaning of what is written, *He drew (vayatzel) upon the spirit that was on him and put it upon the seventy elders* (Num. 11:25), like a candle from which are kindled many candles, yet it remains intact. So Rabbi Shimon bar Yoḥai, the master of lights, illumines all yet the light does not depart from him and remains intact."

On the root *ne'ezal*, see Scholem, *Origins of the Kabbalah*, 447–448.

26. See Daniel C. Matt, "Matnita di-Lan: A Technique of Innovation in the Zohar" in *The Zohar and Its Generation*, ed. Joseph Dan (Mehqerei Yerushalayim be-Mahshevet Yisrael 8) (Jerusalem: Hebrew University, 1989), 123–145 [Hebrew] on the use of the term *Mishnah* in the *Zohar*.

27. BT *Ḥagiga* 12a; see also *Tanḥuma, Shemini* 9.

28. *Sefer ha-Bahir* 160, translation from Matt, *The Essential Kabbalah*, 193. On this important passage see Scholem, *Origins of the Kabbalah*, 136–137. See also Arthur Green, *Seek My Face, Speak My Name: A Contemporary Jewish Theology* (Northvale: Jason Aaronson, 1992), 154–155.

29. *Sefer ha-Bahir* 147, trans. Aryeh Kaplan (Boston: Weiser Books, 1979), 53–54. See also *Bahir* 148. The *Zohar* also employs this myth on numerous occasions in different ways. See, for example, *Zohar* 1:32a; 2:148b–149a.

30. On this curious number, see Maimonides, *Hilkhot Yesodei ha-Torah* 3:8 and especially 3 Enoch, Section 7: "The first man, however, and his generation sat at the entrance to the Garden of Eden so that they might gaze at the bright image of the Shekhinah, for the brilliance of the Shekhinah radiated from one end of the world to the other, 65, 000 times [brighter] than the wheel of the sun." Cited in Peter Schäfer, *The Hidden and Manifest God: Some Major Themes in Early Jewish Mysticism*, trans. Aubrey Pomerance (Albany: State University of New York Press, 1992), 125

31. This term may derive from the Jewish Sufi work *Duties of the Heart*, by Baḥya ibn Pakuda. See Wolfson, *Through a Speculum That Shines*, 171.

32. Moses Maimonides, *Hilkhot Yesodei ha-Torah* 4:7. See also Yosef ben Shalom Askhenazi, a kabbalist with close connections to the zoharic circle, in his *Perush le-parashat Bereshit*, 49: "Just as the eye of the human being sees potentially and will only ever actually

see when accompanied by the light of one of the luminaries, so the eyes of the soul will not actually see until the known light accompanies them. Understand this."

33. Moses Maimonides, *Perek Helek*. From Isadore Twersky, ed. and trans., *A Maimonides Reader* (Springfield: Behrman House, 1972), 412.

34. The desire to attain and radiate the divine light lies at the heart of the zoharic quest as the composition's motto verse suggests: "The en-lightened will shine like the radiance of the sky" (Dan. 12:3). See Hellner-Eshed on facial illumination in *A River Issues from Eden*, 363–367 [Hebrew]. See also Wolfson, *Through a Speculum That Shines*, 270. A well-known story from *Midrash ha-Ne'elam* (*Zohar* 2:14a–15a) that, like our text, recounts the mystical initiation of Rabbi Ḥiyya, notes that Rabbi El'azar "stood and expounded words of mysteries of wisdom and his face lit up like the sun, and his words spread out and soared in the firmament."

35. See *Midrash ha-Ne'elam*, *Zohar Ḥadash*, 15a. The term *karbosa* remains enigmatic.

36. There is wordplay here—people use/*mishtamshin* the sun/*shemesh*.

37. Maimonides in *Hilkhot Yesodei ha-Torah* 3:2 and 3:5 writes that the nine spheres are themselves divided into many spheres totaling eighteen.

38. See especially Canto 15 and Canto 16. On the influence of *Keter Malkhut* on the *Zohar*, see Tishby, *The Wisdom of the Zohar* 1:76.

39. A similar idea can also be found in *Numbers Rabbah* (15:9) without the kabbalistic overlay: "Israel said: *Send forth Your light and Your truth; they will lead me* (Ps. 43:3). Immense is the light of the Blessed Holy One. The sun and the moon illuminate the world eternally. From where do they illuminate? They 'snatch' from the sparks of light above, as it is said, *Sun and moon stand still on high as Your arrows fly in brightness, Your flashing spear in brilliance* (Hab. 3:3). Immense is the light above, that only one hundredth of it is given to the created beings, as it is said, *He knows what (ma, read as meah, hundred) is in the darkness [and light dwells with Him]* (Dan. 2:22). Therefore I made the sun and the moon to shine before you, as it is said, *And God set them in the expanse of the sky to shine upon the earth* (Gen. 1:17)."

40. On this enigmatic phrase, see Meroz, "Zoharic Narratives and Their Adaptations," *Hispania Judaica Bulletin* 3 (2001): 3–63. See 27 note 90. The translation here follows the suggestion of Yehuda Liebes.

41. Cf. *Zohar* 2:14a–15a for another account of Rabbi Ḥiyya's mystical initiation.

42. Scholem, *Major Trends in Jewish Mysticism*, 222.

43. Wolfson, *Language, Eros, Being: Kabbalistic Hermeneutics and Poetic Imagination* (New York: Fordham University Press, 2005), 221.

44. Ibid.

45. On the image of the chain linking the divine and non-divine worlds in the Kabbalah, see Moshe Idel, *Enchanted Chains: Techniques and Rituals in Jewish Mysticism* (Los Angeles: Cherub Press, 2005), 42–53. On the widespread of idea of the Chain of Being, see Lovejoy, *The Great Chain of Being*. See also Arthur Green, *Ehyeh: A Kabbalah for Tomorrow* (Woodstock: Jewish Lights Publishing, 2003), 106–119.

46. Moses de Leon, *Sefer ha-Rimmon*, 181–182. The translation is a combination of Matt, *The Essential Kabbalah*, 26, and Scholem, *Major Trends in Jewish Mysticism*, 223.

Chapter 9. Rabbi Ḥiyya, Rabbi Yose, and the Merchants in the Cave

1. The *Zohar* here seems to have conflated two verses from Jeremiah, 6:20 and 31:16.

2. Liebes, "Zohar and Eros," 81.

3. Eitan Fishbane, "Tears of Disclosure: The Role of Weeping in Zoharic Narrative," *The Journal of Jewish Thought and Philosophy*, 11 (2002): 25–47, especially 25 and notes there. See also Gil Anidjar, *Our Place in Andalus: Kabbalah, Philosophy, Literature in Arab Jewish Letters* (Stanford: Stanford University Press, 2002), 7, 171–172, 188.

4. Hellner-Eshed, *A River Issues From Eden*, 139 [Hebrew].

5. See Nathan Wolski, "Mystical Poetics: Narrative, Time and Exegesis in the Zohar," *Prooftexts* 28 (2008):101–128, for a more detailed discussion.

6. Walter Benjamin, "Theses on the Philosophy of History," in *Illuminations*, ed. Hannah Arendt, trans. Harry Zohn (London: Fontana, 1973), 252.

7. The flight from mysterious assailants on the way is a perhaps a narrative analogue to the series of expositions about exile.

8. See Wolfson, *Langauge, Eros, Being*, 8, on cosmic isotropy and the doctrine of signatures.

9. Cf. *Zohar* 1:145b, 1:249a, 2:174a. See also *Leviticus Rabbah* 29:2; *Pesikta de-Rav Kahana* 23:2; BT *Taanit* 5b.
10. The *Zohar* here seems to have conflated two verses from Jeremiah, 6:20 and 31:16.
11. Cf. *Zohar* 1:120a; 1:5b–6a.
12. The Hebrew word *shav* is read here as *return* rather than as *again* as in the first part of the homily and describes the return of the male aspect of the divine, signified by the Tetragrammaton, to a state of union with the female grade of divinity, the Assembly of Israel, the *Shekhinah*.
13. Symbolizing *gevurah*, the forces of judgment.
14. Zion here symbolizes the divine grade *Yesod*, the divine phallus. See *Zohar* 1:186a.
15. See also *Zohar* 1:72b for similar ironic laments.
16. Cf. *Zohar* 3:76b.
17. See Liebes, "Zohar and Eros." On the significance of meals as an occasion for mystical expositions, see Hecker, *Mystical Bodies, Mystical Meals*, 116–125.
18. See *Zohar* 1:85a where Rabbi El'azar, like Don Quixote, imaginatively transforms an inn into a village castle. See Steven Hutchinson, *Cervantine Journeys* (Madison: University of Wisconsin Press, 1992), 162ff.
19. Cf. BT *Horayot* 13b where a similar expression is used to shame Rabbi Shimon ben Gamliel. Elsewhere in the *Zohar*, though, this term is used without this ironic aspect, e.g., *Zohar* 3:59b.
20. See, for example, BT *Ḥagiga* 15a.
21. See Oded Yisraeli, *The Interpretation of Secrets*, 105–112.
22. See Mishnah *Avot* 2:12: "Make yourself fit to study Torah for it is not yours by inheritance."
23. Symbolizing the last sefirah, *Malkhut*.
24. The male grade of divinity, *Tiferet*.
25. Symbolizing the divine phallus, the conduit of the divine flow, the ninth sefirah, *Yesod*.
26. See *Zohar* 1:219a; 2:169a. Cf. *Zohar* 3:133b *Idra Rabba*.
27. Symbolizing the sefirot *Nezaḥ* and *Hod*.
28. On similar *ars poetica* expressions in the *Zohar* see Hellner-Eshed, *A River Issues From Eden*, 24, 25, 59, 61, 146, 431 [Hebrew]. See also Daniel C. Matt, "New-Ancient Words: The Aura of Secrecy in the Zohar" in *Gershom Scholem's Major Trends in Jewish Mysticism 50 Years After*, ed. Peter Schäfer and Joseph Dan (Tubingen: J.C.B. Mohr, 1993), 181–207. On the fear associated with revealing secrets, see *Zohar* 3:127b, *Idra Rabba*, "Woe if I reveal, woe if I do not reveal"; See also Fishbane, "Tears of Disclosure."

29. Cf. *Zohar* 2:140a where the same verse is interpreted as referring to the arraying and adorning of the black (*shahor*) light of dawn (*shahar*).

30. On the significance of sitting, see Hecker, *Mystical Bodies*, 121–125.

31. See *Zohar* 1:4a.

32. See Hellner-Eshed's detailed analysis of the various stages of the nocturnal delight in *A River Issues From Eden*, 149–176 [Hebrew].

33. See PT *Taanit* 1:1; BT *Sanhedrin* 94a and Rashi there; see also *Zohar* 2:130b.

34. *Masa* means both oracle and burden.

35. The female aspect of divinity, *Malkhut*, the *Shekhinah*.

36. Symbolizing *Yesod*, see note 40 in this chapter.

37. Cf. BT *Megilla* 29a.

38. Beer Sheva, indeed: "the well of seven" is a symbol for the *Shekhinah*, the seventh of the offspring of *Hokhmah* and *Binah*, and the well into which the divine plenty flows.

39. See BT *Pesahim* 2a. Cf. *Zohar* 3:204a–b.

40. *Yesod*, symbolized by "morning" and "good," is filled with "light," the divine influx from above.

41. See Hellner-Eshed, *A River Issues From Eden*, 124–130 [Hebrew], for a discussion of the significance of this concept in the *Zohar*.

42. See *Mekhilta Beshalah* 3:2:23.

43. Wolfson, *Language, Eros, Being*, 25–26.

44. Fishbane, "Tears of Disclosure," 25.

45. See Hellner-Eshed, *A River Issues From Eden*, 22–23, 237–296 [Hebrew].

46. See Liebes, "The Zohar as Renaissance" [Hebrew] and idem, "Zohar and Eros" [Hebrew].

47. Hellner-Eshed, *A River Issues From Eden*, 146 [Hebrew]. This improvisatory character does not mean that zoharic composition is not bound by formal (even rigid) conventions and rules. See Hellner-Eshed, 230.

48. See Wolfson, *Language, Eros, Being*, 37–38.

Chapter 10. The Palace of Love

1. Yehuda Liebes, "Zohar and Eros," 70 [Hebrew]. Two monumental scholarly works have recently been written on the broader theme of Eros in the Kabbalah. See Moshe Idel, *Kabbalah and Eros* (New Haven: Yale University Press, 2005) and Elliot R. Wolfson, *Language, Eros, Being: Kabbalistic Hermeneutics and Poetic Imagination* (New York: Fordham University Press, 2004).

2. On the river that flows from Eden in the *Zohar*, see Hellner-Eshed, *A River Issues From Eden*, 268–296 [Hebrew].

3. Rabbi Nahman of Bratslav beautifully conveys this idea through his image of the heart and the fountain in his famous tale "The Seven Beggars." See Arnold J. Band, trans. *Nahman of Bratslav: The Tales* (New York: Paulist Press, 1978), 268–269.

4. YHVH = *yod, hey, vav, hey.*

5. The two children are *Tiferet* (actually comprised of six sefirot) and *Malkhut.*

6. The male, the female, the male with the female, and the female with the male.

Selected Bibliography

Abrams, Daniel. *The Female Body of God in Kabbalistic Literature: Embodied Forms of Love and Sexuality in the Divine Feminine.* Jerusalem: Magnes Press, 2004. [Hebrew]

———. "The Invention of the Zohar as a Book: On the Assumptions and Expectations of the Kabbalists and Modern Scholars." *Kabbalah: Journal for the Study of Jewish Mystical Texts* 19 (2009): 7–142.

———. "The Zohar as a Book: On the Assumptions and Expectations of the Kabbalists and Modern Scholarship." *Kabbalah: Journal for the Study of Jewish Mystical Texts* 12 (2004): 201–232. [Hebrew]

Altman, Alexander. "The Ladder of Ascension." In *Studies in Mysticism and Religion Presented to Gershom Scholem on His Seventieth Birthday,* edited by E. E. Urbach, R. J. Z. Werblowsky, and C. Wirszubski, 1–32. Jerusalem: Magnes Press, 1967.

Anidjar, Gil. *Our Place in Andalus: Kabbalah, Philosophy, Literature in Arab Jewish Letters.* Stanford: Stanford University Press, 2002.

Ariel, David S. *The Mystic Quest: An Introduction to Jewish Mysticism.* Northvale: Jason Aronson, 1988.

Baer, Yitzhak. *A History of the Jews in Christian Spain,* vol. 1. Translated by Louis Schoffman. Philadelphia: The Jewish Publication Society of America, 1966.

Berger, David. "Miracles and Natural Order in Nahmanides." In *Rabbi Moses Nahmanides: Explorations in His Religious and Literary Virtuosity,* edited by Isadore Twersky, 107–128. Cambridge: Harvard University Press, 1983.

Boyarin, Daniel. *Carnal Israel: Reading Sex in Talmudic Culture.* Berkeley: University of California Press, 1993.

———. *Intertextuality and the Reading of Midrash.* Bloomington: Indiana University Press, 1990.

257

Cole, Peter. *The Dream of the Poem: Hebrew Poetry from Muslim and Christian Spain, 950–1492.* Princeton: Princeton University Press, 2007.

———, trans. *Selected Poems of Solomon Ibn Gabirol.* Princeton: Princeton University Press, 2001.

Dan, Joseph, ed. *The Early Kabbalah.* New York: Paulist Press, 1986.

Davidson, Herbert A. *Alfarabi, Avicenna and Averroes on Intellect: Their Cosmologies, Theories of the Active Intellect and Theories of Human Intellect.* Oxford: Oxford University Press, 1992.

de Leon, Moses. *Sefer ha-Rimmon.* Critically edited and with an introduction by Elliot R. Wolfson. Atlanta: Scholars Press, 1988. [Hebrew]

———. *Sefer Shekel ha-Kodesh.* Critically edited and with an introduction by Charles Mopsik. Los Angeles: Cherub Press, 1996. [Hebrew]

Fishbane, Eitan. "Tears of Disclosure: The Role of Weeping in Zoharic Narrative." *The Journal of Jewish Thought and Philosophy* 11 (2002): 25–47.

Gikatilla, Joseph. *Gates of Light.* Translated by Avi Weinstein. London: AltaMira Press, 1994.

Giller, Pinchas. *Reading the Zohar: The Sacred Text of the Kabbalah.* New York: Oxford University Press, 2001.

Goodman, Lenn E., ed. *Neoplatonism and Jewish Thought.* Albany: State University of New York Press, 1992.

Green, Arthur. *Ehyeh: A Kabbalah for Tomorrow.* Woodstock: Jewish Lights Publishing, 2003.

———. *A Guide to the Zohar.* Stanford: Stanford University Press, 2004.

———. *Seek My Face, Speak My Name: A Contemporary Jewish Theology.* Northvale: Jason Aronson, 1992.

Hadot, Pierre. *Plotinus or The Simplicity of Vision.* Translated by Michael Chase. Chicago: University of Chicago Press, 1993.

Halbertal, Moshe. *By Way of Truth: Nahmanides and the Creation of Tradition.* Jerusalem: Shalom Hartman Institute, 2006. [Hebrew]

Hallamish, Moshe. *An Introduction to the Kabbalah.* Translated by Ruth Bar Ilan and Ora Wiskind-Elper. Albany: State University of New York Press, 1999.

Hecker, Joel. *Mystical Bodies, Mystical Meals: Eating and Embodiment in Medieval Kabbalah.* Detroit: Wayne State University Press, 2005.

Hellner-Eshed, Melila. *A River Issues From Eden: On the Language of Mystical Experience in the Zohar.* Tel Aviv: Am Oved, 2005. [Hebrew]

Huss, Boaz. "The Appearance of *Sefer ha-Zohar*." *Tarbiz* 70 (2001): 507–542. [Hebrew]

————. "The New Age of Kabbalah: Contemporary Kabbalah, the New Age and Postmodern Spirituality." *Journal of Modern Jewish Studies* 6 (2007): 107–125.

————. "A Sage Is Preferable Than a Prophet: Rabbi Shimon bar Yohai and Moses in the Zohar." *Kabbalah: Journal for the Study of Jewish Mystical Texts* 4 (1999): 103–139. [Hebrew]

Idel, Moshe. *Ascensions on High in Jewish Mysticism: Pillars, Lines, Ladders*. Budapest: Central European University Press, 2005.

————. *Enchanted Chains: Techniques and Rituals in Jewish Mysticism*. Los Angeles: Cherub Press, 2005.

————. *Kabbalah and Eros*. New Haven: Yale University Press, 2005.

————. *Kabbalah: New Perspectives*. New Haven: Yale University Press, 1988.

————. *Nocturnal Kabbalists*. Jerusalem: Carmel, 2006. [Hebrew]

Ivry, Alfred L. "Neoplatonic Currents in Maimonides' Thought." In *Perspectives on Maimonides: Philosophical and Historical Studies*, edited by Joel L. Kramer, 115–140. Oxford: Oxford University Press, 1991.

————. "Providence, Divine Omniscience and Possibility: The Case of Maimonides." In *Maimonides: A Collection of Critical Essays*, edited by Joseph A. Buijs, 175–191. Notre Dame: University of Notre Dame Press, 1990.

Jonas, Hans. *The Gnostic Religion*. Boston: Beacon Press, 2001 [1958].

Kaplan, Aryeh, trans. *The Bahir*. Boston: Weiser Books, 1979.

Leibowitz, Yeshayahu. *The Faith of Maimonides*. Translated by John Glucker. Tel Aviv: MOD Books, 1989.

Liebes, Yehuda. *Studies in the Zohar*. Translated by Arnold Schwartz, Stephanie Nakache, and Penina Peli. Albany: State University of New York Press, 1993.

————. "Zohar and Eros." *Alpayyim* 9 (1994): 67–119. [Hebrew]

————. "The *Zohar* as Renaissance." *Daat* 46 (2001): 5–11. [Hebrew]

————. "The Zohar's Relation to the Land of Israel." In *Zion and Zionism Amongst the Jews of Spain and the Orient*, edited by Z. Harvey et al., 31–44. Jerusalem: Misgav Yerushalayim, 2002. [Hebrew]

Loberbaum, Yair. *Image of God: Halacha and Agada*. Tel Aviv: Schocken Books, 2004. [Hebrew]

Lovejoy, Arthur O. *The Great Chain of Being: A Study of the History of an Idea*. Cambridge: Harvard University Press, 1933.

Maimonides, Moses. *The Guide of the Perplexed.* Translated by Shlomo Pines. Chicago: University of Chicago Press, 1963.

Matt, Daniel C. *The Essential Kabbalah: The Heart of Jewish Mysticism.* San Francisco: Harper, 1995.

———. "New-Ancient Words: The Aura of Secrecy in the Zohar." In *Gershom Scholem's Major Trends in Jewish Mysticism, 50 Years After,* edited by Peter Schäfer and Joseph Dan, 181–207. Tubingen: J.C.B. Mohr, 1993.

———. "*Matnita di-Lan*: A Technique of Innovation in the Zohar." In *The Zohar and Its Generation,* edited by Joseph Dan, 123–145. (Mehqerei Yerushalayim be-Mahshevet Yisrael 8). Jerusalem: Hebrew University, 1989. [Hebrew]

———. *Zohar: The Book of Enlightenment.* New York: Paulist Press, 1983.

———, trans. *The Zohar—Pritzker Edition,* vols. 1–4. Stanford: Stanford University Press, 2004, 2004, 2006, 2007.

McGinn, Bernard. "The God beyond God: Theology and Mysticism in the Thought of Meister Eckhart." *Journal of Religion* 61 (1981): 1–19.

Meroz, Ronit. "Zoharic Narratives and Their Adaptations." *Hispania Judaica Bulletin* 3 (2001): 3–63.

Pagels, Elaine. *The Gnostic Gospels.* New York: Vintage Books, 1989.

Pagis, Dan. "'And drink thy wine with joy': Hedonistic Speculation in Three Wine Songs by Samuel Hannagid." In *Studies in Literature Presented to Simon Halkin,* edited by E. Fleischer, 133–140. Jerusalem: Magnes Press, 1973. [Hebrew]

Pechter, Mordechai. "Between Night and Day." In *The Zohar and Its Generation,* edited by Joseph Dan, 311–346. Jerusalem: Hebrew University, 1989. [Hebrew]

Plotinus. *The Enneads.* Translated by Stephen MacKenna. London: Penguin Books, 1991.

Raffel, Charles M. "Providence as Consequent Upon the Intellect: Maimonides' Theory of Providence." *AJS Review* 12 (1987): 25–71.

Ravitzky, Aviezer. "Samuel Ibn Tibbon and the Esoteric Character of the Guide of the Perplexed." *AJS Review* 6 (1981): 87–123.

Schäfer, Peter. *The Hidden and Manifest God: Some Major Themes in Early Jewish Mysticism.* Translated by Aubrey Pomerance. Albany: State University of New York Press, 1992.

Scheindlin, Raymond P. *The Gazelle: Medieval Hebrew Poems on God, Israel and the Soul.* Oxford: Oxford University Press, 1991.

———. *Wine, Women and Death: Medieval Hebrew Poems on the Good Life.* Philadelphia: Jewish Publication Society, 1986.

Schippers, Arie. *Spanish Hebrew Poetry and The Arabic Literary Tradition: Arabic Themes in Hebrew Andalusian Poetry*. Leiden: Brill, 1994.

Scholem, Gershom. *Major Trends in Jewish Mysticism*. New York: Schocken Books, 1946.

———. *On the Kabbalah and Its Symbolism*. Translated by Ralph Manheim. New York: Schocken Books, 1965.

———. *On the Mystical Shape of the Godhead*. Translated by Joachim Neugroschel. New York: Schocken Books, 1991.

———. *Origins of the Kabbalah*. Edited by R. J. Zwi Werblowsky and translated by Allan Arkush. Philadelphia: The Jewish Publication Society, 1987.

———. "The Paradisic Garb of Souls and the Origin of the Concept of Haluka de-Rabbanan." *Tarbiz* 24 (1955): 290–306. [Hebrew]

———. *Zohar: The Book of Splendor*. New York: Schocken Books, 1949.

Schwartz, Dov. "The Debate Over Maimonides' Theory of Providence in Thirteenth-Century Jewish Philosophy." *Jewish Studies Quarterly* 2 (1995): 185–196.

Sherwin, Byron L. *Kabbalah: An Introduction to Jewish Mysticism*. Lanham: Rowman and Littlefield Publishers, 2006.

Tishby, Isaiah. *The Wisdom of the Zohar*, 3 vols. Translated by David Goldstein. London: The Littman Library of Jewish Civilization, 1989.

Twersky, Isadore. *A Maimonides Reader*. Springfield: Behrman House, 1972.

Urbach, Ephraim E. *The Sages: Their Concepts and Beliefs*. Translated by Israel Abrahams. Cambridge: Harvard University Press, 1975.

Wineman, Aryeh. *Mystic Tales from the Zohar*. Princeton: Princeton University Press, 1998.

Wolfson, Elliot R. "Beautiful Maiden Without Eyes: *Peshat* and *Sod* in Zoharic Hermeneutics." In *The Midrashic Imagination: Jewish Exegesis, Thought and History*, edited by Michael Fishbane, 155–203. Albany: State University of New York Press, 1993.

———. "Forms of Visionary Ascent as Ecstatic Experience in the Zoharic Literature." In *Gershom Scholem's Major Trends in Jewish Mysticism, 50 Years After*, edited by Peter Schäfer and Joseph Dan, 209–235. Tubingen: J.C.B. Mohr, 1993.

———. *Language, Eros, Being: Kabbalistic Hermeneutics and Poetic Imagination*. New York: Fordham University Press, 2005.

———. "The Left Contained in the Right: A Study in Zoharic Hermeneutics." *AJS Review* 11 (1986): 27–52.

————. *Through a Speculum That Shines: Vision and Imagination in Medieval Jewish Mysticism.* Princeton: Princeton University Press, 1994.

Wolski, Nathan. "Don Quixote and Sancho Panza were walking on the way: El Caballero Andante and the Book of Radiance." *Shofar: An Interdisciplinary Journal of Jewish Studies* 27 (2009): 24–47.

————. "Mystical Poetics: Narrative, Time and Exegesis in the Zohar." *Prooftexts* 28 (2008): 101–128.

Wolski, Nathan, and Merav Carmeli. "Those Who Know Have Wings: Celestial Journeys with the Masters of the Academy." *Kabbalah: Journal for the Study of Jewish Mystical Texts* 16 (2007): 83–114.

Yisraeli, Oded. *The Interpretation of Secrets and the Secret of Interpretation: Midrashic and Hermenutic Strategies in Sabba de-Mishpatim of the Zohar.* Los Angeles: Cherub Press, 2005. [Hebrew]

Index

263

Index of *Zohar* Passages